INTRODUCTION TO SUMERIAN

DANIEL A FOXVOG

LECTURER IN ASSYRIOLOGY (RETIRED)

UNIVERSITY OF CALIFORNIA AT BERKELEY

Revised June 2014

CONTENTS

PREFACE	3
THE SUMERIAN WRITING SYSTEM	4
TABLE OF SYLLABIC SIGN VALUES	16
PHONOLOGY	18
NOUNS AND ADJECTIVES	23
THE NOMINAL CHAIN	28
PRONOUNS AND DEMONSTRATIVES	31
SUMMARY OF PERSONAL PRONOUN FORMS	38
THE ADNOMINAL CASES: GENITIVE AND EQUATIVE	39
THE COPULA	46
ADVERBS AND NUMERALS	51
THE ADVERBAL CASES	54
INTRODUCTION TO THE VERB	61
DIMENSIONAL PREFIXES 1: INTRODUCTION	69
DIMENSIONAL PREFIXES 2: DATIVE	73
DIMENSIONAL PREFIXES 3: COMITATIVE, ABLATIVE-INSTRUMENTAL, TERMINATIVE	78
CORE PREFIXES: ERGATIVE, LOCATIVE-TERMINATIVE, LOCATIVE	83
THE VENTIVE ELEMENT	90
RELATIVE CLAUSES: THE NOMINALIZING SUFFIX -a	95
PREFORMATIVES (MODAL PREFIXES)	102
THE IMPERATIVE	109
IMPERFECTIVE FINITE VERBS	117
PARTICIPLES AND THE INFINITIVE	127
APPENDIX: CHART OF VERBAL PREFIX CHAIN ELEMENTS	150
APPENDIX: THE EMESAL DIALECT	151
INDEX	152
EXERCISES	153

PREFACE

> Entia non sunt multiplicanda
> praeter necessitatem
>
> William of Ockham

This grammar is intended primarily for use in the first year of university study under the guidance of a teacher who can describe the classic problems in greater detail, add current alternative explanations for phenomena, help the student parse and understand the many textual illustrations found throughout, and provide supplementary information about the history of the language and the culture of early Mesopotamia. A few exercises have been provided to accompany study of the lessons, some artificial, others drawn from actual texts. Both require vocabulary lookup from the companion Elementary Sumerian Glossary or its equivalent. Upon completing this introduction, the student will be well prepared to progress to sign learning and reading of texts. Konrad Volk's A Sumerian Reader (Studia Pohl Series Maior 18, Rome, 1997-) is a good beginning.

This introduction may also be of benefit to those who have already learned some Sumerian more or less inductively through the reading of simple royal inscriptions and who would now like a more structured review of its grammar, with the help of abundant textual illustrations, from something a bit more practical and pedagogically oriented than the available reference grammars.

Cross-references have often been provided throughout to sections in Marie-Louise Thomsen's earlier standard The Sumerian Langauge (Copenhagen, 1987^2), where additional information and further examples can often be found for individual topics. A newer restatement of the grammatical system is Dietz Otto Edzard's Sumerian Grammar (Leiden, 2003). An up to date quick overview is Gonzalo Rubio's "Sumerian Morphology," in Alan S. Kaye (ed.), Morphologies of Asia and Africa II (2007) 1327-1379. Pascal Attinger's encyclopedic Eléments de linguistique sumérienne (Fribourg, 1993) is a tremendously helpful reference but beyond the reach of the beginner. Abraham H. Jagersma's new revolutionary and monumental Descriptive Grammar of Sumerian (2010) is now available for download on the Web and will eventually be published by Oxford University Press.

For standard Assyriological abbreviations used in this introduction see the Abbreviations for Assyriology of the Cuneiform Digital Library Initiative (CDLI) on the Web. The standard academic online dictionary is the Electronic Pennsylvannia Sumerian Dictionary. The chronological abbeviations used here are:

OS	Old Sumerian period	(2500-2350 BC)
OAkk	Old Akkadian (Sargonic) period	(2350-2150 BC)
Ur III	3rd Ur Dynasty (Neo-Sumerian) period	(2150-2000 BC)
OB	Old Babylonian period	(1900-1600 BC)

For those who may own a version of my less polished UC Berkeley teaching grammar from 1990 or earlier, the present version will be seen to be finally comprehensive, greatly expanded, hopefully much improved, and perhaps worth a serious second look. My description of the morphology and historical morphophonemics of the verbal prefix system remains an idiosyncratic, somewhat unconventional minority position. Jagersma's new description, based in many respects upon a subtle system of orthographic and morphophonological rules, is now popular especially in Europe, and it may well become the accepted description among many current students of Sumerian grammar.

This annual revision has made some improvements to textual examples and added new scholarly references. The book's pagination however remains essentially the same.

> Guerneville, California USA
> June 2014

THE SUMERIAN WRITING SYSTEM

I. TRANSLITERATION CONVENTIONS

A. Sign Diacritics and Index Numbers

Sumerian features a large number of homonyms — words that were pronounced similarly but had different meanings and were written with different <u>signs</u>, for example:

/du/   'to come, go'

/du/   'to build'

/du/   'to release'

A system of numerical subscripts, and diacritics over vowels representing subscripts, serves to identify precisely which sign appears in the actual text. The standard reference for sign identification remains R. Labat's Manuel d'Epigraphie akkadienne (1948-), which has seen numerous editions and reprintings. Y. Rosengarten's Répertoire commenté des signes présargoniques sumériens de Lagaš (1967) is indispensible for reading Old Sumerian texts. R. Borger's Assyrisch-babylonische Zeichenliste (AOAT 33/33a, 1978) is now the modern reference for sign readings and index numbers, although the best new sign list for OB Sumerian literary texts is the Altbabylonische Zeichenliste der sumerisch-literarischen Texte by C. Mittermayer & P. Attinger (Fribourg, 2006). Borger's index system which is used here is as follows:

<u>Single-syllable signs</u>	<u>Multiple-syllable signs</u>	
du (= du$_1$)	muru	
dú (= du$_2$)	múru	Note that the diacritic always falls on the FIRST VOWEL of the word!
dù (= du$_3$)	mùru	
du$_4$ etc.	muru$_4$	

There is variation in the systems employed in older signlists for multiple-syllable signs, especially in Labat. In the earliest editions of his signlist which may still be encountered in libraries, Labat carried the use of diacritics through index numbers 4-5 by shifting the acute and grave accents onto the first syllable of multiple-syllable signs:

murú   (= muru$_2$)

murù   (= muru$_3$)

múru   (= muru$_4$)

mùru   (= muru$_5$)

4

This would not be a problem except for a number of signs which have long and short values. For example, the sign túk can be read /tuk/ or /tuku/. Labat gives the latter reading as túku, which then does not represent tuku$_4$, but rather tuku$_2$, i.e. túk(u)! Borger's AbZ system, used here and in later editions of Labat, is more consistent, placing the diacritics on the first syllable of multi-syllable signs, but using them only for index numbers 2 and 3.

New values of signs, pronunciations for which no generally accepted index numbers yet exist, are given an "x" subscript, e.g. da$_x$ 'side'.

Note, finally, that more and more frequently the acute and grave accents are being totally abandoned in favor of numeric subscripts throughout. This, for example, is the current convention of the new Pennsylvania Sumerian Dictionary, e.g. du, du$_2$, du$_3$, du$_4$, etc. Since the system of accents is still current in Sumerological literature, however, it is vital that the beginner become familiar with it, and so it has been maintained here.

B. Upper and Lower Case, Italics, and Brackets

In unilingual Sumerian contexts, Sumerian words are normally written in lower case roman letters. Upper case (capital) letters (CAPS) are used:

1) When the exact meaning of a sign is unknown or unclear. Many signs are polyvalent, that is, they have more than one value or reading. When the particular reading of a sign is in doubt, one may indicate this doubt by choosing its most common value and writing this in CAPS. For example, in the sentence KA-ĝu$_{10}$ ma-gig 'My KA hurts me' a body part is intended. But the KA sign can be read ka 'mouth', kìri 'nose' or zú 'tooth', and the exact part of the face might not be clear from the context. By writing KA one clearly identifies the sign to the reader without committing oneself to any of its specific readings.

2) When the exact pronunciation of a sign is unknown or unclear. For example, in the phrase a-SIS 'brackish water', the pronunciation of the second sign is still not completely clear: ses, or sis? Rather than commit oneself to a possibly incorrect choice, CAPS can be used to tell the reader that the choice is being left open.

3) When one wishes to identify a non-standard or "x"-value of a sign. In this case, the x-value is immediately followed by a known standard value of the sign in CAPS placed within parentheses, for example da$_x$(Á) 'side'.

4) When one wishes to spell out the components of a compound logogram, for example énsi(PA.TE.SI) 'governor' or ugnim(KI.KUŠ.LU.ÚB.ĜAR) 'army'.

In bilingual or Akkadian contexts, a variety of conventions exist. Very commonly Akkadian words are written in lower case roman or italic letters with Sumerian logograms in CAPS: a-na É.GAL-šu 'to his palace'. In some publications one also sees Sumerian words written in spaced roman letters, with Akkadian in either lower case roman letters or *italics*.

Determinatives, unpronounced indicators of meaning, are written with superscripts in Sumerological literature, or, often, in CAPS on the line in Akkadian contexts: ^{giš}hašhur or ĜIŠ.HAŠHUR. They are also sometimes seen written lower case on the line separated by periods: ĝiš.hašhur.

Partly or wholly missing or broken signs can be indicated using square brackets, e.g. lu[gal] or [lugal]. Partly broken signs can also be indicated using half-brackets. A sign presumed to have been omitted by the ancient scribe is indicated by the use of <angle> brackets, while a sign deleted by a modern editor is indicated by double angle <<angle>> brackets.

C. Conventions for Linking Signs and Words

<u>Hyphens and Periods</u>

In Akkadian contexts, hyphens are always used to transliterate Akkadian, while periods separate the elements of Sumerian words or logograms. In Sumerian contexts, periods link the parts of compound signs written in CAPS, and hyphens are used elsewhere, e.g.:

        énsi(PA.TE.SI)   'governor'
        ^{kuš}É.ÍB-ùr   'shield'
        an-šè   'towards heaven'

Problems can arise, however, when one attempts to formulate rules for the linking of the elements in the chain formations characteristic of Sumerian. The formal definition of a Sumerian word remains difficult (cf. J. Black, "Sumerian Lexical Categories," Zeitschrift für Assyriologie 92 [2002] 60ff. and G. Cunningham, "Sumerian Word Classes Reconsidered," in Your Praise is Sweet. A Memorial Volume for Jeremy Black [London, 2010] 41-52.) Consequently, we only transliterate Sumerian sign by sign; we do not usually transcribe "words." Verbal chains consist of stems and affixes always linked together into one unit. But nominal chains often consist of adjectives, appositions, dependent genitive constructions, and relative clauses beside head nouns and suffixes, and the linking or separation of various parts of nominal chains in unilingual Sumerian contexts is very much subject to the training and habits of individual scholars. One rule of thumb is: the longer the the chain, the less likely its parts will be linked with hyphens. The main criterion at work is usually clarity of presentation.

    Components of nominal compounds are normally linked:

        dub-sar   'tablet writer' = 'scribe'

Adjectives were always in the past joined to the words they modify, but most scholars now write the adjective as a separate word:

        dumu-tur or dumu tur 'child small' = 'the small child'

Verbal adjectives (past participles) are now also rarely linked:

        é-dù-a or é dù-a 'house that was built' = 'the built house'

The two parts of a genitive construction are today never linked unless they are components of a compound noun:

        é lugal-la 'the house of the king'   {é lugal+ak}
        zà-mu   'edge of the year' = 'the new year' {zà mu+ak}

In the absence of a universally accepted methodology, one must attempt to develop one's own sensitivity to how Sumerian forms units of meaning. Our systems of linking signs and words are intended only to help clarify the relationships between them and to aid in the visual presentation of the language. The writing system itself makes no such linkages and does not employ any sort of punctuation. One should take as a model the usual practices of established scholars. One should also try to be consistent.

Plus (+) and Times (x) in Sign Descriptions

When one sign is written inside (or, especially in older texts, above or below) another sign, the resulting new sign may be described by writing both components in CAPS, with the base sign and added sign separated by an "x":

    KAxA   MOUTH times WATER = naĝ 'to drink'

If the reading/pronunciation of such a sign also happens to be unknown, this, by necessity, will actually be the standard way to transliterate it:

    IRIxA   CITY times WATER = 'the city IRIxA'

Two signs joined closely together, especially when they share one or more wedges in common or have lost some feature as a result of the close placement, are called <u>ligatures</u>. Some ligatures also feature an archaic reversal of the order of their components. The parts of ligatures are traditionally linked with a "plus" character, although some scholars will also use a period:

    GAL+LÚ   BIG plus MAN = lugal 'king'

    GAL+UŠUM BIG plus SERPENT = ušumgal 'dragon'

    SÌG+UZU   HIT plus FLESH = túd 'to beat, whip'

    ZU+AB = abzu '(mythical) subterranean ocean, abyss'

    EN+ZU = suen 'Suen (the moon god)'

More complicated compound signs may feature a number of linked elements, with parentheses marking subunits, e.g.:

    DAG+KISIM$_5$x(UDU.MÁŠ) = amaš 'sheepfold'

Colon

In publications of archaic or Old Sumerian texts in which the order of signs is not as fixed as in later scribal tradition, a colon may be used to tell the reader that the order of the signs on either side of the colon is reversed in actual writing, e.g. za:gìn for written GÌN-ZA instead of normal za-gìn 'lapis lazuli'. Colons can also be used to indicate that the proper order of signs is unknown. Thus a transliteration ba:bi:bu would signify:

"I have no idea which sign comes first, second or third!"

II. ORIGIN AND DEVELOPMENT OF THE SIGN SYSTEM

D. Schmandt-Besserat has demonstrated that cuneiform writing per se developed rather abruptly towards the end of the 4th millennium from a system of counting tokens that had long been in use throughout the Ancient Near East. Our oldest true texts, however, are the pictographic tablets that come from level IVa at Uruk (ca. 3100 BC). Other archaic texts come from later Uruk levels, from Jemdet Nasr, and from Ur (1st Dynasty, ca. 2700 BC). Many of these old documents are still difficult to read, but much new progress has recently been made. By ca. 2600 BC the texts become completely intelligible and feature a developing mixed logographic and syllabic cuneiform writing system.

> The term "pictogram (pictographic)" is used exclusively to refer to the signs of the archaic texts, in which "pictures" were drawn on clay with a pointed stylus. The terms "ideogram (ideographic)" and "logogram (logographic)" are interchangeable and refer to signs which represent "ideas" or "words" respectively, as opposed to signs which represent syllabic values or mere sounds. Logogram is the term used by modern Sumerologists.

Signs depicting concrete objects form the ultimate basis of the archaic system. They may represent whole objects:

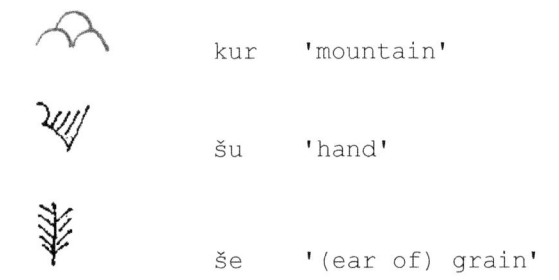

    kur   'mountain'

    šu   'hand'

    še   '(ear of) grain'

or significant parts of objects:

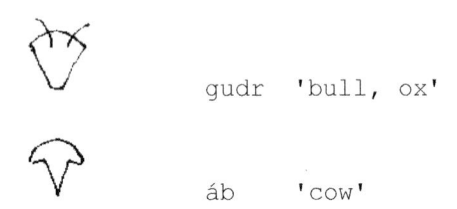

    gud_r   'bull, ox'

    áb   'cow'

Other signs were a bit more abstract, but are still comprehensible:

    a   'water'

    ĝi$_6$ 'night'

Many other archaic signs, however, are either too abstract or, oddly enough, too specific and detailed, for us to identify as yet. The large number of often minutely differentiated signs characteristic of the archaic texts suggests that an attempt was made to produce one-to-one correspondences between signs and objects. This system no doubt soon became unwieldy, and, moreover, could not easily express more abstract ideas or processes. Therefore, alternative ways of generating signs were developed.

gunû and *šeššig* Signs

One method of generating new signs was to mark a portion of a base sign to specify the object intended. The marks are called by the Akkadian scribes either *gunû*-strokes (from Sumerian gùn-a 'colored, decorated') or *šeššig*-hatchings (due to the resemblance of the strokes to the early cross-hatched form of the Sumerian sign for grain, še). Compare the following two sets of signs:

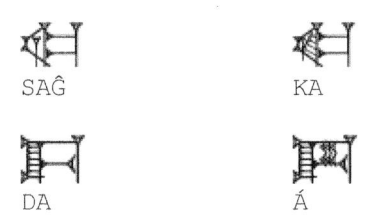

SAĜ   KA

DA   Á

In the first set, the base sign is saĝ 'head'. Strokes over the mouth portion produces SAĜ-*gunû*, to be read ka 'mouth'. In the second set, the base sign is da 'side' (i.e., a shoulder, arm and hand). Hatchings over the arm portion produces DA-*šeššig*, to be read á 'arm'.

Compound Signs

New signs were generated by combining two or more signs:

1) Doubling or even tripling the same sign:

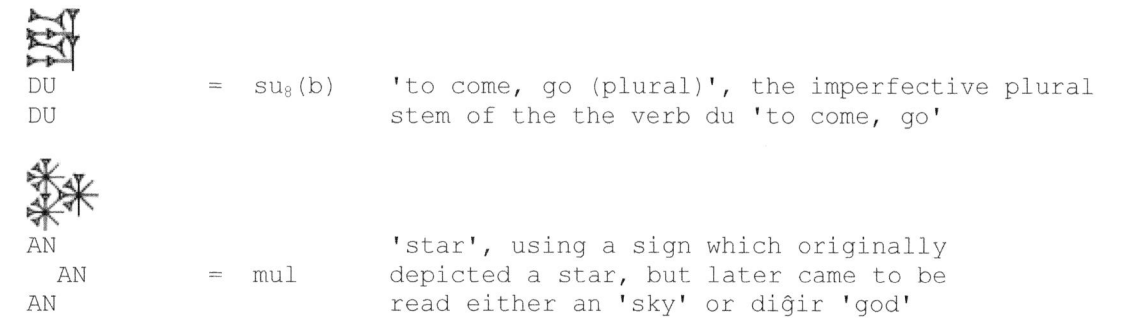

   DU   = su₈(b)   'to come, go (plural)', the imperfective plural
   DU   stem of the the verb du 'to come, go'

   AN   'star', using a sign which originally
     AN   = mul   depicted a star, but later came to be
   AN   read either an 'sky' or diĝir 'god'

2) Combining two (or more) different signs to produce a new idea by association of ideas:

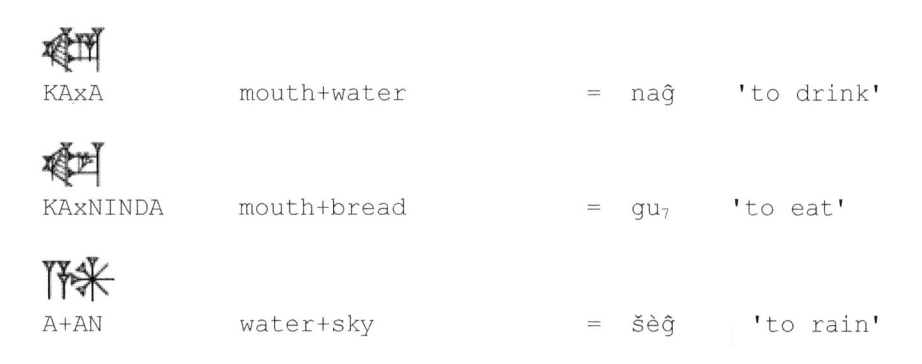

   KAxA   mouth+water   = naĝ   'to drink'

   KAxNINDA   mouth+bread   = gu₇   'to eat'

   A+AN   water+sky   = šèĝ   'to rain'

NÍĜINxA   encircled area+water   = ambar   'marsh'

NÍĜINxBÙR   encircled area+hole   = pú   'well'

MUNUS+UR   female+dog   = nig   'bitch'

3) Adding to a base sign a <u>phonetic indicator</u> which points to the pronunciation of a word associated in meaning with the base sign:

KAxME   mouth+<u>me</u>   = eme   'tongue'

KAxNUN   mouth+<u>nun</u>   = nundum   'lip'

EZENxBAD   walled area+<u>bad</u> = bàd   'city wall'

UD.ZÚ.BAR   sun+<u>zubar</u>   = zubar/zabar 'bronze'

<u>Polyvalency</u>

The most important new development by far was the principle of <u>polyvalency</u>, the association of semantically related "many values" with a particular sign, each with its own separate pronunciation. This became a very productive and simple method of generating new logographic values. For example:

    apin 'plow'   can also be read   uru$_4$ 'to plow'
                                       engar   'plowman, farmer'
                                       àbsin   'furrow'

    ka   'mouth'   can also be read   kìri   'nose'
                                       zú   'tooth'
                                       inim   'word'

    pa   'branch' can also be read   ĝidri   'scepter'
                                       sìg   'to hit'
                                       ugula   'foreman'

    utu   'sun'   can also be read   ud   'light, day, time'
                                       babbar   'shining, white'
                                       àh   'dried, withered'

    an   'sky'   can also be read   diĝir   'god, goddess, deity'

Determinatives

To help the reader decide which possible value of a polyvalent sign was intended by the writer, the use of determinatives arose. A determinative is one of a limited number of signs which, when placed before or after a sign or group of signs, indicates that the determined object belongs to a particular semantic category, e.g. wooden, reed, copper or bronze objects, or persons, deities, places, etc. Determinatives were still basically optional as late as the Ur III period (2114-2004). When Sumerian died as a spoken language, they became obligatory. Determinatives were presumably not to be pronounced when a text was read, and to show that they are not actually part of a word we transliterate them, in unilingual Sumerian context at least, as superscripts. To use the example of the 'plow' sign above, the polyvalent sign APIN is read

    apin - if preceded by a 'wood' determinative: ^{giš}apin 'plow'

    engar - if preceded by a 'person' determinative: ^{lú}engar 'plowman'

but uru$_4$ 'to plow' or àbsin 'furrow' elsewhere, depending upon context.

Rebus Writing and Syllabic Values

At some point rebus writings arose, where the sign for an object which could easily be drawn was used to write a homophonous word which could not so easily be depicted, especially an abstract idea. For example, the picture of an arrow, pronounced /ti/, became also the standard sign for ti 'rib' as well as for the verb ti(l) 'to live'. The adoption of the rebus principle was a great innovation, but it adds to the difficulty of learning the Sumerian writing system, since meanings of words thus written are divorced entirely from the original basic shapes and meanings of their signs.

With the expansion of the rebus principle the development of syllabic, or purely phonological, values of signs became possible. For example, the logograms mu 'name' or ga 'milk' could now be used to write the verbal prefixes mu- 'hither, forth' or ga- 'let me', that is, grammatical elements which were not really logograms, but, rather, indicated syntactic relationships within the sentence. A regular system of syllabic values also made possible the spelling out of any word — especially useful when dealing with foreign loanwords, for which no proper Sumerian logograms existed.

Finally, a limited set of some ninety or so Vowel, Consonant-Vowel, and Vowel-Consonant syllabic values formed the basis of the Akkadian writing system, modified somewhat from the Sumerian to render different sounds in the Akkadian phonemic inventory and then expanded over time to produce many new phonetic and even multiple-syllable values (CVC, VCV, CVCV).

The Sumero-Akkadian writing system was still in limited use as late as the 1st century A.D.; the last known texts are astronomical in nature and can be dated to ca. 76 A.D. The system thus served the needs of Mesopotamian civilizations for a continuous span of over 3200 years - a remarkable achievement in human history.

III. ORTHOGRAPHY

The fully developed writing system employs logograms (word signs), syllabic signs (sound values derived from word signs), and determinatives (unpronounced logograms which help the reader choose from among the different logographic values of polyvalent signs) to reproduce the spoken language. Some now speak of the received system as logophonetic or logosyllabic in character.

Logograms

Many Sumerian logograms are written with a single sign, for example a 'water'. Other logograms are written with two or more signs representing ideas added together to render a new idea, resulting in a compound sign or sign complex which has a pronunciation different from that of any of its parts, e.g.:

    KAxA   > naĝ 'to drink' (combining KA 'mouth' and A 'water')

    Á.KALAG > usu 'strength' (combining Á 'arm' and KALAG 'strong')

Such compound logograms should be differentiated from compound words made up of two or more logograms, e.g.:

    kù-babbar 'silver'   (lit. 'white precious metal')

    kù-sig$_{17}$ 'gold'   (lit. 'yellow precious metal')

    ur-mah   'lion'   (lit. 'great beast of prey')

    za-dím   'lapidary' (lit. 'stone fashioner')

Logograms are used in Sumerian to write nominal and verbal roots or words, and in Akkadian as a kind of shorthand to write Akkadian words which would otherwise have to be spelled out using syllabic signs. For example, an Akkadian scribe could write the sentence 'The king came to his palace' completely syllabically: *šar-ru-um a-na e-kal-li-šu il-li-kam*. He would be just as likely, however, to use the common Sumerian logograms for 'king' and 'palace' and write instead LUGAL *a-na* É.GAL-*šu il-li-kam*.

Syllabic Signs

Syllabic signs are used in Sumerian primarily to write grammatical elements. They are also commonly used to write words for which there is no proper logogram. Sometimes this phonetic writing is a clue that the word in question is a foreign loanword, e.g. sa-tu < Akkadian *šadû* 'mountain'.

Texts in the Emesal dialect of Sumerian feature a high percentage of syllabic writings, since many words in this dialect are pronounced differently from their main dialect (Emegir) counterparts. For example, Emesal ka-na-áĝ = Emegir kalam 'nation', Emesal u-mu-un = Emegir en 'lord'. We also occasionally encounter main dialect texts written syllabically, but usually only from peripheral geographical areas such as the Elamite capital of Susa (in Iran) or northern Mesopotamian sites such as Shaduppum (modern Tell Harmal) near Baghdad.

Syllabic signs are occasionally used as glosses on polyvalent signs to indicate the proper pronunciations; we normally transliterate glosses as superscripts as we do determinatives, for example: èn ba-na-tar[ar] 'he was questioned'. An early native gloss may rarely become fixed as part of the standard writing of a word. The best example is the word for 'ear, intelligence', which can be written three different ways, two of which incorporate full glosses:

    1)   The sign ĝeštug is written: PI

2) The sign ĝéštug is written: $^{geš-túg}PI$

3) The sign ĝèštug is written: $^{geš}PI^{túg}$

Determinatives

Determinatives are logograms which may appear before or after words which categorize the latter in a variety of ways. They are orthographic aids and were presumably not pronounced in actual speech. They begin to be used sporadically by the end of the archaic period. While they were probably developed to help a reader chose the desired value of a polyvalent sign, they are often employed obligatorily even when the determined logogram is not polyvalent. For example, while the wood determinative ĝiš may be used before the PA sign to help specify its reading ĝidri 'scepter', rather than, e.g., sìg 'to hit', ĝiš is also used before hašhur 'apple (tree or wood)' even though this sign has no other reading. Other common functions are to help the reader distinguish between homonymous words, e.g. ad 'sound' and ^{giš}ad 'plank' or between different related meanings of a word, e.g. nú 'to sleep' but ^{giš}ĝèšnu(NÚ) 'bed'.

The following determinatives are placed BEFORE the words they determine and so are referred to as pre-determinatives:

Determinative	Meaning	Category
I (abbr. ^{m})	one, (item)	personal names (usually male)
lú	man, person	male professions
munus (abbr. ^{f})	woman, female	female names and professions*
diĝir (abbr. ^{d})	god	deities
dug	pot	vessels
gi	reed	reed varieties and objects
ĝiš	tree, wood	trees, woods and wooden objects
i₇ (or íd)	watercourse	canals and rivers
kuš	skin	leather hides and objects
mul	star	planets, stars and constellations
na₄	stone	stones and stone objects
šim	aromatic, resin	aromatic substances
túg (or tu₉)	garment	(woolen) garments
ú	grass	grassy plants, herbs, cereals
iri	city	city names (previously read uru)
uruda	copper	copper (and bronze) objects
uzu	flesh	body parts, meat cuts

*An Akkadian invention, not actually attested in Sumerian texts (P. Steinkeller, Or 51 [1982] 358f.)

The following determinatives are placed AFTER the words they determine and so are referred to as post-determinatives:

ki	place	cities and other geographic entities
ku₆	fish	fish, amphibians, crustaceans
mušen	bird	birds, insects, other winged animals
nisi(g)	greens	vegetables (the obsolete reading sar 'garden plot' is still also seen)
zabar	bronze	bronze objects (often combined with the pre-determinative uruda)

Long and Short Pronunciations of Sumerian Roots

Many Sumerian nominal and verbal roots which end in a consonant drop that consonant when the root is not followed by some vocalic element, i.e., at the end of a word complex or nominal chain or when followed by a consonantal suffix. For example, the simple phrase 'the good child' is written dumu-du$_{10}$, and it was presumably actually pronounced /dumu du/. When the ergative case marker -e 'by' is added, however, the same phrase was pronounced /dumu duge/. We know this is so because the writing system "picks up" the dropped consonant of the adjective and expresses it linked with the vowel in a following syllabic sign: dumu-du$_{10}$-ge. This hidden consonant is generally referred to by the German term <u>Auslaut</u> 'final sound', as in "the adjective du$_{10}$ has a /g/ Auslaut."

Our modern signlists assign values to such signs both with and without their Auslauts, thus giving both a "long" and "short" value for each sign, e.g.:

dùg,	du$_{10}$	'good'	kudr,	ku$_5$	'to cut'
dug$_4$,	du$_{11}$	'to do'	níĝ,	nì	'thing'
gudr,	gu$_4$	'bull, ox'	šag$_4$,	šà	'heart, interior'

In the older literature the long values were generally used everywhere; the phrase 'by the good child' would thus have been transliterated dumu-dùg-ge. But this has the disadvantage of suggesting to the reader that an actual doubling of the consonant took place, and, in fact, many names of Sumerian rulers, deities and cities known from the early days of Assyriology are still found cited in forms containing doubled consonants which do not reflect their actual Sumerian pronunciations, e.g. the goddess Inanna, rather than Inana, or the king Mesannepadda, rather than Mesanepada, etc. After World War II, Sumerologists began to bring the transliteration of Sumerian more in line with its actual pronunciation by utilizing the system of short sign values which is still preferred by the majority of scholars, although there is now a tendency to return to the long values among Old Sumerian specialists. Certainly it was the short values that were taught in the Old Babylonian scribal schools, to judge from the data of the Proto-Ea signlists (see J. Klein & T. Sharlach, Zeitschrift für Assyriologie 97 [2007] 4 n. 16). Eventually one must simply learn to be comfortable with both the long and short values of every sign which features an <u>amissible</u> final consonant, though at first it will be sufficient just to learn the short values together with their Auslauts, e.g. du$_{10}$(g), ku$_5$(dr), etc.

If hidden Auslauts create extra problems in the remembering of Sumerian signs or words, the rules of orthography offer one great consolation: a final consonant picked up and expressed overtly in a following syllabic sign is a good indication as to the correct reading of a polyvalent sign. For example, KA-ga can only be read either ka-ga 'in the mouth' or du$_{11}$-ga 'done', whereas KA-ma can only be read inim-ma 'of the word'.

Probably basically related to the preceding phenomenon is the non-significant doubling of consonants in other environments. For example, the verbal chain analyzed as mu+n+a+n+šúm 'he gave it to him' can be found written both as mu-na-an-šúm or mu-un-na-an-šúm, just as the phrase an+a 'in the sky' can be written an-a or an-na. Despite the inconsistency, such redundant writings can again provide help in the correct reading of polyvalent signs: AN-na can only be read an-na 'in the sky', while AN-re can only be read diĝir-re 'by the god'.

Direction of Writing

A shift in the reading and writing of signs took place sometime between the end of the Old Babylonian period (1600 BC) and ca. 1200 BC according to current theory, although at least one modern scholar places the onset of the change as early as ca. 2500 BC.

In the archaic pictographic texts signs were written from the top to the bottom of a column, and the pictures of objects represented by each sign are seen in their normal physical orientation. By 1200 BC signs were being written consistently left to right in a line, with the the orientation of signs now shifted 90 degrees counterclockwise. In a signlist such as Labat's one will see the shift shown as having taken place sometime between the Archaic and Ur III periods, although a monumental inscription such as the law code stele of the later OB king Hammurapi, ca. 1750, still clearly shows the original direction of writing. Modern practice is to continue to publish cuneiform texts and to read cuneiform in the left to right orientation for all periods except for the earliest, even though this practice may be anachronistic for the middle 3rd to early 2nd millennium texts that form the classical Sumerian corpus. For a description of this phenomenon see S. Picchioni, "The Direction of Cuneiform Writing: Theory and Evidence," Studi Orientali e Linguistici 2 (1984-85) 11-26; M. Powell, "Three Problems in the History of Cuneiform Writing: Origins, Direction of Script, Literacy," in Visible Language XV/4 (1981) 419-440; and M. Fitzgerald, "pisan dub-ba and the Direction of Cuneiform Script," CDLI Bulletin 2003:2 (Internet).

IV.   READING CUNEIFORM

In summary, any particular Sumerian sign may have three kinds of uses:

1)   It will usually have one or more logographic values, each with a different pronunciation. A single value may itself have more than one meaning, just as an English word may have more than one common meaning. Sumerian expresses the human experience with a relatively limited word stock; one must continually strive to develop a feeling for the basic meaning of any particular Sumerian word and how it can be used to convey a range of ideas for which modern languages use different individual words.

2)   One of the logographic values of a sign may function as a determinative.

3)   One or more of the logographic values may function as a syllabic sign.

For example, the sign AN can represent:

- the logogram an in the meaning 'sky, heaven'

- the logogram an in the meaning 'high area'

- the logogram an in the meaning '(the sky-god) An'

- the logogram diĝir 'god, goddess'

- the determinative (^{d}) for deities, as in ^{d}en-líl '(the god) Enlil'

- the syllable an, as in mu-na-an-šúm 'he gave it to him'

- the syllable am$_6$ (in Old Sumerian), as in lugal-am$_6$ 'he is king'

REMEMBER: A WORD WHICH FEATURES AN AMISSIBLE AUSLAUT DROPS ITS
                  FINAL CONSONANT WHEN IT IS NOT FOLLOWED BY A VOWEL.

TABLE OF SYLLABIC SIGN VALUES: V, CV, VC

Syllables shown linked are written with the same sign.

VOWELS: a   i   e   u   ú
              'à   ì   ù   u₈

STOPS: CV   Voiced   Voiceless

  Labials   ba | bi   bé | | bu | pa | pi   pe | | pu |
                       bí

  Dentals   da | di   de | | du | ta | ti   te | tu
                        dè(NE)
                     | dì |

              | (d)rá | | (d)re6 |

  Velars   ga | gi   ge | + gu   ka | ki   ke | ku
                     | gé | gú | ke4 |
                     | gi4   ge4 |

STOPS: VC

  Labials   aB | iB   eB | uB
                     | íB   éB |
                                              ┌─────────────────────────┐
                                              │ Voiced versus voice-   │
                                              │ less values are not   │
                                              │ distinguished by   │
                                              │ separate VC signs.   │
  Dentals   aD | iD   eD | uD   │   │
                                              │   B = b or p   │
                                              │   D = d or t   │
                                              │   G = g or k   │
  Velars   aG | iG   eG | uG   │   Z = z or s   │
                                              └─────────────────────────┘

FRICATIVES

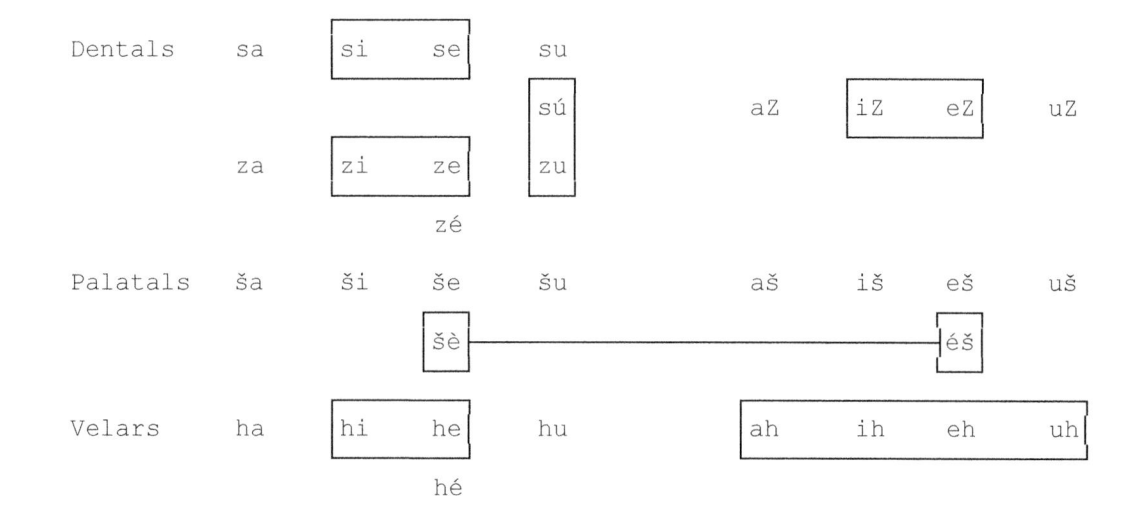

Dentals	sa	si	se	su				
				sú		aZ	iZ	eZ	uZ
	za	zi	ze	zu				
			zé					

Palatals	ša	ši	še	šu		aš	iš	eš	uš
			šè				éš		

Velars	ha	hi	he	hu		ah	ih	eh	uh
			hé						

NASALS

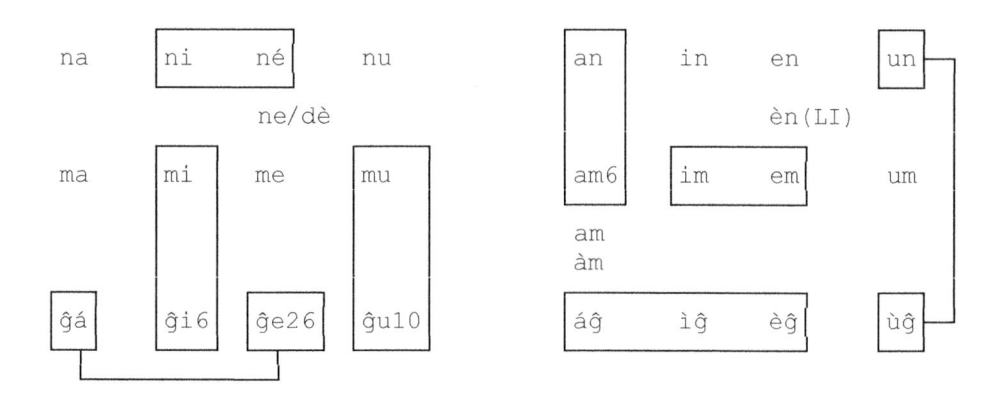

	na	ni	né	nu		an	in	en	un
		ne/dè						èn(LI)	
	ma	mi	me	mu		am6	im	em	um
						am			
						àm			
	ĝá	ĝi6	ĝe26	ĝu10		áĝ	ìĝ	èĝ	ùĝ

LIQUIDS

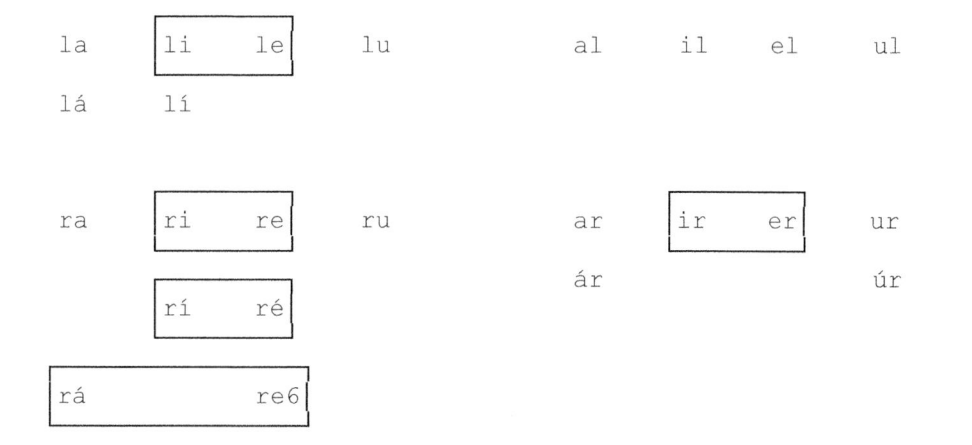

	la	li	le	lu		al	il	el	ul
	lá	lí							

	ra	ri	re	ru		ar	ir	er	ur
		rí	ré			ár			úr
	rá		re6						

PHONOLOGY

What is known about the pronunciation of Sumerian has come down to us very much filtered through the sound system of Akkadian, the latter itself determined only by comparison with the better known phonemic systems of other Semitic languages.

> A phoneme is a minimal speech sound (phone), or a small group of related sounds (allophones), which is capable of signaling a difference in meaning. In English, /b/ and /p/ are separate phonemes because they can differentiate two otherwise identical words, for example "bit" versus "pit." A phoneme can have several different pronunciations (allophones, phonological realizations) and still be recognized as "the same sound." For example, when spoken at normal conversational speed English "ten" and "city" feature two different "t" sounds. "City" has a flapped "d" a bit like the "r" in Spanish pero. Every language has a limited number of vocalic and consonantal phonemes which together constitute its unique phonemic inventory. Phonemes are indicated by slashes /b/, phones by square brackets [b].

The Akkadian scribal schools produced signlists and vocabularies which spelled out syllabically how Sumerian signs or words were to be pronounced. These syllabic spellings are the basis of our understanding of the Sumerian sound system, but they are essentially only Akkadian pronunciations of Sumerian vocables. Sounds or distinctions between sounds which did not exist in the Akkadian phonemic inventory were spelled out as best as possible, as the Akkadian speakers heard or understood them.

For example, the essential difference between the sounds that we transcribe as /b/ vs. /p/ or /d/ vs. /t/ and /g/ vs. /k/ might well have been one of minus or plus aspiration rather than a voiced vs. voiceless contrast as in English, e.g. [p] vs. [pʰ].

> Aspiration refers to a following slight puff of air. Voicing refers to the vibration of the vocal cords. A "b" is voiced, a "p" is voiceless. Unlike English, voiceless stops in French or Dutch, for example, are unaspirated.

But Akkadian, like English, probably featured only the latter phonemic contrast, and voiced vs. voiceless is how Akkadian speakers no doubt distinguished and pronounced the Sumerian sounds. Our standard transcription of the Sumerian sound system should thus be regarded as only an approximation of how Sumerian was actually pronounced.

VOWELS (§4-15)

Vowels definitely known to have phonemic status include /a/, /e/, /i/ and /u/. A few scholars, most notably S. Lieberman, have posited the existence of an /o/ phoneme, but this idea has not yet gained general acceptance. How the four standard vowels actually sounded in all phonological environments will never be known. By convention we pronounce them with roughly European values, as in Spanish or German; English speakers should by all means avoid English long (alphabet) pronunciations:

> /a/ always as in "father", never as in "day" or "bat"
> /e/ as in "play" or "pet", never as in "she"
> /i/ as in "tree" or "tip", never as in "lie"
> /u/ as in "who" or "hood", never as in "use"

Sumerian had no true phonemic diphthongs such as /aw/ or /oy/. but there are indications of /y/ or /w/ semivowel glides between vowels, e.g. written mu-e-a-áĝ possibly pronounced as /m(u)weyaĝ/. A /y/ representing an /n/ before a root may lie behind writings such as ba-e-√ or ba-a-√ for ba-an-√ or ì-a-√ for in-√ in Ur III and OB texts.

When transcribing words Sumerologists will sometimes separate neighboring vowels with an apostrophe, as in the personal name written a-a-kal-la but transcribed A'akala. This convention is only for legibility; it does not indicate here the presence of a Sumerian

18

glottal stop, a catch or hiatus produced at the back of the throat, as between the two English words "I am" when pronounced slowly and distinctly.

Edzard, 2003 13f., claims the existence of vowel length within roots. See now a more nuanced discussion of vowel quality and length by E.J.M. Smith in Journal of Cuneiform Studies 59 (2007) 19-38. Elsewhere, length usually seems to be only allophonic, serving to take the place of another sound. In Pre-Old Babylonian period Sumerian compensatory lengthening exists, most often the lengthening of a vowel to compensate for the loss of a following /n/. Thus an Ur III text might write in-gi-ì (presumably pronounced [ingi:] with or without nasalization) instead of in-gi-in (a colon [:] indicates lengthening of a preceding sound).

Certain vocalic elements will undergo regular sorts of modifications in specific grammatical and phonological environments. For the pattern of i/e vowel harmony in Old Sumerian Lagaš verbal prefixes see Thomsen §7. In all periods both progressive or anticipatory assimilation (conditioned by a preceding sound) and regressive or lag assimilation (conditioned by a following sound) are common in many environments, generally following predictable patterns.

Thomsen's discussion of vowel "contraction" (§14f.) is inadequate. The phenomena she describes have never been studied rigorously and as a whole, and will certainly turn out to be better described in terms of replacement or deletion of vowels rather than contraction. Specific assimilation, elision, and deletion phenomena will be described individually as they are encountered throughout this grammar.

CONSONANTS (§16-30)

The consonantal phonemes of Sumerian are conventionally represented as follows:

STOPS AND NASALS		Voiced	Voiceless	Nasal	Uncertain Articulation
	Labial	b	p	m	
	Dental	d	t	n	dr
	Velar	g	k	ĝ	
	Glottal		(ʔ)		
FRICATIVES	Dental	z	s		
	Palatal		š		
	Velar		h (IPA [x])		
	Glottal		(H) (IPA [h])		
LIQUIDS		l	l₂	r	

Stops

Stops are consonant sounds which feature an interruption or stopping of the air stream. As mentioned earlier, Sumerian stops may originally have featured a contrast other than voiced vs. voiceless, probably unaspirated vs. aspirated. This contrast is the source of some differing Akkadian spellings for the same Sumerian word, and since modern scholarship is based heavily upon Akkadian lexical materials the student will consequently encounter transliteration variations even in current Sumerological literature. In scholarly works one will find, for example, both gag and kak as spellings for the noun 'peg' or both bàr and pàr for the verb 'to spread out'. P. Steinkeller maintains that "Sumerian roots did not have (what is traditionally transliterated as) voiceless consonants in the final position" (ZA 71, 27; cf. I. J. Gelb MAD 2², 32f.). Accordingly the final stops permitted are thus only /b d g/ and not /p t k/, and one should, for example, read gag rather than kak at least in older Sumerian texts. This rule is not rigorously observed in later periods, nor is it reflected in Sumerological literature.

The Phoneme /dr/

Most scholars now accept the existence of a phoneme /dr/, also spelled /ď/ or /ř/. Edzard 2003, 18f. proposes instead /r/ with a caret (^). The pronunciation is still uncertain. It was first thought to be a biarticulated stop. More recently, Yang Zhi, in Journal of Ancient Civilizations 2 (Changchun [1987] 125) suggested that "The presence of an /s/ in the spelling of this city name [Adab, properly pronounced as /ud^rubu/] — especially in texts outside of Sumer (Ebla and Ugarit) — probably indicates that the consonant /*dr/ was a (retroflex?) fricative which was perceived in these areas as /s/ or at least closer to /s/ than to /r/ or /d/." In §3.3.2 of his forthcoming new grammar, Jagersma argues for an affricate of the shape [ts^h], the aspirated counterpart of the phoneme we transliterate as /z/ but he claims was pronounced as an unaspirated voiceless [ts]. J. Black in RA 84 (1984) 108f., 117, summarized previous scholars' views concerning /dr/ and concluded that the writings which illustrate it "may be evidence of a sound change in progress (rhotacism) whereby intervocalic /-d-/ became /-r-/, or of synchronic alternation resulting from allophony" and that "There is no need to assume an 'extra' sound which is neither [d] nor [r]."

/dr/ has been identified in final position in a dozen or so words, thanks to a special Sumerian orthographic convention. When a word ending with /dr/ takes a grammatical suffix featuring a vowel /a/ or /e/, the combination of /dr/ and the following /a/ or /e/ will properly be written with a DU sign, to be read either rá or re₆ respectively. Thus gudr+a(k) 'of the ox' is written gud-rá while gudr+e 'by the ox' is written gud-re₆. (If /dr/ is indeed an actual phoneme, we should in fact probably be transcribing the DU sign as drá and dre₆ in such cases, but rá and re₆ remain the standard writings.) In the Akkadian-speaking environment of the Old Babylonian school texts the phoneme usually resolves itself orthographically as a simple /d/ sound or occasionally as /r/.

The /dr/ phoneme may well occur in initial or medial position in other words, but at present there is no equally obvious way to identify such occurrences with certainty. Candidates for initial /dr/ include dù 'to build', based on the existence of its variant sign values dù/rú, also de₅(g)/ri(g) 'to fall, fell', and du₇/ru₅ 'to gore'. See P. Steinkeller, Journal of Near Eastern Studies 46 (1987) 56 n. 5 and Journal of Cuneiform Studies 35 (1983) 249f.

The Velar Nasal /ĝ/

The velar nasal [ŋ], as in English "sing," is now frequently transliterated as a /g/ capped by a caret (^) symbol, a composite character which can be found in the character sets of modern word processors. More ideal is a /g/ capped by a tilde (~) symbol, but as yet this character is generally available only in typeset books and journals or in linguistically oriented academic word processing programs like Notabene Lingua.

The Akkadian sound system did not feature this phoneme, and the Akkadian lexical texts consequently spelled out Sumerian signs or words containing it only approximately, usually rendering it with a /g/, sometimes also with an /n/ or /m/, also with /ng/ or /mg/. As a result, the existence of the phoneme /ĝ/ was deduced only a few decades ago, and Sumerologists are only now beginning to use the symbol ĝ in close transliteration to distinguish the nasal /ĝ/ from the stop /g/. The practice is still not yet universal, and so, for example, balaĝ 'harp' or saĝ 'head' are frequently still written simply balag and sag, especially by Akkadologists. Note that in a number of Sumerian words now known to contain /ĝ/ the phoneme may also be found transcribed as an /n/ or /m/. For example, one finds the words kíĝ 'work', huĝ 'to rent' or alaĝ 'figure' still generally written kin, hun, and alam or alan in current publications, including signlists, although a sign value kíg, or even better proper kíĝ, is now beginning to be seen. Medial /ĝ/ is also seen regularly written ng or mg in a few words, most notably dingir for diĝir 'god' or nimgir for niĝir 'herald'. When learning Sumerian it is vital to learn to write and pronounce correctly all words containing this phoneme, regardless of the older spellings encountered in the literature.

It is now clear that /ĝ/ is a common phoneme in Sumerian, and that it can occur in any position in a word. In English, on the other hand, the sound occurs only in medial or final position, and some practice may be needed to pronounce it smoothly when it begins a word, as in ĝá-e 'I' or ĝuruš 'adult male'.

The presence of an /ĝ/ in final position is most clearly seen when the word is followed by a suffixed /a/ or /e/, in which case proper Sumerian orthography employs the sign ĜÁ to write a syllable composed of /ĝ/ and the following vowel. If the vowel is /a/, ĜÁ represents the sound /ĝa/ and we transliterate it as ĝá. If the vowel is /e/, the same sign is used, but we must transliterate it as ĝe$_{26}$ instead. Compare the participle bùluĝ+a 'nurtured' written bùluĝ-ĝá with the infinitive bùluĝ+e+d+e 'to nurture' written bùluĝ-ĝe$_{26}$-dè. The sign value ĝe$_{26}$ is relatively new and is only now coming into general use. In older literature one will find only the sign value ĝá, regardless of context. For completeness one must also mention the rare value ĝe$_8$(NE) seen in Emesal contexts.

We now know that to render the syllable /ĝu/ the Sumerians used the sign MU, and so current scholars transliterate the sign as ĝu$_{10}$ when the value featuring the velar nasal is required. Unfortunately, in all but the newest Sumerological literature the frequent 1st sg. possessive pronoun -ĝu$_{10}$ 'my' will still be found written -mu, and once again the student must be aware of an older writing of a sign while now carefully distinguishing between, and pronouncing properly, its correct values; thus, for example, mu 'name', but mu-ĝu$_{10}$ (wr. MU-MU) 'my name'. To complicate matters, the writing -mu of the possessive pronoun is actually correct in some contexts. /ĝu/ is the proper pronunciation for the word 'my' in Emegir, the main dialect of Sumerian, while /mu/ is the pronunciation in Emesal, the so-called women's dialect, which is also used in Sumerian liturgical texts.

To spell out words containing the initial syllable /ĝi/ or /ĝe/ the Sumerians employed the MI sign, to which consequently we have now assigned the values ĝi$_6$ and ĝe$_6$. To spell out words featuring the syllable /aĝ/, /eĝ/ or /iĝ/ the sign used was ÁĜ, now given the values èĝ and ìĝ alongside áĝ. For the syllable /uĝ/ the sign used was UN, with the value ùĝ. Thus, for example, the Emesal dialect equivalent of the Emegir dialect word /halam/ 'to obliterate' was pronounced /ĝeleĝ/, and the latter was normally written out syllabically as ĝe$_6$-le-èĝ. See the Table of Syllabic Sign Values on p. 17 for an overview of the orthographic treatment of the phoneme /ĝ/.

Fricatives

We assume that the Sumerian sibilants /s/ and /z/ were pronounced approximately as in English, although A. Jagersma now describes /z/ as an unaspirated affricate [ts]. The phoneme /š/ is the sound "sh" as in "wish."

> Fricatives refer to sounds produced by friction of the air stream against parts of the mouth or throat. A sibilant is a fricative produced in the front or middle of the mouth which has a hissing quality, like "s" or "f." A velar or glottal fricative is produced further back in the mouth or throat. An affricate combines a stop with a following fricative, like [ts] or [dz].

The phoneme usually transliterated as /h/ in Sumerological contexts is the sound written "ch" in German "doch," i.e. a voiceless velar fricative [x]. In Akkadian contexts and in typeset publications it can be transliterated as an h with a breve below it, but in unilingual contexts, as in this grammar, the diacritic can be omitted since, until very recently at least, the existence of a voiceless glottal fricative [h] phoneme, as in English "house," has not been accepted for Sumerian. Note, however, that D.O. Edzard 2003 (pp. 19-20) has tried to build a case for the existence of a kind of glottal "barrier" phoneme, perhaps a true [h], symbolized as /H/ and P. Attinger and a few others now symbolize as a glottal stop [ʔ]. Jagersma 2010 now accepts both [h] and [ʔ].

Liquids

The precise pronunciations of the liquids are uncertain. The /r/ phoneme could have

been trilled or flapped, as in Spanish perro vs. pero, or it could even have been a
voiced velar fricative as is found in German or French. It was certainly not pronounced
like the English /r/ which is a retroflexed vowel rather than a consonant.

Sumerian may have had two kinds of /l/ phonemes. The primary /l/ phoneme was probably
pronounced approximately as it is in English, but this is only an assumption; several
types of lateral resonants occur among the world's languages. The second /l/ phoneme may
be evidenced thus far only in final position and in only a few words. We have no real
idea of how it was actually pronounced. It is indicated orthographically by the use of
the sign LÁ rather than LA when a word ending with it is followed by an /a/ vowel as in
líl+a(k) 'of the air' written líl-lá. This second /l/ phoneme is never given any
distinguishing diacritic in our literature. It occurs only rarely, primarily in the
words líl 'air', gibil 'new', pél 'to spoil', and $di_4(l)$-$di_4(l)$-lá/la 'little ones,
children' (a specialized pronunciation variant of *tur-tur-ra), and perhaps also in ul,
túl, dul/dul_4 and in a few more poorly attested roots. Palatalization [l^y] is suggested
by writings such as é-ki-tuš-akkil-ìa(NI)-ni (Gudea 75 rev. 1) or lá(LAL)-ìa 'surplus'.
Note also the (etymological) /l/ and /n/ variation in certain words, e.g. lú versus the
old noun formative nu- or lagal versus nagal 'vizier'. M. Yoshikawa, Acta Sumerologica
12 (1990) 339-344, offers arguments discounting the existence of a second /l/ phoneme.
Jagersma 2010 also denies its existence.

STRESS-RELATED PHENOMENA

Since J. Krecher's groundbreaking "Verschlusslaute und Betonung im Sumerischen," AOAT 1
(1969) 157ff., little further work has been accomplished on stress in Sumerian and its
effects on word structure. Common pronunciation modifications in Sumerian that are
probably stress related are instances of aphaeresis, syncope, or apocope, that is,
deletion of sounds at the beginning, middle or the ends of words. Compare the variants
ù-sún/sún 'wild cow', or ù-tu(d)/tu(d) 'to give birth'. Examples of deleted sounds
within reduplicated words are the adjectives dadag 'pure' < dág-dág or zazalag
'shining' < zalag-zalag. P. Steinkeller (Third-Millennium Texts in the Iraq Museum
(1992) 47) following E. Sollberger has recently reaffirmed a nice solution to the
problem of the proper pronunciation of the word for 'goat', which had long been read ùz
but currently is read ud_5 to account for instances with a following -da sign. The long
form of the word can be understood as /uzud/, which, when followed by a vowel becomes
/uzd/, e.g. uzud+a > /uzuda/ > /uzda/ written ùz-da. When no vowel follows, /uzud/ may
well reduce to /uz/, whence the standard sign value ÙZ. A reading ud_5 would therefore
not be strictly necessary, though it is attested in Proto-Ea 875 and so must be regarded
as the standard OB value. A similar example may be the adjective commonly written
kalag-ga 'strong', but which is probably better understood as a syncopated form
kalag+a > /kalga/, in which case we should now regularly transliterate kal-ga. A
slightly different phenomenon is the deletion of intervocalic nasals in pairs of sign
values such as sumun/sun 'old', súmun/sún 'wild cow', sumur/súr 'angry', nimin/nin_5
'forty', umuš/$uš_4$ 'understanding', tumu/tu_{15} 'wind', etc. The phenomenon of sound
deletion, some of which may be due to stress patterns, could be much more extensive
in Sumerian than the conservative logographic writing system has led us to believe.

EMESAL DIALECT   (§559-566)

In addition to the main dialect of Sumerian called eme-gi_7(r) or eme-gir_{15} 'native
tongue', there existed a female dialect or sociolect called eme-sal 'thin/fine tongue',
used mainly for direct speech of female deities and in religious lamentations and
liturgical texts recited by the gala priest recorded from the Old Babylonian to Late
Babylonian periods. As briefly indicated above, it is differentiated from the main
dialect mainly by regular sound changes, occasionally also by substitutions of different words altogether. See Manfred Schretter, Emesal-Studien (Innsbruck, 1990) for
an exhaustive treatment of the subject and R. Borger in AOAT 305 (2003) 622f. a full list
of attested eme-sal words. See further the appendix to this grammar on p. 151.

NOUNS, ADJECTIVES AND ADVERBS

NOUNS AND NOMINAL COMPOUNDS (§47-78)

Words that can be classed as nouns in Sumerian, which can function as heads of nominal chains (see next lesson), include primary nouns like dumu 'son, child', or é 'house, temple', and a number of verbal roots employed as nouns such as bar 'exterior', u_5 'cabin', ti 'life', bùru 'hole', or ba 'allotment'. The stock of primary nouns was relatively limited, and the language relied instead upon a large number of different types of nominal compounds to render experience, including most notably:

1) Compounds formed by juxtaposition of primary nouns such as an-ki 'heaven and earth', saĝ-men 'head crown', é-kur 'house (that is a) mountain' (the temple of the god Enlil in Nippur), ka-làl 'mouth (that is) honey', an-úr 'heaven base' > 'horizon', an-šà 'heaven center', kalam-šà 'country interior', é-šà 'house interior', iri-bar 'city exterior' > 'suburb', é-muhaldim 'house (having a) cook' > 'kitchen'.

2) Compounds consisting of one or more nouns and a participle such as dub-sar 'tablet writer > scribe', za-dím 'stone fashioner' > 'lapidary', balaĝ-di 'harp player', gu_4-gaz 'cattle slaughterer', kisal-luh 'courtyard cleaner', ki-ùr 'place (of) leveling)' > 'terrace', ki-tuš 'place (of) dwelling' > 'residence', sa-pàr 'net (of) spreading' > 'casting net', ĝír-udu-úš 'knife (of) sheep killing', lú-éš-gíd 'man (of) rope pulling' > 'surveyor', á-dah 'one who adds an arm' > 'helper'. See the final lesson on participles for other such examples.

3) Compounds consisting of a noun and a common adjective such as é-gal 'big house' > 'palace', dub-sar-mah 'chief scribe', kù-sig_{17} 'yellow silver' > 'gold'.

4) Abstract nouns derived by means of the abstracting prefix nam- such as nam-lugal 'kingship', nam-mah 'loftiness', nam-ti(l) 'life', nam-úš 'death', nam-dumu 'children (as a group)', nam-um-ma 'old (wailing) women (as a group)'.

5) Compounds featuring the productive formative níĝ- 'thing' or the obsolete formative nu- 'person' (< lú), such as níĝ-gi-na 'verified thing' > 'truth, law', níĝ-gig 'bitter/sore thing, sacrilege', níĝ-sa_{10} 'buying thing' > 'price', nu-bànda 'junior (boss-)man' > 'overseer', nu-$kiri_6$(-k) 'man of the orchard' > 'orchard-keeper', or nu-èš(-k) 'man of the shrine' > 'priest', the last two being genitive constructions.

6) Words which are in origin actually short phrases but which function syntactically as nouns, such as the frozen nominalized verbal forms ì-du_8 'he opened' > 'gate-keeper' and in-dub-ba 'that which was heaped up here' > 'demarcation mound' (see Sjöberg, Or 39 [1970] 81), or the frozen cohortative verbal forms ga-ab-šúm 'let me give it' > 'seller', gan-tuš 'let me live here' > 'tenant'. Genitive phrases are common, e.g. gi-nindana(-k) 'reed of one nindan (length) > 'measuring rod', or zà-mu(-k) 'edge of the year' > 'New Year'. Many occupation names are genitive phrases such as lú-ur_5-ra(-k) 'man of the loan' > 'creditor', or niĝir-sila(-k) 'herald of the street', as are many proper nouns, e.g. ^{d}nin-ĝír-su(-k) 'Lord of Girsu' (chief male deity of the capital city of the state of Lagaš).

7) Participles with clear verbal meanings used as substantives such as íl 'porter'.

Gender (§37)

Sumerian features a kind of grammatical gender which has nothing to do with the natural gender categories masculine vs. feminine. Instead, nouns are viewed as either <u>personal</u>, referring to individual human beings, whether singular or plural, or <u>impersonal</u>, generally referring to persons viewed as a group (collectives), animals, places, or things. Some grammars use the terminology "animate" vs. "inanimate," which can be misleading, since the impersonal category is used not only for lifeless objects, but also for animals, groups of persons, and "objectified" individual persons referred to scornfully or dismissively such as slaves — all of which are certainly animate, living things.

The personal vs. impersonal distinction is made evident mainly in certain 3rd person pronoun forms, in the plural marking of nouns, and in the marking of personal dative objects. In the pronominal paradigms where the distinction is maintained, the personal category is nearly always signalled by the presence of a consonantal element /n/, the impersonal by the element /b/. The original difference between these elements was one of <u>deixis</u> (pointing, demonstrating), /n/ designating near-deixis 'this one here', and /b/ <u>far-deixis</u> 'that one there'.

> As in many other languages, the 3rd person pronominal forms probably developed from demonstratives. The Sumerian pronominal suffix -bi, in fact, functions both as a possessive pronoun 'its, their' and as a demonstrative 'this, that', and the demonstrative suffix -ne 'this' and independent demonstrative pronoun ne-e(n) are certainly related to the possessive suffix -(a)ni 'his, her' and probably also to the personal plural locative-terminative verbal infix -ne- 'by/for them' and the nominal personal plural marker -(e)ne.

<u>Number</u> (§65-77)

Sumerian nouns may be understood as singular, plural, or collective (referring to items or individuals viewed as a group) in number. It is important to note that the language is flexible and does not always show a plural form where we might expect it. In addition, Sumerian features a great deal of redundancy in the marking of grammatical relations, and so, for example, if a subject is already marked as plural by a verbal affix, an explicit nominal marker of the plural can be omitted from the subject noun with no loss of meaning, and vice versa. To summarize the marking of number on nouns:

No Mark	The noun is usually singular, but may also be understood as plural or collective; information supplied by the verb or by the context will help to clarify. A number of nouns are intrinsically collective, for example érin 'workers, troops' or ugnim 'army'. In Old Sumerian texts collectives are very common, varying with plural forms; compare the occupation written ugula íl (collective) varying with ugula íl-ne (plural), both meaning 'foreman of porters'.
Reduplicated Noun	The noun is plural, and the notion conveyed is possibly something akin to "all individual persons or items," for example en-en 'all the lords, every single lord'.
Reduplicated Adjective	Reduplication of adjectives may serve the same function as reduplication of nouns, as in diĝir-gal-gal 'all the great gods'. Such a form probably represents an abbreviation of an underlying doubly reduplicated form diĝir-gal diĝir-gal, a construction that is rare but definitely occurring.
Plural Suffix -(e)ne	An explicit mark of the plural of personal nouns only (note that it features the personal gender deictic element /n/); it never occurs with animals or things. The basic form of the suffix seems to have been simply -ne; -e-ne properly appears only when a preceding noun ends in a consonant. This rule breaks down by the Old Babylonian period, however, where the epenthetic /e/ vowel may appear even when it is not needed to separate the initial /n/ of the suffix from a preceding consonant. Thus lugal-e-ne 'kings' and dumu-ne 'sons' are correctly written, while OB lú-ù-ne (< lú-e-ne) 'persons' is a common but hypercorrect writing (the epenthetic vowel often assimilates to a preceding vowel). The converse is true in

	Old Sumerian: -ne often appears where -e-ne is expected. Finally, -(e)ne may co-occur with plural reduplication, e.g. en-en-né-ne 'all the lords', lugal-lugal-ne 'all the kings'.
Adj. Suffix -hi-a	A past participle meaning 'mixed'. Reserved usually for assortments or mixtures of animals or things, for example: u₈ udu-hi-a 'assorted ewes and rams' or anše-hi-a 'various donkeys (of different ages or sexes)'.

Several examples:

> 0.0.4 dabin <u>àga-ús-ne</u> gu₄-da ì-da-gu₇   {àga-ús+(e)ne}
> 4 (ban) barley meal was eaten by the guards with (-da-) the oxen
> (Nik I 130 1:1-3 OS)
> Here "guards" is written explicitly plural.
>
> 0.0.3 dabin <u>àga-ús</u> é-gal-la ì-gu₇
> 3 (ban) barley meal was eaten by the guards in (-a) the palace
> (Nik I 131 1:4-2:1 OS)
> Here "guards" is a collective.
>
> lú šuku dab₅-ba-ne   {dab₅+a+(e)ne}
> The men who (-a) took subsistence allotments
> (HSS 3, 2 1:2 OS)

ARTICLES

Sumerian has no articles, either definite ("the") or indefinite ("a"). Thus the noun lugal may be translated 'the king', 'a king', or just 'king' as required by the context.

ADJECTIVES (§79-83)

<u>Forms of Adjectives</u>

Simple adjectives like gal 'big', tur 'small', mah 'great', or ĝen 'ordinary' are basically verbal roots functioning as noun modifiers: iri gal 'the big city', dumu tur 'the small child'. In form they are perfective participles (described in the final lesson).

Another common kind of adjective, also in form a (past) participle, can be produced from verbal stems using the nominalizing (relativizing) suffix -a, for example é dù-a 'the house which was built' > 'the built house'.

A third kind of adjective regularly takes the same suffix -a, even though these seem to function as simple adjectives without any recognizable past participial meaning, for example kalag-a 'strong, mighty'. Whether this -a is indeed identical with the nominalizing suffix -a is still a matter of occasional controversy.

Finally, common adjectives may also occasionally take the suffix -a, but even after J. Krecher's major 1978 study (Or 47, 376-403, see Thomsen §80), it is ordinarily difficult to sense a difference in meaning between an adjective with and without -a, for example zi(d) vs. zi-da 'righteous, faithful'. That the distinction may be one of lesser or greater "determination" or "definiteness," for example lú du₁₀(g) 'a good man' vs. lú du₁₀-ga 'the good man', cannot be convincingly demonstrated. If the adjectival suffix -a is truly identical with the nominalizing particle -a, then the contrast may consist in whatever slight difference in meaning can be discerned between a simple adjective as a kind of present participle 'good man' and a past participle lú du₁₀-ga 'the man who is/was good', or the like.

tigi níĝ du₁₀(-ga) Constructions

Related to the problem of adjectives marked with the suffix -a are appositional attributive constructions which employ the term níĝ 'thing' between a head noun and a modifying adjective that often, though not always, features the suffix -a. A good example is the poetic expression tigi níĝ du₁₀-ga 'tigi-hymn which is a good thing' = 'the good tigi-hymn'. Following are three examples featuring adjectival roots with suffix -a and a níĝ which seems to serve only a stylistic purpose. The fourth example shows the same construction with kalag, which regularly takes the suffix -a:

    dím-ma níĝ sa₆-ga   {sa₆(g)+a}
    excellent judgment
    (Šulgi B 10 Ur III)

    ĝišbun níĝ du₁₀-ga mu-un-na-an-ni-ĝál   {du₁₀(g)+a}
    He produced a fine banquet there (-ni-) for her (-na-)
    (Iddin-Dagan A 204 OB)

    asila níĝ húl-húl-la-šè   {húl+húl+a}
    amidst very happy rejoicing
    (RIME 4.3.7.3 Sumerian 74 OB)

    uruda níĝ kal-ga   {kal(a)g+a}
    Strong Copper
    (Debate Between Copper and Silver passim OB)

Multiple adjectives

A noun can be qualified by multiple adjectives (as well as other attributives), including participles (marked with -a), within a nominal chain, for example:

    anše tur mah
    donkeys small and big
    (Nik I 203 iv 1 OS)

    sá-du₁₁ kas gíg du₁₀-ga-kam   {du₁₀(g)+a+ak+am}
    it is (-am) a regular offering of (-ak) good black beer
    (TSA 34 3:10 OS)

    (lú) zu-a kal-la-ni   {zu+a kal+a+(a)ni}
    (persons) who were known and dear to him
    (Lugalbanda and Enmerkar 5 OB)

Reduplication of Adjectives

Adjectives are often reduplicated, and it seems clear that this reduplication may signify either intensification of the adjectival idea or plurality of the modified noun (as noted above). Thus diĝir gal-gal might indicate 'the very great god' or 'the great gods.' Many common adjectives reduplicate to indicate intensity, e.g. kal 'precious' vs. kal-kal 'very precious', or šen 'clean', vs. šen-šen 'very clean, immaculate'. Occasionally one encounters such revealing syntax as péš ĝiš-gi níĝ kun sù kun sù-da 'canebrake mice, things with very long tails' (Nanna's Journey 275 OB), where one might otherwise expect just níĝ kun sù-sù-da. Since adjectives are basically verbal roots, the plural reduplication of roots commonly seen in verbal forms is naturally to be expected also in adjectives. Cf. further the plural past participle de₅-de₅-ga 'collected ones (dead animals)' or níĝ-gi-na 'right thing, law' {gi(n)+a} vs. níĝ-gi-gi-na 'all the laws' (Gudea Statue B 7:38 Ur III). Some textual examples:

```
4 ninda-bàppir gal-gal  1 ninda-bàppir tur-tur
4 extra-big beer-breads, 1 extra-small beer-bread
(Genava 26, 53 3:2-3 OS)
```
Reference to a single bread makes the meaning unambiguous.

```
1 giš ù-suh₅ gal-gal
1 very large pine
(VS 27, 44, 1:1 OS)
```
Reference to a single pine makes the meaning unambiguous.

```
dim gal-gal ki-a mi-ni-si-si
Many (very) big mooring poles he sank into the earth
(Gudea, Cyl A 22:11 Ur III)
```
Verb shows plural reduplication, but the adjective is ambiguous.

```
2 mùd gaz-gaz-za                                              {gaz-gaz+a}
2 smashed m.-vessels
(DP 488 2:2 OS)
```
Unclear: plural reduplication or 'smashed to bits'?

In languages like Sumerian which show reduplicated nominal or verbal roots, color terms tend to be reduplicated. See the discussion by M. Civil, EBLA 1975-1985 (1987) 155 n. 32. In early texts some color adjectives are explicitly reduplicated. For the term 'white' the reduplicated pronunciation continues into later periods, though with a change in the writing: OS bar₆-bar₆ > OB babbar(BAR₆). The term 'black' on the other hand was rarely written reduplicated: gíg-gíg. More frequent was the writing gíg which is probably always to be read giggi(GÍG). Compare common OB ku₁₀-ku₁₀ (or kúkku)) 'dark'. Other color terms are only sometimes reduplicated in later periods, e.g. si₁₂-si₁₂(SIG₇) vs. sig₇(-ga) 'yellow/green',, or gùn-gùn(-na) vs. gùn(-na) 'multi-colored, dappled'. A few non-color adjectives are also standardly reduplicated, notably ku₇-ku₇ 'sweet', dadag 'pure' (< dág-dág), zazalag (< zalag-zalag) 'shining, clean'.

Transliterating Adjectives

In older text editions adjectives are regularly transliterated linked with hyphens to the nouns they modify. In modern editions more and more scholars are beginning to omit the hyphens and transliterate adjectives as words separate from their head nouns. Both conventions have drawbacks. Linking the adjective aids in analysis and translation by emphasizing the structure of the nominal chain involved, but linking can also produce awkwardly long chains and can tend to obscure the notion of what is a word in Sumerian. As of the 2013 revision, this grammar will follow the new convention and show adjectives, including past participles marked with suffix -a, usually unlinked in transliteration except in compound nouns, whether standard or ad hoc, or in proper nouns (names of persons, temples, fields, and the like).

REMEMBER: THE PERSONAL GENDER CATEGORY REFERS TO PERSONS VIEWED
                 INDIVIDUALLY, WHETHER SINGULAR OR PLURAL.

                 THE IMPERSONAL GENDER CATEGORY REFERS TO PERSONS VIEWED
                 AS A GROUP, TO SLAVES, TO ANIMALS, AND TO THINGS.

THE NOMINAL CHAIN

An ordinary Sumerian verbal sentence or clause will feature a verbal complex and one or more nominal complexes which correspond to such English syntactic categories as subject, object, indirect object, and adverbial or prepositional phrases. Because these complexes are partly agglutinative linkages of stems and affixed grammatical elements, they have come to be referred to as chain formations or simply chains. The next several lessons will discuss the component elements of nominal chains.

All nominal chains consist minimally of two elements: a head noun (simple, compound, or reduplicated) and a case marker which indicates the relationship between the head noun and the other parts of the sentence. The head noun may be modified by several other elements which, if present, fall between it and the case marker in a definite sequence. The position of each permitted class of element in the nominal chain is referred to as its rank order within the chain. The ordering of elements in the most basic type of nominal chain is as follows:

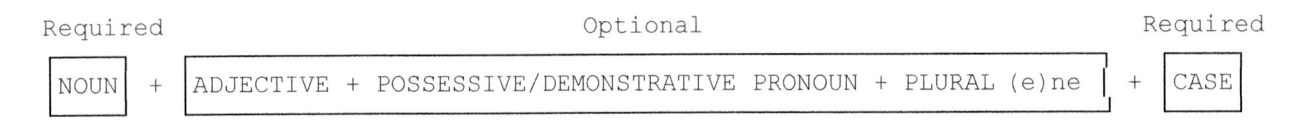

Required   Optional   Required

| NOUN | + | ADJECTIVE + POSSESSIVE/DEMONSTRATIVE PRONOUN + PLURAL (e)ne | + | CASE |

An independent pronoun may take the place of a noun in a nominal chain, but no modification of the pronoun is permitted. Such chains are therefore always quite short, taking the form:

| PRONOUN + CASE |

In all subsequent illustrations of simple nominal (and verbal) chains, grammatical analyses will be shown as sequences of lexical and grammatical elements linked by pluses (+); the expected orthographic realizations will be shown as sequences of sign values linked by hyphens (-). In all illustrations of grammatical phenomena throughout this grammar, pay particular attention to the ways in which stems and agglutinative grammatical affixes combine and affect each other phonologically, and how each resulting chain is finally represented by the writing system. Below, for example, you will note that the final /i/ vowel of the possessive and demonstrative suffixes -(a)ni and -bi is regularly deleted before the plural marker -(e)ne, and that the initial /a/ or /e/ of the suffixes -(a)ni or -(e)ne is not present when the preceding element ends in a vowel.

As you begin, be careful also to note also regular orthographic conventions such as the optional non-significant "picking up" of a final consonant of a root in a syllabic sign used to write a following vowel, e.g. gal+a > gal-la rather than gal-a, or the choice of one sign rather than another in the writing of the same syllable in different grammatical contexts. In what context below, for example, does one find the written sign value né(NI) rather than ne, or bé(BI) rather than bi? What grammatical information is conveyed by these different writings? It is highly likely that certain Sumerian orthographic practices were designed intentionally to supply clues to correct understanding of forms!

Chain Elements	Written Realization	Case and Optional Affixes
dumu+∅	> dumu 'the son' (subject)	absolutive case (-∅)
dumu+(a)ni+∅	> dumu-ni 'his/her son'	possessive + absolutive

dumu+(a)ni+e	>	dumu-né 'by his/her son'	possessive + ergative case (-e)
dumu+bi+e	>	dumu-bé 'by that son'	demonstrative + ergative
dumu+(e)ne+Ø	>	dumu-ne 'the sons'	plural + absolutive
dumu dumu+Ø	>	dumu dumu 'all the sons'	reduplication + absolutive
dumu+tur+ra	>	dumu tur-ra 'for the small son'	adjective + dative case (-ra)
dumu+tur+(a)ni+Ø	>	dumu tur-ra-ni 'his/her small son'	adjective + possessive + absolutive
dumu+tur+bi+ra	>	dumu tur-bi-ra 'for that small son'	adjective + demonstrative + dative
dumu+tur+(e)ne+ra	>	dumu tur-re-ne-ra 'for the small sons'	adjective + plural + dative
dumu+(a)ni+(e)ne+ra	>	dumu-né-ne-ra 'for his/her sons'	possessive + plural + dative
dumu+tur+bi+(e)ne+da	>	dumu tur-bé-ne-da 'with those small sons'	adjective + demonstrative + plural + comitative case (-da)

When analyzing longer nominal chains it is sometimes helpful to think of a chain as a concatention of subunits, each unit, when modified by a following element, forming with that element a new, larger unit which then may be modified by another following element, and so forth. To illustrate, the last example above can be progressively built up as follows:

{dumu + tur}	small son
{{dumu + tur} + bi}	that small son
{{{dumu + tur} + bi} + (e)ne}	those small sons
{{{{dumu + tur} + bi} + (e)ne} + da}	with those small sons

The analysis of a nominal chain becomes a bit more difficult when the head noun is further modified, either by a genitive construction or when the ADJECTIVE slot in the chain is filled by more complex attributives such as relative clauses or other types of appositions. Such expanded types of nominal chain will be seen in later discussions of the genitive case marker and of the nominalizing suffix -a.

Keep in mind that the head noun of a nominal chain need not be a single noun. It can be a nominal compound such as those described in the previous lesson, a noun pluralized by reduplication such as diĝir diĝir 'all the gods', an <u>asyndetic</u> compound of two different nouns such as an ki 'heaven (and) earth' or ama ad-da 'mother (and) father', or an apposition such as iri úri^{ki} 'the city Ur'. For example:

dub-sar tur-re-ne	the junior scribes
en en-bi	all those lords

an ki-a	in (-a) heaven and earth
ama ad-da-ni	his mother and father
iri Lagaš^ki-a	in the city Lagaš

Bahuvrihi modifiers

Another very common type of modification of the head noun in Sumerian is the bahuvrihi attributive. This term from Sanskrit grammar means '(having or characterized by) much rice' and describes _paratactic_ phrases such as lugal á dugud, which is to be translated not 'king who _is_ a weighty arm' (apposition) but rather 'king who _has_ a weighty arm'. Likewise é bur sa₇-sa₇ is a 'temple having many beautifully formed bur vessels', or uĝ saĝ-gíg-ga 'the people having Black Heads' = the Sumerians.

Copula-final chains

A nominal chain will sometimes end with an enclitic copula (one of Sumerian's two verbs "to be"). When this occurs, the copula can replace the final case marker, and the relationship of that chain to the rest of the sentence will be indicated by the verbal chain or must be inferred from context. See the later lesson on the copula.

A copula may also follow a case marker, often with short adverbial expressions as in ana+šè+(a)m ('what' + terminative case + copula 'it is') > a-na-šè-àm 'it is for what' = 'why?', or in predicative genitive constructions such as ĝá+ak+am ('I' + genitive case + 'it is') > ĝá-kam 'it is of me' = 'it is mine'. Compare ki-siki-bi-ta-me 'they (the women) are (-me) from (-ta) that place of wool (weaving)' (HSS 3, 24 6:11 OS).

Preposed adjectives

Adjectives virtually always follow the nouns they modify, in accordance with their rank-order position within the nominal chain. One frequent exception occurs in literary texts, where the adjective kù(g) 'holy' can be found preceding the name of a divinity or even an epic hero: kù ᵈinana(k) 'Holy Inana', kù lugal-bàn-da 'Holy Lugalbanda' (Lugalbanda and Anzu 351/353). Perhaps kù here is better described as a foregrounded (emphasized) adjective standing in apposition to a following noun: 'the holy one, Inana'. This poetic form must be kept distinct from personal names which are genitive constructions of the form kù-ᵈDN(-ak) 'Silver of (a Divine Name)', which have Akkadian parallels of the shape _kasap-DN_. See G. Marchesi, _LUMMA_ (Padova, 2006) 73 n. 384.

REMEMBER: A PROPER NOMINAL CHAIN REGULARLY ENDS WITH A CASE MARKER!

THE PARTS OF A NOMINAL CHAIN ALWAYS APPEAR IN A FIXED ORDER. KEEP THIS RANK ORDER FIRMLY IN MIND!

PRONOUNS AND DEMONSTRATIVES

Early Sumerian texts preserve only a relatively small number of basic pronouns; most plural forms are conspicuously absent. Fuller paradigms can be reconstructed from the later literary and grammatical texts produced in the Akkadian scribal schools, but the traditions behind these sources are uncertain and the forms they display often seem fanciful or otherwise doubtful.

Many Sumerian pronominal forms appear to be historically related, and some are obviously secondary, especially 1st and 2nd plurals (see, for example, the independent pronoun paradigm below). Such secondary forms may have originated by analogy with the fuller paradigms of Akkadian. A few may even have been the work of Akkadian scribes who, unhappy with the more limited Sumerian patterns, filled in the paradigms with artificial forms of their own creation. Whatever the source, some pronominal forms are only attested from periods in which Sumerian was no longer a living language — in some cases only in scholastic grammatical texts — and these must be viewed with caution. In other cases forms are as yet not attested or probably never existed at all.

In the various pronominal paradigms detailed throughout this introduction and also gathered together for ease of comparison in the Summary of Personal Pronoun Forms at the end of this lesson, pronominal elements which are theoretically predictable but not yet actually or reliably attested are indicated by a question mark (?), while elements which the general pattern of the language seems to preclude entirely are indicated by a dash (—).

INDEPENDENT PRONOUNS (§90-99)

The following are the standard citation forms:

```
   Sg  1   ĝá-e   (older ĝe₂₆)        I, me                        (or ĝe₂₆-e)
       2   za-e   (older zé)          you
       3p  e-ne   (older a-ne)        he, him, she, her           (OB also èn)

   Pl  1   me-en-dè-en                (it is) we, us
       2   me-en-zé-en                (it is) you
       3p  e-ne-ne  (older a-ne-ne)   they (personal), them
```

Like nouns, independent pronouns can appear as heads of nominal chains and take case postpositions to indicate their relationship to the rest of the sentence. The Summary of Personal Pronoun Forms illustrates how they combine phonologically and orthographically with following case markers. Note that what appears to be the demonstrative (or ergative?) suffix -e seems to have been historically added onto the later forms of some of these pronouns. This -e element probably had an original determining or topicalizing function. In view of the 2nd person sg. form zé, found in the Gudea inscriptions, it is possible that the normal citation form of the 1st sg. should actually be read ĝe₂₆-e (just ĝe₂₆ in Gudea), in earlier periods at least. Alternately, the two forms may be historical elisions: /ĝae/ > /ĝe:/, /zae/ > /ze:/. The 3rd person forms a-ne and a-ne-ne are found in the Gudea texts and earlier. Finally, the 1st and 2nd plurals are merely free-standing forms of the enclitic copula: -me-en-dè-en 'we are', -me-en-zé-en 'you are'.

Since the affixes of the verbal complex are already capable of expressing most required pronominal ideas, the independent pronouns are generally used only for emphasis or clarity. The chief exception is their use in nominal sentences, especially combined with the genitive and the copular verb "to be" in predicative genitive constructions, e.g. níĝ-bi ĝá-a-kam 'that thing is (-am) mine', for which see the next lesson.

Note in passing that the interjection ga-na 'Up! Come on!' found in the Gudea cylinders usually read by students, is not related either to the 1st sg. independent pronoun or to the verb ĝen 'to come'.

POSSESSIVE SUFFIXES (§101-110)

The Form of the Possessive Pronouns

The Summary of Personal Pronoun Forms illustrates how the possessive suffixes combine with following case markers (be aware that most plural forms are hypothetical). See also Thomsen §105-106. I would add the following notes and alternative explanations to Thomsen's description of these elements:

The main task involved in learning the possessive suffixes is recognizing the ways in which they combine with following elements, the singular forms in particular since many plurals are rarely, if ever, attested in the living stages of the language. You will recall from the discussion of the rank order of the nominal chain that the elements which can follow possessives in a nominal chain include only the personal plural marker -(e)ne, the case markers, and/or the enclitic copula. Compare the paradigms of the possessive pronouns plus following absolutive, ergative, and locative case markers:

```
          ABSOLUTIVE (-Ø)        ERGATIVE    (-e)         LOCATIVE (-a)
                                 LOC.-TERM.  (-e)

Sg 1    -ĝu₁₀       my           -ĝu₁₀        by my        -ĝá         in my
   2    -zu         your         -zu          by your      -za         in your
   3p   -(a)ni      his/her      -(a)né       by his/her   -(a)na      in his/her
   3i   -bi         its          -bé          by its       -ba         in its

Pl 1    -me         our          -me          by our       -me-a       in our
   2    -zu-ne-ne   your (pl.)   -zu-ne-ne    by your      -zu-ne-ne-a in your
   3p   -(a)ne-ne   their        -(a)ne-ne    by their     -(a)ne-ne-a in their
```

The first column shows the standard citation forms of the possessive pronouns. The mark of the absolutive, the case of the subject or patient, is a zero morph (i.e. no overt suffix, conventionally represented by the symbol Ø).

Note that the mark of BOTH the ergative and the locative-terminative cases is -e. In normal orthography -e seldom appears in any clear, obvious form after possessives. Exceptions do occur, for example such writings as -(a)-ni-e in the royal inscriptions of Gudea (ca. 2120 BC), probably to be transliterated rather as -(a)-né-e. In the Ur III Shulgi hymns (originals composed ca. 2075 BC) we find -ĝu₁₀-u₈ < -ĝu₁₀-e, i.e. an assimilation of -e to the preceding /u/ vowel and a possible lengthening: /ĝue/ > /ĝuu/ pronounced [ĝu:]. On the whole, however, one normally cannot distinguish between possessives with and without a following -e, and a nominal chain showing only a possessive at the end could therefore represent either a syntactic subject/patient (absolutive case) or an ergative agent or a locative-terminative indirect object. Thus the phrase lugal-ĝu₁₀ could represent either 'my king' {lugal+ĝu₁₀+Ø} or 'by my king' {lugal+ĝu₁₀+e}. Keep in mind, then, that if a sentence seems to lack a needed ergative or locative-terminative case marker it may well be hidden in a possessive suffix.

Related to this phenomenon is the matter discussed by Thomsen in §107. As the Table of Syllabic Sign Values (p. 16f. above) shows, the NI and BI signs can also be read né and bé; the choice of values is entirely up to the reader of a text. Though it is not universal practice, in this grammar the presence of a presumed case marker -e after the possessive suffixes -ni and -bi will consistently be indicated by the transliterations -né and -bé. Thus lugal+ani+Ø 'his king (subject)' should be transliterated as lugal-a-ni, but lugal+ani+e 'by his king' (ergative) as lugal-a-né. For the deletion of the /i/ vowels in the 3rd person sg. ergative and locative-terminative forms compare the possessive pronouns + personal pl. element paradigm shown immediately below.

The locative case is marked by the suffix -a. Like ergative and locative-terminative -e it properly replaces the /u/ and /i/ vowels of the singular possessive pronouns, but unlike them it always appears overtly after the /e/ vowels of the plural possessive pronouns. In fact, the locative should never elide to any preceding vowel regardless of the context. Exceptions to the standard paradigm do occur, however, especially in connection with the pronominal suffixes -(a)ni and -bi. Compare two nearly exactly parallel Gudea passages, Statue B 8:34-37 and Cylinder B 18:1-3. The first shows the two terms zà-ba 'at its edge' and é-bi-a 'within its temple' while the second writes the same forms, conversely, as zà-bi-a and é-ba. The variation must be stylistic.

Thomsen (§104) believes that the initial /a/ vowel of the 3rd sg. and pl. forms -(a)ni and -(a)ne-ne is *deleted* before vowels. It is the view here, rather, that the basic shapes of the pronouns are -ni and -ne-ne respectively, and that an epenthetic or helping vowel /a/ is *inserted* before them whenever a preceding stem ends in a consonant. Compare the similar use of /e/ in the personal plural marker -(e)ne. These helping vowels are regularly written in classical OB Sumerian, but are frequently omitted, at least in writing, in earlier periods. Thus, a Pre-Sargonic or Gudea text may write lugal-ni 'his king' or lugal-ne 'kings', while the later Akkadian scribes will adhere to the rules and regularly write lugal-a-ni and lugal-e-ne. Having lost contact with the practices of the spoken language, later scribes even begin to regard the helping vowels as required parts of the suffixes and often write helping vowels where they are not needed, as in lú-ù-ne instead of lú-ne < lú+(e)ne 'men, persons'. Do not yield to the temptation of adjusting early, apparently "defective" writings by inserting an /a/ or /e/ into your transliterations of actual text, e.g. lugala-ni, lugal(a)-ni, or lugal-(e)ne. The Sumerians probably pronounced the helping vowels, but they felt no need to write them consistently, and neither should we. Transliterate as written: lugal-ni, lugal-ne, etc.

In reading texts one will encounter the possessive chain -zu-ne as well as the paradigmatic 2nd person pl. possessive suffix -zu-ne-ne. Do not confuse them; they render different ideas. -zu-ne-ne is the proper possessive pronoun, which usually occurs with a sg. head noun, e.g. dumu+zunene > dumu-zu-ne-ne 'your (pl.) son'. -zu-ne represents a 2nd person sg. -zu suffix plus the personal pl. element -(e)ne, and it indicates a plural personal noun, for example dumu+zu+(e)ne > dumu-zu-ne 'your (sg.) sons'.

The rank order of the nominal chain permits the insertion of a personal plural marker between a possessive suffix and a following case marker. The plural marker -(e)ne combines with the singular possessives as follows (plural suffixes plus -(e)ne are, to my knowledge, unattested, barring a few erroneous -ne-ne-ne forms):

	SINGULAR		PLURAL	
1	lugal-ĝu$_{10}$	my king	lugal-ĝu$_{10}$-ne	my kings
2	lugal-zu	your king	lugal-zu-ne	your kings
3p	lugal-a-ni	his/her king	lugal-a-né-ne	his kings
3i	lugal-bi	its/their king	lugal-bé-ne	its kings

Note that the epenthetic vowel /e/ of the plural marker -(e)ne does not appear after the /u/ vowel of the 1st and 2nd person forms. Conversely, the /i/ vowel of the 3rd sg. personal -(a)ni and impersonal -bi is deleted, and /e/ does appear after the resulting consonantal elements /n/ and /b/. Compare the similar phenomena in the possessive pronoun plus ergative case paradigm above. The same deletion of /i/ occurs when -(a)ni or -bi are followed by the genitive (-ak) or locative (-a) postpositions (producing -(a)na or -ba, see next lesson), and these deletion patterns provide good illustrations of the view held throughout this grammar that in Sumerian the preponderance of grammatical information is conveyed principally by consonantal elements, associated vowels serving in many contexts only prosthetically or epenthetically — i.e. as helping or anaptictic sounds at the beginning or in the middle of words respectively — to initiate or separate consonantal elements and so to render them pronounceable.

Uses of the Possessive Pronouns

In addition to literal possession, these pronouns can also indicate a more general referential connection between the possessor and the possessed.

(1) They can indicate a subjective genitive relationship:

    ki-áĝ-ĝá-ni-me-en
    You are (-me-en) her beloved (i.e. the one loved by her).
    (Enmerkar and Ensuhgirana 277 OB)

(2) They can indicate an objective genitive relationship:

    a-ba-a ĝá-gin₇ búr-búr-bi mu-zu
    Who like me will know its revealing (i.e. the revealing of it)?
    (Šulgi C 111 Ur III)

    á-tuku hul-ĝál érim-du-bé-ne tu₁₀-tu₁₀-bi kè(AK)-dè
    Its mighty, evil-doing, inimical ones: in order to perform their smiting
    (i.e. the smiting of them)
    (Civil, JCS 21, 29 1:46-48 Ur III)

(3) They can indicate kinds of indirect object relationships:

    nam-ti-il níĝ-gig-ga-ni hé-a
    May life be his hurtful thing (i.e. be hurtful to him)!
    (Urnamma 28 2:13-14 Ur III)

    ᵈen-líl-le sipa ᵈur-ᵈnamma-ra ki-bala érim-ĝál-la-né si mu-na-an-sá
    Enlil put in order for Ur-Namma his hostile rebel lands (i.e. those
    hostile to him)
    (Urnamma B 14 Ur III)

    inim é-gal-kam inim-ĝar-bi nu-mu-tùm
    It is a command of the palace.
    He shall not bring up its complaint (i.e. a complaint about it)!
    (Sollberger, TCS 1, 130:10-11 Ur III)

    tukum-bi Ur-àm-ma sipa nam-érim-bi ù-un-ku₅ dub-bi zi-re-dam
    If Ur'amma the shepherd has sworn an oath about this, its tablet (i.e. the
    one concerning this) is to be canceled
    (Fish, Cat 533:7-10 Ur III)

    nin₉ bàn-da-ĝu₁₀-gin₇ ír-ĝu₁₀ hé-še₈-še₈
    May you weep my tears (i.e. tears concerning me) like my little sister!
    (Dumuzi's Dream 14 OB)

arhuš-ĝu₁₀ igi-ni-šè hu-mu-ra-ab-bé
May you say my mercy (i.e. mercy <u>for</u> me) before him!
(Hallo, AOAT 25, 218:36 Larsa letter)

ĝá-e ús-sa-zu-me-en
I am your follower (i.e. the one who follows <u>after</u> you)
(Enmerkar and Ensuhgirana 278 OB)

é-gal-la-na níĝ-gu₇ la-ba-na-ĝál tuš-ù-bi nu-ub-du₇   {tuš+e+bi+Ø}
In his palace there was nothing for him to eat,
its dwelling (i.e. dwelling <u>in</u> it) was not suitable there
(Lament over Sumer and Ur 307)

(4) They can indicate an even more tangential connection or relationship:

a-ĝu₁₀ šà-ga šu ba-ni-du₁₁
You put my seed (i.e. the seed for the begetting of me) in the womb
(Gudea, Cyl A 3:8 Ur III)

alaĝ-na-ni mu-tu nam-šita-e ba-gub
He created his stone figure (i.e. a figure of himself) and set it up for prayer
(Gudea Statue M 2:7-3:2 Ur III)

iri-na ú-si₁₉-ni zà-bi-a mu-da-a-nú   {mu+n+da+n+nú}
In his city, his unclean ones (i.e. those unclean with respect to him)
he made lie out away from him (mu-da-) at (-a) its edges
(Gudea Cyl B 18:1)

ᵍᶦˢtir-zu mes kur-ra hé-em
ᵍᶦˢgu-za-bé é-gal lugal-la-ke₄ [me]-te hé-em-mi-ib-ĝál
May your forests be of mountain mes-trees!
May their chairs (i.e. ones made of them) be fit for the king's palace!
(Enki and the World Order 221f. OB)

DEMONSTRATIVE ELEMENTS (§133-138)

    -bi   'that, this'   -bi functions both as the 3rd sg. impersonal possessive suffix and as the most commonly used demonstrative, and so it can be translated 'its, their, this, that, those' depending upon context. The demonstrative sense is probably the more basic, referring to far-deixis, 'that one there', though frequently its demonstrative force is more general: 'the pertinent or relevant one'; in certain contexts it has been compared to our article "the" (P. Steinkeller, Sale Documents p. 34 n. 59, p. 93 n. 271).

    -ne   "this"   -ne indicates near-deixis, 'this one here'. -ne is rare; do not confuse it with the personal plural suffix -(e)ne. This demonstrative also occurs as an independent pronoun ne-en, ne-e, or just ne (compare the copular form ne-me 'these are they' in Steinkeller, Sale Documents No. 45:10 Ur III), or níĝ ne-e '(who has done) this thing' in Ur-Namma Hymn A 156). For a possible origin note ne-e = níĝ-e = Akk. *an-[nu-ú]* 'this' (Emesal Vocabulary III 157 in MSL IV 42), which identifies ne-e as the Emesal pronunciation of the main dialect word meaning 'this thing', also the writing ne-dé-a for usual níĝ-dé-a 'marriage gifts' in Codex Ur-Namma 349.

-ri	'that one there'	-ri indicates remoteness in space or time, 'that one yonder, way over there, way back then'. Compare the later lexical equivalent *nesû* 'to withdraw, recede'. Non-lexical references are somewhat rare except in stereotyped phrases. It occupies the position of an adjective in the nominal chain, e.g. u₄-ri-a 'on that remote day, in olden times'. The connection of this -ri with a homophonous suffix, the so-called Isolating Postposition -ri, remains unclear (see M. Green, JCS 30 (1978) 145).
-e	'this, the'	-e seems to have a a near-deixis or determining force, '(as for) this one'. Like its counterpart -ri, it functions as an adjective, especially in standard expressions built on the noun gú 'river bank', e.g. gú-ri-ta ... gú-e-ta 'from yonder side, over there ... from this side, over here' (Enlil and Sud 70 OB).
-še	'that nearby'	-še is a rare suffix known mainly from lexical sources. It may have the sense 'near one's adressee' (M. Civil & R. Biggs, RA 60 (1966) 7).
ur₅	'this (one)'	This is an independent impersonal pronoun, occurring especially in such phrases as ur₅-gin₇ 'like this, thus' or ur₅-šè(-àm) '(it is) because of this'.

INTERROGATIVE PRONOUNS (§111-127)

The basic interrogative pronouns are a-ba 'who?' (personal), a-na 'what?' (impersonal), and me-a 'where?'. They normally occur with case markers and/or the copula to form a variety of interrogative expressions. The commonest such expressions include (-am is the 3rd sg. enclitic copula 'he/she/it is'):

a-ba-àm	it is who?	=	who is it?
a-na-aš/šè(-àm)	(it is) for what?	=	why?
a-na-àm	it is what?	=	why?
a-na-gin₇(-nam)	(it is) like what?	=	how?
me-a	in where?	=	where?
me-šè	towards where?	=	whither?
me-ta	from where?	=	whence?
cf. en-na-me-šè, en-šè	to until?	=	how long?

REFLEXIVE EXPRESSIONS (§129-132)

ní 'self' can occur either as a self-standing noun as in the compound verb ní - te(n) 'to cool oneself, relax', or modified by a possessive suffix as in ní-zu 'yourself'. It is often combined with a possessive suffix and dimensional case postposition to produce adverbial expressions such as:

ní-ba	in itself
ní-bi-ta	by itself
ní-bi-šè	for itself

Used with genitive -ak it may be translated '(one's) own' as in é ní+ĝu₁₀+ak+a > é ní-ĝá-ka 'in (-a) the house of (-ak) my self' > 'in my own house'.

A related expression is built on the nominal phrase ní-te (var. me-te) 'approaching oneself'. It occurs in 3rd person expressions such as:

```
ní-te-ni          himself, herself          {ní-te+(a)ni+Ø}
ní-te-né          by himself, herself       {ní-te+(a)ni+e}
ní-te-ne-ne       by themselves             {ní-te+(a)nene+e}
ní-te-na          his/her own               {ní-te+(a)ni+ak+Ø}
ní-te-a-ni-ta     by his own free will      {ní-te+(a)ni+ta}
```

INDEFINITE ADJECTIVE (§128)

The indefinite adjective na-me 'any' functions as a neutral term and may be translated positively or negatively depending upon whether the verbal form with which it occurs is positive or negative, e.g. lugal na-me nu-um-ĝen 'some king did not come > no king came'. It often modifies lú 'person', níĝ 'thing', ki 'place', or u₄ 'day, time':

```
lú na-me          some(one), any(one), no (one), none
níĝ na-me         something, anything, nothing
ki na-me          somewhere, nowhere
u₄ na-me          sometime, never
```

Since it is often used elliptically, e.g. <lú> na-me, it has also been described as an indefinite pronoun. Like other adjectives, it may be transliterated either linked with a hyphen to a preceding head noun or left as a self-standing word. And like other adjectives it will normally appear in a nominal chain ending in a case marker, e.g. ki na-me-šè 'to some/no other place' (TCS 1, 77:5 Ur III), é-a še na-me nu-ĝál 'there is not any barley in the house' (MVN 11, 168:13 Ur III).

RELATIVE PRONOUNS

The following nouns or interrogative pronouns can function as virtual relative pronouns in contexts discussed in the lesson on relative clauses and the nominalizing particle -a:

```
lú        the person (who)
níĝ       the thing (which)
ki        the place (where)
a-ba      (the one) who
a-na      (that) which
```

For an analysis of these terms as head nouns rather than formal relative pronouns, see F. Karahashi, "Relative Clauses in Sumerian Revisited. An Interpretation of lú and níĝ from a Syntactic Point of View," AV Jeremy Black (2010) 165-171.

REMEMBER: A NEEDED ERGATIVE OR LOCATIVE-TERMINATIVE POSTPOSITION -e
             MAY BE HIDDEN IN A PRECEDING POSSESSIVE PRONOUN!

             THE POSSESSIVE PRONOUN -bi 'ITS, THEIR' ALSO REGULARLY
             FUNCTIONS AS A DEMONSTRATIVE 'THIS, THAT'!

SUMMARY OF PERSONAL PRONOUN FORMS

INDEPENDENT PRONOUNS (§91)

	Absolutive & Ergative (Ø/e)	Dative (ra/r)	Dimensional (da/ta/šè)
1	ĝá-e (ĝe₂₆-e)	ĝá-(a)-ra/ar*	ĝá-(a)-da
2	za-e (older zé)	za-(a)-ra/ar*	za-(a)-da
3p	e-ne (older a-ne)	e-ne-ra/er	e-ne-da
1	me-en-dè-en	—	—
2	me-en-zé-en	—	—
3p	e-ne-ne (older a-ne-ne)	e-ne-ne-ra/er	e-ne-ne-da

*An -e- or assimilated -a- vowel may occur between the pronouns and case markers in 1st and 2nd sg. forms.

POSSESSIVE PRONOUNS (§101-110)

	Absolutive (Ø)	Erg./Loc.-Term. (e)	Dative (ra)	Terminative (šè)
1	-ĝu₁₀	-ĝu₁₀	-ĝu₁₀-ra/ur	-ĝu₁₀-šè/uš
2	-zu	-zu	-zu-ra/ur	-zu-šè/uš
3p	-(a)-ni	-(a)-né	-(a)-ni-ra/ir	-(a)-ni-šè/iš
3i	-bi	-bé	-bi-ra/ir	-bi-šè/iš
1	-me	-me	-me-ra/(er?)	-me-šè
2	-zu-ne-ne	-zu-ne-ne	-zu-ne-ne-ra/er	-zu-ne-ne-šè
3p	-(a)-ne-ne	-(a)-ne-ne	-(a)-ne-ne-ra/er	-(a)-ne-ne-šè

	Genitive (ak)	Locative (a)	Dimensional (da/ta/šè)	Plural ((e)ne)
1	-ĝá	-ĝá	-ĝu₁₀-da	-ĝu₁₀-ne
2	-za	-za	-zu-da	-zu-ne
3p	-(a)-na	-(a)-na	-(a)-ni-da	-(a)-né-ne
3i	-ba	-ba	-bi-da	-bé-ne
1	-me	-me-a	-me-da	?
2	-zu-ne-ne	-zu-ne-ne-a	-zu-ne-ne-da	?
3p	-(a)-ne-ne	-(a)-ne-ne-a	-(a)-ne-ne-da	?

Note that many plural forms are reconstructed or attested only in OB or later grammatical texts.

THE ADNOMINAL CASES: GENITIVE AND EQUATIVE

The ten suffixed case markers of Sumerian are conventionally referred to as postpositions since they stand after the nouns to which they refer, in contrast to the English prepositions which render similar ideas but which stand before the nouns to which they refer. The case postpositions fall into two broad categories.

The genitive and equative cases indicate relationships between one noun (or pronoun) and another and so may be described as <u>adnominal</u> in function. The remaining cases are <u>adverbal</u> in function, serving to indicate relationships between nouns and verbs. Since they only relate substantives, the genitive and equative cases are marked only by nominal postpositions. The adverbal cases, which mark verbal subjects, agents, and objects, and convey locational or directional ideas, are, by contrast, marked not only by nominal postpositions, but often also by corresponding affixes in verbal forms (the ergative and dimensional prefixes and the subject/patient affixes). When a sentence or clause features both a phrase marked with an adverbal postposition and a corresponding verbal affix, the verbal affix can be said to repeat or <u>resume</u> in the verbal complex information previously stated in the nominal part(s) of the sentence.

THE GENITIVE CASE (§161-168)

<u>The Genitive Construction</u>

The genitive postposition links two nouns to form a genitive construction, resulting in an expanded nominal chain which, like any other, may include the usual adjectival, pronominal or plural modifiers, and which must ultimately end with a case marker. Thus in a sense the genitive postposition can be said always to co-occur with another case marker — the only postposition that may ordinarily do so. The genitive postposition is therefore a different sort of syntactic element, but it is nevertheless conventionally referred to as a case marker.

All regular genitive constructions consist basically of three components: (1) a nomen regens or "ruling/governing noun"; (2) a nomen rectum or "ruled/governed noun"; (3) and the genitive postposition -ak 'of'.

The head nouns of both the <u>regens</u> and <u>rectum</u> may be modified by adjectives or other attributives, possessive or demonstrative pronouns, and plural markers — subject to certain restrictions in the ordering of elements. Returning to the discussion of the rank order of the nominal chain, the following represents the structure of a basic expanded nominal chain featuring a single genitive construction (cf. Thomsen §46):

REGENS	RECTUM	GEN	REGENS MODIFIERS	CASE
noun + adj	noun + adj + poss/dem + plural + ak		poss/dem + plural	case

The rectum (with its genitive marker) can be thought of as a kind of secondary adjectival modifier of the regens, standing between any primary adjectival element and any following possessive or demonstrative pronoun and/or personal plural marker. Study both the structure and the phonological and orthographic shapes of the following examples (deletion of the final /k/ of the genitive will be discussued below):

    {é} + {lugal+ak} + Ø > é lugal-la
                                   The house of the king

    {é} + {lugal+ak} + a > é lugal-la-ka
                                     In (-a) the house of the king

```
{dumu} + {lugal+ani+ak} + e  >  dumu lugal-a-na-ke₄
                                   By (-e) the son of his king

{šeš tur} + {lugal mah+ak} + ene + Ø  >  šeš tur lugal mah-a-ke₄-ne
                                            The young brothers of the lofty king

{šeš tur} + {lugal mah+zu+ak} + bi + ene + Ø  >  šeš tur lugal mah-za-bé-ne
                                                    Those young brothers of
                                                    your lofty king
```

Multiple Genitive Constructions

A Sumerian nominal chain can feature a second or, less commonly, even a third embedded genitive construction, although a third genitive is never graphically indicated. In such cases, one genitive construction becomes the new rectum of another construction, and the genitive postpositions accumulate at the end of the chain:

```
regens + {regens + rectum + ak} + ak
regens + {regens + {regens + rectum + ak} + ak + (ak)}
```

For example:

```
é dumu+ak+Ø                       >  é dumu
                                        The house of the son

é dumu lugal+ak+ak+Ø              >  é dumu lugal-la-ka
                                        The house of the son of the king

é dumu lugal úri(m)^ki+ak+ak+ak+Ø  >  é dumu lugal úri^ki-ma-ka
                                         The house of the son of the king of Ur
```

A chain featuring a double or triple genitive construction could theoretically become quite complex if its components were extensively qualified, but in practice adjectival or pronominal qualification tends towards a minimum in such forms, presumably for the sake of clarity. If such qualification is desired, the language can make use of an anticipatory genitive construction (described below) to help break a long chain into more manageable subsections.

Form of the Genitive Postposition

The genitive postposition in its fullest form takes the shape /ak/. It is, however, subject to special phonological rules depending upon the elements which precede or follow it. More formally, it can be described as a morphophoneme //AK// with four phonemic realizations depending upon its phonological environment, that is, whether it is preceded or followed by a vowel (V), a consonant (C), or a zero morph — i.e. by a word-boundary (#) — which functions phonotactically like a consonant. It is pronounced as follows:

```
/ak/  in environ-  C__V    é lugal+ak+a  > é lugal-a-ka    In (-a) the king's house
      ment

/k/   in environ-  V__V    é dumu+ak+a   > é dumu-ka       In the son's house
      ment

/a/   in environ-  C__C    é lugal+ak+šè > é lugal-a-šè    To (-šè) the king's house
      ment         C__#    é lugal+ak+Ø  > é lugal-a       The king's house

/Ø/   in environ-  V__C    é dumu+ak+šè  > é dumu-šè       To the son's house
      ment         V__#    é dumu+ak+Ø   > é dumu          The son's house
```

Stated less formally, /a/ is retained when a consonant precedes, and /k/ is retained when a vowel follows.

There are a few exceptions to the above scheme. First, in the V_# environment, very rarely /a/ unexpectedly appears instead of /Ø/, probably to resolve a possible ambiguity. For example, using the above illustration é dumu-a might be written instead of é dumu. Second, in pre-Old Babylonian orthography the presence of a /k/ was apparently considered a sufficient sign of a genitive, and an otherwise needed /a/ is often not written, although it was possibly pronounced, e.g. é lugal-ka rather than é lugal-la-ka. In older texts, even a noun's Auslaut can fail to appear, for example ùnu-kam 'it is (-am) of the cattle herdsman' rather than expected ùnu-da-kam < unud+ak+am, as in Nik I 220 ii 4. In the earlier stages of this predominately logographic writing system often only the most significant elements were spelled out; the rest could be left for the native speaker to supply.

When a genitive directly follows a possessive pronoun, the vowels /u/ and /i/ of the sg. pronouns do not appear, and -ak thus behaves as it always does when following consonants. But following the final /e/ of the plural pronouns -ak behaves as expected:

```
Sg 1    -ĝu₁₀+ak+Ø      >   -ĝá         of my
   2    -zu+ak+Ø        >   -za         of your
   3p   -(a)ni+ak+Ø     >   -(a)-na     of his, her
   3i   -bi+ak+Ø        >   -ba         of its, their (coll.)

Pl 1    -me+ak+Ø        >   -me         of our
   2    -zunene+ak+Ø    >   -zu-ne-ne   of your
   3p   -(a)nene+ak+Ø   >   -(a)-ne-ne  of their (personal)
```

For example: ká iri+ĝu₁₀+ak+Ø   >   ká iri-ĝá
                                           The gate of my city

               ká iri+ĝu₁₀+ak+šè   >   ká iri-ĝá-šè
                                           To (-šè) the gate of my city

               é mah lugal+(a)nene+ak+Ø > é mah lugal-la-ne-ne
                                           The lofty house of their king

               é mah lugal+(a)nene+ak+a > é mah lugal-la-ne-ne-ka
                                           In (-a) the lofty house of their king

Note that the possessive pronoun -bi 'its/their' and the demonstrative suffix -bi 'that' are the same element and so follow the same phonological rules. Thus ká tùr+bi+ak > ká tùr-ba can be translated either 'the gate of its/their pen' or 'the gate of that pen'.

Genitive and Locative Compared

When a locative case postposition -a is suffixed to a possessive pronoun, the /u/ and /i/ vowels of the singular pronouns are again deleted, and the resulting forms thus look PRECISELY THE SAME as the genitive forms when no other vocalic suffix follows which will cause the /k/ of the genitive to appear. The two paradigms differ, however, in the plural, where locative -a always appears while the /a/ of the genitive is always deleted. Compare the following possessive pronoun + locative paradigm with the preceding possessive + genitive paradigm:

```
Sg  1   -ĝu₁₀+a    >   -ĝá              in my
    2   -zu+a      >   -za              in your
    3p  -ani+a     >   -(a)-na          in his, her
    3i  -bi+a      >   -ba              in its, their (collective)

Pl  1   -me+a      >   -me-a            in our
    2   -zunene+a  >   -zu-ne-ne-a      in your
    3p  -anene+a   >   -(a)-ne-ne-a     in their (personal)
```

Thus the nominal chain é-za can represent either "of your house" {é+zu+ak} or "in your house" {é+zu+a}, and one must rely upon context to decide which meaning is appropriate. Compare a fuller form featuring both a genitive and a locative: é lugal-za-ka "in the house of your king" {é lugal+zu+ak+a} where the vocalic locative marker causes the /k/ of the genitive to be pronounced. Contrast, on the other hand, a chain such as é lugal-za-šè, which ends in the terminative case marker -šè "towards." Here again -za- can only be analyzed as pronoun plus genitive even though the final /k/ is not visible; a locative is impossible since only the genitive can be followed by another case marker. Thus analyze é lugal+zu+ak+šè "to the house of your king."

Irregular Genitive Patterns

There are four noteworthy uses of the genitive which do not conform to the strict REGENS + RECTUM + AK pattern:

1. ANTICIPATORY GENITIVE (§164). Here the rectum precedes the regens, and the regens is marked by a possessive suffix in agreement with the rectum:

     lugal+ak diĝir+(a)ni+Ø   >   lugal-la diĝir-ra-ni   Of the king his god =
                                                           The god of the king

     udu+ak lugal+bi+Ø   >   udu lugal-bi   Of the sheep its owner =
                                                           The owner of the sheep

The anticipatory genitive is an EXTREMELY common Sumerian construction, used not only as a stylistic alternative to the ordinary genitive construction, but also to help simplify more complex nominal chains by breaking them into more manageable subsections. It is also a pattern that is REGULARLY missed by the beginner and so one which should be kept firmly in mind in the early stages of study.

2. GENITIVE WITHOUT REGENS (§167). Here the regens has been deleted and is merely understood: úri(m)^ki+ak > úri^ki-ma "he of Ur, the Urimite," standing for an underlying <dumu> úri^ki-ma "son/citizen of Ur" or <lú> úri^ki-ma "man of Ur." Compare Old Sumerian DP 119 4:6 where previously listed personnel are summarized as Géme-^dBa-ú-ka-me "they are (personnel) of Geme-Ba'u(-k)"; many parallel texts actually write the expected lú. This sort of elliptical genitive construction is common in gentilics (terms referring to ethnic origin or national identity), as above, in names of occupations, and in connection with certain types of subordinate clauses which will be discussed later apropos of the nominalizing suffix -a and the syntax of relative clauses.

3. PREDICATIVE GENITIVE. Here a genitive without regens is used with a form of the copular verb "to be" to generate predicates of nominal sentences or clauses. (A nominal sentence is an "X = Y" sentence in which the subject is identified with a predicate noun, pronoun, or adjective, as in "Šulgi is king," "the king am I," or "the king is great.")

This construction is especially common with independent pronouns but can also occur freely with nouns, e.g. é-bi šeš-gal-a-kam 'that house is the elder brother's. The following independent pronoun paradigm features the 3rd sg. copular element /am/ "it is"; an extra written -a- vowel is common in the 1st and 2nd person singular forms:

```
Sg 1   ĝá+ak+am      >   ĝá-(a)-kam      it is of me, it is mine
   2   za+ak+am      >   za-(a)-kam      it is yours
   3p  ene+ak+am     >   e-ne-kam        it is his/hers

Pl 1   —
   2   —
   3p  enene+ak+am   >   e-ne-ne-kam     it is theirs
```

The regens underlying such constructions can be thought of as a repeated subject deleted by a syntactic rule to avoid redundancy, for example:

    kù-bi   <kù> ĝá-a-kam   That silver is <silver> of me =
                                                  That silver is mine

    lú-ne   <lú> iri-ba-kam   This man is <a man> of that city =
                                                    This man is of that city

4. GENITIVE AS IMPLICIT AGENT (§166). A genitive can be used in several different contexts to imply an agent, as in older epithets of the form:

    dumu tud+a an+ak+Ø > dumu tu-da an-na   child born of (the god) An =
                                                                            child born by An

Textual instances:

    maš apin-lá è-a PN engar-kam   {engar+ak+am}
    They are (-am) the lease-tax goats brought in of (i.e. by) PN the farmer
    (Nik I 183 1:3-5 OS)

    udu gu₇-a PN kurušda-kam   {kurušda+ak+am}
    They are sheep used of (i.e. by) PN the animal fattener
    (Nik I 148 5:2-4 OS)

    gù-dé-a lú é dù-a-ke₄   {dù+a+ak+e}
    By (-e) Gudea, the man of the built house (i.e. the one who built it)
    (Gudea Cyl A 20:24 Ur III)

This older participial construction with an agent implied by a genitive often occurs in royal inscriptions in alternation with a much more common and more widely used pattern in which the agent is explicitly marked by the ergative postposition -e. This more productive second pattern, which will be mentioned again in the description of Sumerian relative clauses, is referred to as the Mesanepada Construction, after the name of an early king which illustrates it:

    mes an+e pà(d)+a > mes an-né pà-da   Youth chosen by An

Lastly a caution: The beginning student should keep in mind that that most proper names are actually short phrases, and many common divine and royal names are actually genitive constructions which are not always obvious from their usual citation forms, for example:

    ᵈnin-ĝír-su   <   ᵈnin ĝirsu+ak   Queen of (the city) Ĝirsu
    ᵈnin-hur-saĝ   <   ᵈnin hursaĝ+ak   Queen of the Mountains
    ᵈnin-sún   <   ᵈnin sún+ak   Queen of the Wild Cows

ᵈinana	<	ᵈnin an+ak	Queen of Heaven
ᵈdumu-zi-abzu	<	ᵈdumu-zi abzu+ak	Good Child of the Abzu
ur-ᵈnamma	<	ur ᵈnamma+ak	Dog of (the goddess) Namma

When such genitive-based names are followed by vocalic grammatical markers, the /k/ of the inherent genitive naturally reappears, a common source of confusion the first few times it is encountered, for example:

ᵈnin+ĝirsu+ak+e	>	ᵈnin-ĝír-su-ke₄	by (-e) Ningirsu(-k)
dumu ur-ᵈnamma+ak+ak+e	>	dumu ur-ᵈnamma-ka-ke₄	by the son of Ur-Namma(-k)
a-šà ᵈnin+sún+ak+ak(+ak)	>	a-šà ᵈnin-sún-na-ka	of the field of Ninsuna(-k)

A similar confusion can also arise when one first encounters nouns with an intrinsic /k/ Auslaut, i.e. stems that end with an amissible consonant /k/ which, like that of the genitive marker, is regularly deleted when no vowel follows, for example:

énsi(k)+Ø	>	ensí	the governor (subject)
dumu énsi(k)+ak+e	>	dumu énsi-ka-ke₄	by the son of the governor
ka(k)+a/ak	>	ka-ka	in (-a) or of (-ak) the mouth

In the second phrase, the presence of two /k/ sounds may, at first glance, suggest the presence of two genitive markers, an incorrect analysis since only one complete genitive construction (regens + rectum + ak) can be accounted for. The last word could be taken for a reduplicated noun.

* * * * *

THE EQUATIVE CASE (§214ff.)

Like the genitive, the equative case indicates a relationship between nouns or pronouns. Also like the genitive, it is marked only by a nominal postposition; it has no corresponding infix in the verbal chain. It has the basic meaning "like, as," but in subordinate relative clauses (discussed in a later lesson) it can take on temporal adverbial meanings such as "just as," "at the same time as," "as soon as," "during," "while." It is also seen in a variety of standard adverbial expressions such as ur₅-gin₇ 'like this, thus' or húl-la-gin₇ 'happily', or a-na-gin₇ 'like what, how'.

The equative is most often written with the sign GIM, traditionally read simply -gim. There is good evidence, however, that it is more properly to be read -gin₇ and some indication as well that the final /n/ could be dropped. Thus the sign GIM has also been read in the past -gi₁₈ or -ge₁₈ by a few earlier scholars. The problem of determining the actual pronunciation arises owing to the existence of a number of conflicting syllabic writings, including: -gi-im, -gi-in, -ge-en, -gi/ge, -ki/ke, or -gé/ke₄ (the last three instances represent single signs with two possible readings). For a nice discussion of all these forms see now D. Frayne, Royal Inscriptions of Mesopotamia, Early Periods 1 (2008) 95.

The pronunciation may have varied with time and place, and so we will merely follow the current convention of reading the equative as -gin₇ and leave the question of its precise pronunciation in different times and places open. Examples:

ama-ni-gin₇	like her mother
dumu-saĝ lugal-la-gin₇	like the first-born son of the king
a-ba za-e-gin₇	who (is) like you?"

REMEMBER: A GENITIVE CONSTRUCTION = REGENS + RECTUM + AK!

THE /a/ OF THE GENITIVE POSTPOSITION IS LIABLE TO DELETION,
BUT THE LOCATIVE POSTPOSITION -a IS NEVER DELETED!

THE ANTICIPATORY GENITIVE IS THE ONE OF COMMONEST AND
MOST COMMONLY OVERLOOKED SYNTACTIC PATTERNS OF SUMERIAN!

THE COPULA

There are two verbs "to be" in Sumerian. The first is the proper verbal root ĝál 'to be present, to exist'. The second is a syntactic element with the form /me/ or /m/ whose basic function is copular, that is, which marks predicates of non-verbal or <u>nominal sentences</u>. It indicates an identity between two substantives or between a substantive and an adjective, linking them as subject and predicate, as, for example, "I am the king" or "the king is mighty" or most generally "X = Y." Since it only indicates an identity, it conveys no notion of tense, and can be translated "is/are," "was/were," or "will be" according to context. The copula occurs most often as an <u>enclitic</u>, an unstressed element which must always be suffixed to another word, properly the second (predicate) part of a nominal sentence. In simple contexts a copula is optional and often omitted.

THE ENCLITIC COPULA (§541-546; §108)

The enclitic copula is conjugated, and its paradigm is that of the verbal subject (to be discussed in detail later). Note that in this paradigm the 3rd person sg. serves for both personal and impersonal/collective subjects, while the 3rd person plural is reserved for personal subjects only.

1	me + (e)n	>	-me-en	I am	
2	me + (e)n	>	-me-en	you are	
3p/i	m + ∅	>	-(V)m/-àm	he/she/it is; they are	-am₆ in OS
1	me + (e)nden	>	-me-en-dè-en	we are	
2	me + (e)nzen	>	-me-en-zé-en	you are	
3p	me + (e)š	>	-me-eš	they (personal) are	

An old question in the description of the copula forms is whether the /e/ vowel which appears in all of the non-3rd sg. pronominal elements should be analyzed as belonging to a copular stem /me/, or belonging to the pronominal elements, i.e. -en, -eš, etc. If the former, then the /e/ of the stem /me/ is deleted in the 3rd sg. form. If the latter, then the copular stem is just /m/ in all forms. In view of the variant /me/ which can appear in finite copulas (see below), the easiest solution is to posit two allomorphs, /m/ and /me/, which occur in different contexts. This is the position taken here. In keeping with the general hypothesis in this grammar that meaning is primarily carried by consonantal elements in the systems of Sumerian grammatical affixes, I would maintain that here, as is also the case when these subject pronouns occur in finite verbal forms, the /e/ is an epenthetic or helping vowel which is placed between consonantal elements to render them pronounceable and that the verbal subject paradigm is then formally just: -(e)n, -(e)n, -∅, -(e)nden, -(e)nzen, -(e)š. Note that the symbol ∅ here again indicates a zero morph, i.e the 3rd sg. verbal subject marker has no overt representation.

When a word or grammatical suffix preceding the 3rd sg. copula also ends in a consonant, an epenthetic vowel /a/ serves to separate that consonant and the the following copular stem /m/. The resulting form is written -àm(A.AN) (or -am₆(AN) before the time of Gudea), e.g. lugal-àm 'he is king'. The syllable /am/ could also be joined with a preceding consonant in a closed-syllable sign Cam, e.g. lugal-lam (the doubling or "picking up" of the /l/ in the final sign is only an orthographic convention), though such a form is more often seen written with two syllables: lugal-la-àm. When the preceding consonant is the /k/ of the genitive postposition -ak, the /k/ and the copula are usually written together using the KAM sign: ak+m > -a-kam. For example, é lugal-la-kam 'it is the house of the king'.

When a vowel precedes the 3rd sg. copula there is no need to insert an epenthetic vowel /a/ before the /m/, as in dumu-zu-um 'he is your son' or ama-ni-im 'she is his mother', but in later texts one occasionally sees a hyper-correct -àm written here as well. At least some later scribes apparently lost sight of the phonotactic rules and came to regard -àm as the mark of the 3rd sg. copula in all contexts.

In Old Sumerian the 3rd pl. form is usually written just -me, rather than -me-eš, although the full form is known, e.g. sagi-me-eš 'they are cupbearers' (CT 50, 36 7:8). The writing -me-éš (or -me-eš) begins to appear regularly in the later Ur III period.

In Gudea and other Ur III texts, where final /n/ is not always written in a variety of contexts, the 1st or 2nd sg. copula can be written as just -me rather than -me-en. See textual examples at the bottom of this page.

Study the following nominal sentences:

ĝá-e lugal-me-en	I (emphasized) am the king
za-e ir₁₁-me-en	You (emphasized) are a slave
ur-ᵈnamma lugal-àm	Ur-Namma is king
nin-bi ama-ni-im	That lady is his mother
ad-da-ni šeš-zu-um	His father is your brother
lú tur-e-ne šeš-me-eš	The young men are brothers
é-zu gal-la-àm	Your house is big
munus-bi ama lugal-a-kam	That woman is the mother of the king
é-bi ĝá-a-kam	That house is mine (lit. of me)

In the preceding simple illustrations the subjects and predicates are not marked for case (alternately, all might be said to stand in the unmarked absolutive case). Since copular constructions are non-verbal, they may ordinarily feature no adverbal case markers, but predicates can indeed be marked for the adnominal equative case, e.g. lú-bi lugal-gin₇-nam {lugal+gin₇+am} 'that man is like a king'.

When the subject of a copular sentence or clause is an independent pronoun, it is regularly deleted, though it can be retained for emphasis: ⟨ĝá-e⟩ lugal-me-en 'I am king'. On the other hand, the copula can be combined with a pronominal subject to provide a particularly strong emphasis: ĝá-e-me-en lugal-me-en 'I am I, I am the king!' = 'It is indeed I who am the king!'

Some textual examples:

ama nu-tuku-me ama-ĝu₁₀ zé-me   {nu+tuku+me+n} {zé+me+n}
a nu-tuku-me a-ĝu₁₀ zé-me
I am one who has no mother - you are my mother!
I am one who has no father - you are my father!
(Gudea Cyl A 3:6-7 Ur III)

zé-e-me maškim-a-ni hé-me   {zé-e+me+n} {hé+me+n}
It is you who must be his inspector!
(Sollberger, TCS 1, 128:6-7 Ur III}

PN PN₂-ra zi lugal ĝá-e-me ha-na-šúm   {ĝá/ĝe₂₆-e+me+n} {hé+na+Ø+šúm+Ø}
(By the) life of the king,   {dative -ra is resumed by -na-}
it was indeed I who gave PN to PN₂!
(TCS 1, 81:3-7 Ur III)

ADDITIONAL FUNCTIONS OF THE COPULA

The copula frequently serves to mark off appositions or parenthetical insertions within sentences, as in ᵈšul-gi-re lugal-àm é-gal in-dù 'Shulgi(r), (he being) the king, built the palace'.

It can represent strong emphasis in the view of A. Falkenstein (see discussion and references in NSGU II pp. 36-37 ad No. 22:11). A possible example of such a use is:

>   1 sìla mun-àm ka-ka-né ì-sub₆-bé
>   1 quart of salt it shall be that will be rubbed onto her mouth
>   (Ur-Nammu Code §25 Ur III)

Occurrences of the copula at the end of sentences or clauses generally seem likewise to mark off parenthetical or emphasized information, but this usage is usually difficult to understand and is thus often disregarded in translation.

W. Heimpel studied the use of the copula to mark a comparison, varying with the equative postposition -gin₇ 'like' (Studia Pohl Series Minor 2 (1968) 33-36). For the copula as such a similative particle compare a Sumerian-Akkadian bilingual lexical entry where Sum. -àm = Akk. *ki-ma* 'like' (Proto-Aa 8:2, MSL 14, 89).

Some examples for study:

>   udu ab-ba-ĝá 180-àm ù gáb-ús-bi
>   The sheep of my father, they being 180, and their herdsman
>   (NSGU 138:8 Ur III)

>   PN-àm ma-an-šúm bí-in-du₁₁
>   "It was PN, he (-n-) gave it to me (ma-)," he declared regarding it (bí-)
>   (NSGU 127:4-5)

>   PN géme PN₂-kam, é-šu-šúm-ma ì-zàh-àm, buru₁₄-ka PN₃-e in-dab₅
>   PN, being a slave of PN₂ — she having fled to the Ešušuma —
>   was caught by PN₃ during the (time of) harvest
>   (NSGU 214:29-33)

>   u₄ inim lugal nu-ù-da-šub-ba-àm ba-sa₁₀-a   {nu+n+da+šub+Ø+a+am}
>   When he was sold — the king's word not having been *laid down* concerning him
>   (NSGU 71:12-13)

>   PN PN₂-[da] nam-dam-šè-àm da-ga-na nu-ù-nú-a   {nu+n+nú+Ø+a}
>   That PN had not lain in (-n-) the bedroom with PN₂, as in a married state
>   (NSGU 22:9-11)

>   gù-dé-a šà ᵈnin-ĝír-su-ka u₄-dam mu-na-è   {ud+am}
>   For Gudea the meaning of Ninĝirsu came forth like daylight
>   (Gudea Cyl A 12:18-19 Ur III)

>   muš mah-àm a-e im-diri-ga-àm
>   It was like a great snake, one that came floating in on the water
>   (Gudea Cyl A 15:26)

THE FINITE COPULA (§536-540)

The copula can also function as a quasi-finite verb, rather than an enclitic, with the addition of a verbal prefix, often a preformative such as the precative hé- 'may, let' or the negative nu- 'not'. Common forms include:

hé-em or hé-àm	may he/she/it be!	{hé+m+Ø}	(abbreviated as hé-a or hé)
nu-um or nu-àm	he/she/it is not	{nu+m+Ø}	(abbreviated as nu)
nu-me-eš	they are not	{nu+me+š}	

Example:

    kù-bi hé-a še-bi hé-a, ki PN-ta šu la-ba-an-ti-a   {hé+a(m)+Ø}
    Whether it be that silver or that barley —
    that he had not received it from (the place of) PN ...
    (NSGU 208:26-28)

Some have described the negated finite copula instead as a negative enclitic copula, linking it in transliteration to the preceding head noun, e.g. saĝ-nu 'he is not a slave' (e.g. P. Steinkeller, Third-Millennium Texts (1992) p. 30).

Copular subordinate clauses, formed by suffixation of the nominalizing (relativizing) particle -a, are often used to convey the notion "although, even though." In this context, the copular stem allomorph /me/ appears in all forms, and the neutral vocalic prefix ì- is often employed to render the form finite when no other verbal prefix is present:

    á nun ĝal zà-še-ni-šè húl-la ì-me-en-na-ke₄-eš   {i+me+(e)n+a+ak+eš}
    Because I was one showing great strength, delighting over his strong thighs,
    (Šulgi A 27 OB) (= elliptical <nam> ...-a-ak-eš)

    ur-saĝ ug₅-ga ì-me-ša-ke₄-éš   {i+me+(e)š+a+ak+eš}
    Because they were slain heros
    (Gudea Cyl A 26:15)

    lú igi-na sukkal nu-me-a   {nu+me+Ø+a}
    The person in front of her, though he was not a minister,
    (Inana's Descent 291 OB)

    kur-gal ᵈen-líl-da nu-me-a
    Without Great Mountain Enlil
    (Enlil Hymn A 109 OB)

    ùĝ-bi šika ku₅-da nu-me-a bar-ba ba-e-si
    Its people, though they were not broken potsherds, filled its outskirts
    (Lamentation over Ur 211 OB) (-e- resumes -a)

    é-ki saĝa e-me-a   {i+me+Ø+a}
    Eki, though he used to be the temple administrator,
    (CT 50, 26 3:5-6 OS with Lagaš vowel harmony)

One occasionally encounters finite copulas with odd shapes, including forms in which a finite copular stem is conjugated using an added enclitic copular suffix, e.g.

    pi-lu₅-da u₄-bi-ta e-me-am₆   {i+me+am+Ø}
    It was as the custom was in former times
    (Ukg 4 7:26-28 OS, variant has e-me-a)

    sug hé-me-àm
    Truly it had become as a swamp
    (Ur-Namma 27 1:10 Ur III)

^I^PN dumu PN₂ gudu₄ — nu-mu-kuš ì-me-àm — PN₃ dumu PN₄ gudu₄-ke₄ ba-an-tuk
PN, daughter of PN₂ the gudu₄-priest — she being a widow —
was married by PN₃ son of PN₄ the gudu₄-priest
(NSGU 6:2-4 Ur III)

šeš-ĝu₁₀ ᵈnin-ĝír-su ga-nam-me-àm   {gana+me+(a)m+Ø}
Hey, that was in fact my brother Ninĝirsu!
(Gudea Cyl A 5:17 Ur III)
ga-na is an interjection here employed as a prefix.

šu al-la nu-ù-da-me-a-aš   {nu+n+da+me+Ø+a+šè}
Since the hand of (the official) Alla was not (involved) with him
(NSGU 43:4 Ur III)
Here the copula is construed as a completely regular finite verb.

THE PREFORMATIVE nu- AS A FINITE VERB

nu- 'not', which as a preformative normally negates verbal forms, is occasionally
employed as a finite verbal root with either copular or existential meaning, often in
constructions featuring a minimal verbal prefix used primarily to make the form finite.
A common form is V+nu+Ø > in-nu "it was not', with which compare the OB grammatical text
entry in-nu = Akk. *ú-la* 'not (being)' (MSL 4, 164:24). See other examples with prefixes
other than ì- in ETCSL and Thomsen §364.

    lú-še lugal-ĝu₁₀ in-nu.   lú-še lugal-ĝu₁₀ hé-me-a
    That man over there was not my king. Indeed, were that man my king ...
    (Gilgameš and Aga 70-71 OB)

    kur dilmun^ki [(...)] x in-nu
    The land of Dilmun [...] did not exist
    (Emerkar and the Lord of Aratta 12 OB)

    kù ad-da ì-nu
    If there be no silver of (i.e. belonging to) Adda
    (OSP 2, 47 rev. 2 OAkk)

REMEMBER: A COPULA NORMALLY LINKS THE TWO HALVES
                   OF A NOMINAL "X = Y" SENTENCE.

                   A COPULA MAY ALSO INDICATE AN EMPHASIS OR COMPARISON
                   OR SET OFF A PARENTHETICAL INSERTION.

                   THE BASIC VERBAL SUBJECT PARADIGM IS
                   -(e)n, -(e)n, -Ø, -(e)nden, -(e)nzen, -(e)š.

ADVERBS AND NUMERALS

ADVERBS (§84-89)

Adverbs of Manner

Simplex adverbs such as English "fast" or "well" are fairly rare in Sumerian. There are only a limited number of bare adjectival (verbal) roots which can function with adverbial force, e.g. mah 'loftily', gal 'greatly', tur '(in a) small (way)', or hul 'evilly'. These non-marked adverbs are enumerated by J. Krecher in ASJ 9 (1987) 74 and Attinger, Eléments de linguistique sumérien (1993) §105d. Otherwise, Sumerian renders adverbial ideas mainly by means of adverbial expressions ending in case markers. The commonest of these are short phrases consisting usually of only a bare adjectival or verbal root, or a verbal root with a nominalizing (relativizing) -a suffix, followed most often by:

(a) the locative-terminative -e 'by'. Compare the regular use of -e with infinitives discussed in the final lesson, and note that -e often elides to a previous vowel.

    húl-la-e   happily   < húl to be happy
    húl-húl-e   very happily   < ditto

(b) the terminative -šè (or -éš/eš/aš/iš) 'to, as'. Attinger Eléments §105 now calls this the "adverbiative" marker /eš(e)/, distinct from the terminative marker /še/. See further V. Meyer-Lauvin in AV Attinger (2012) 215ff.

    gal-le-eš   greatly, well   < gal big, great
    sud-rá-šè   distantly, by far   < sudr to be far away, distant
    ul-šè   forever   < ul ancient

(c) the sequence -bi-šè (3rd sg. pronoun + terminative)

    gal-bi-šè   greatly, well   < gal big, great
    téš-bi-šè   together   < téš each, single

(d) -bi This last may be a shortened form of -bi-šè, but it is more likely that the sign BI should be read instead as -bé, i.e. the suffix -bi plus a locative-terminative case marker -e which provides the adverbial force in place of the terminative.

    bíl-la-bé   feverishly   < bíl to be hot
    búr-ra-bé   openly   < búr to free, loosen
    diri-bé   surpassingly   < diri(g) to surpass
    gibil-bé   newly   < gibil to be new
    húl-la-bé   happily   < húl to be happy
    lipiš-bé   angrily   < lipiš anger
    téš-bé   all of them   < téš each, single
    ul$_4$-la-bé   quickly   < ul$_4$ to hurry

That the suffix -bi is merely the 3rd sg. impersonal possessive pronoun -bi used with a less evident deictic meaning is suggested by the somewhat rarer adverbial expressions formed by means of other possessive pronouns, for example:

    dili-né   he alone, by himself
                            (impersonal: dili-bé they alone)
    dili-zu-šè   by yourself
    diri-zu-šè   more than you
    silim-ma-né   he being well   {silim+a+(a)ni+e}
    min-na-ne-ne   the two of them, both of them   (mìn+(a)nene+e}
                            (impersonal: min-na-bé both of them)
    húl-la-né/na   he joyfully (cf. Yuhong, NABU 1990/3, 86)

Temporal, Causal, and Localizing Adverbial Expressions (§184; 101; 205)

These are ordinary nominal chains ending in dimensional case postpositions, i.e. the locative -a 'in', ablative -ta 'from', terminative -šè 'to', or locative-terminative -e 'by, at'. In this case the suffix -bi is once again more obviously deictic in meaning, and other possessive pronouns are regularly employed. Common examples include:

ĝi₆-a	in/during the night	
itu-da	in a month, monthly	{itud+a}
u₄-ba	on that day, at that time, then	{ud+bi+a}
u₄-bi-ta	since that time, afterwards	
u₄-da	in/on the day, today; when, if	{ud+a}
u₄-dè	by day	{ud+e}
bar-zu-šè	because of you, for your sake	
mu-bi-šè	because of that, instead of that, about that	
nam-bi-šè	for the sake of that, on the occasion of that	
igi-na	in front of him	
igi-bé	at its front, at the fore	
igi-šè	to the front, to the fore, before	
gaba-bi-šè	facing, opposing, or confronting it	
eger-bé	behind that, after that (locally and temporally)	
eger-bi-ta	since then, thereafter	
eger-(r)a	afterwards	
ki-a	in place, here	
ki-ba	in this place, here	
ki-bi-šè	to that place, thither	
ki-ta	from the place, thence	
ki-ĝá	in/at my place, with me	{ki+ĝu₁₀+a}
šà-ba	in the middle of it, inside it	
šà-bi-ta	out of it, from it	
ugu-bi-a	on top of it	
zà-ba	at it's edge, beside it	

See the lesson on relative clauses for similarly formed adverbial subordinate clauses, and note the subordinating conjunctions such as tukumbi 'if' and en-na 'until'.

Interrogative Expressions

A list of adverbial expressions based on interrogative pronouns such as a-na-šè 'why?' will be found in the lesson dealing with pronouns and demonstratives.

Sentence Adverbs

The origins of terms which Thomsen calls Modal Adverbs (§149) are uncertain, and the following should be learned as independent words:

ì-ne-éš	now	
a-da-al/lam	now	
i-gi₄-in-zu	as if, as though	(wr. igi-zu in Gudea) (B. Alster in Fs. Georg Molin (1983) 122f. suggests instead 'know (this) for sure!' < *i-gin-zu.)

52

NUMERALS (§139-142)

Cardinal Numbers

1	aš, diš, (dili)	60	ĝéš(d)	(wr. DIŠ)
2	min, mìn	600	ĝeš(d)u	(wr. U+DIŠ)
3	eš$_5$			
4	limmu, límmu	3600	šár	
5	ía	36000	šár'u	(wr. ŠÁRx(UxKASKAL))
6	àš			
7	inim, umun$_5$			
8	ussu			
9	ilimmu			
10	u			

Ordinal Numbers

Ordinals are formed in the first instance by use of the genitive /ak/ followed by the copula /am/, e.g. u$_4$ 2-kam 'second day'.

This construction can be extended by the addition of a second genitive /ak/ often with a following locative -a, viz.

2-kam-ma	the second (one)
2-kam-ma-ka	for the second time
u$_4$ 2-kam-ma-ka	on the second day

For a clear and up-to-date description of numerals, including important data from the Ebla texts and discussion of other numerical constructions, see Edzard 2003, pp. 61-67.

Numerical Expressions

Cardinal numbers can be combined with possessive pronouns and case markers to generate adverbial expressions, e.g.

aš-a-né, aša-né	alone, by himself	{aš+(a)ni+e}
min-na-ne-ne	the two of them	{min+(a)nene+Ø}
dili-bé, dili-bi-šè	alone, by itself/themselves	

The adjectives didli (< dili-dili) 'several, various, miscellaneous' and hi-a 'mixed, assorted' are often found qualifying nouns especially in administrative texts, e.g.

lú didli-e-ne	the various men
lú-igi-nigin2 didli	miscellaneous inspection personnel
anše-hi-a	assorted donkeys

Multiplication is indicated by use of the term a-rá 'time(s)', e.g.

mu ^{d}nanna kar-zi-da a-rá 2-kam-aš é-a-na ba-an-ku$_4$ {2+ak+am+šè}
Year Nanna of the Good Quay entered his temple for the second time
(Formula for the 36th regnal year of Šulgi of Ur, -n- resumes -a)

REMEMBER: ADVERBS ARE USUALLY SHORT NOMINAL CHAINS ENDING IN
              CASE MARKERS, MOST OFTEN -e, -eš, -šè, -bé OR -bi-šè

THE ADVERBAL CASES

ABSOLUTIVE -∅ (§38-42; 169)

The absolutive case is unmarked, or more theoretically is marked by a zero morph, symbolized as -∅. This is the case of the sentence subject or patient (defined in the lesson introducing the verb).

ERGATIVE & LOCATIVE-TERMINATIVE -e (§170-174)

As Thomsen observed (§170), one may regard the postposition -e as the mark of "one case with two functions, whose relationship, however, is not entirely clear." Similarly, G. Steiner (ASJ 12, 145 n. 39) speaks of ergative and adessive -e, morphologically identical but functionally differentiated. G. Cunningham (AV J. Black [2010] 47) states: "The ergative case marker can be analyzed as a further grammaticalization, the directive (also referred to as the locative-terminative) being lexically bleached from a meaning such as 'in(to) contact with' to performing the more abstract function of marking the subject of a transitive verb." Jagersma 2010 §7.3 states that the ergative "is not only homonymous but also cognate with the directive case marker." However one wishes to phrase it, this is essentially the position taken in this grammar, and only if their underlying (or historical) identity is understood can we then feel free to speak of the ergative and the locative-terminative as if they were two separate cases. Compare the two quite different functions of the ablative-instrumental case (below). Most scholars have preferred to treat them as distinctly different homophonous cases, even if they possibly split off from a single case at some time in the past.

As the mark of the ergative case, -e refers to the agent, the doer or causer of a verbal event, "by" whom or "because" of which the event takes place. Referred to as the agentive in older literature, scholars now call this case the ergative, following modern linguistic practice for languages like Sumerian whose subject/object marking system is primarily ergative/absolutive in character, rather than the more familiar nominative/accusative orientation which is basic to our Indo-European languages.

As the mark of the locative-terminative case, -e refers to a locality or an object 'by, next to, at' or 'on, upon, onto, over' which the event takes place. This sense can be quite general, and it is sometimes helpful to translate the locative-terminative first as 'with respect to' or 'regarding', and only then to attempt to define the directional or loca-tional idea more precisely with the help of the context. Some scholars have referred to this case as the allative (early Jacobsen), adessive (Steiner, later Jacobsen, Attinger), or directive (Edzard, Krecher, Jagersma, Zólyomi). It combines functions of allative ("to, onto"), adessive ("near, at, by"), locative ("on") and terminative ("to the end point") cases, and so to avoid limiting the range of meaning the less specific traditional term locative-terminative is retained here.

The locative-terminative also has a number of more specialized uses. Most importantly, it marks an otherwise dative object when that object is an impersonal noun: lugal-ra 'to the king' but é-e 'to the house'. Conversely, it will be seen later that a dative is used instead of an ergative to mark a second personal agent in a causative sentence. Thus, there is an intimate syntactic connection between dative and ergative/locative-terminative rection, one whose full implications are only now becoming better understood.

The locative-terminative is often used to form adverbial expressions (a use shared with terminative -šè, see below). For example: húl-la-e 'happily', téš-e 'all together, as one', u$_4$-dè 'by day', ul$_4$-ul$_4$-la-e 'hurriedly', ur$_5$-re 'in this fashion, thus'.

The locative-terminative is the case normally found with the so-called infinitive. It serves either to link the infinitive as a kind of indirect object with the main verb of the sentence, or to produce a more general kind of adverbial clause. For examples see the lesson on participles and infinitives.

The locative-terminative can function as a kind of weak demonstrative or determining element. In this use it is probably related to the near-dexis demonstrative suffix -e. See the lesson dealing with demonstrative pronouns. This is probably also the function which has sometimes been described as *casus pendens* -e (Latin 'hanging case', i.e. a case without a direct syntactic connection with a verb) or even 'vocative' -e, in which the marker serves to anticipate a following specification or to topicalize or focus attention upon the marked noun (or pronoun): lugal-e 'with respect to the king', 'as for the king', 'the king in question'. For examples see P. Attinger, Eléments de linguistique sumérienne (1993) §112a or C. Woods, Acta Sumerologica 22 (2000) 322f.

The locative-terminative occurs in distributive phrases especially in conjunction with the ablative-instrumental postposition -ta, e.g. ĝuruš-e 10 sìla-ta '(rations) per/for (-e) a worker 10 quarts each (-ta)'. Finally, like the terminative (see below) it can also, rarely, mark the second member of a comparison with impersonal nouns (the personal dative serves this function with personal nouns and pronouns): é-bi é-gal lugal-a-ke₄ gal-àm 'that temple is bigger than (i.e. big with respect to) the king's palace'.

-e often does not appear in writing when preceded by a vowel, especially another /e/, but exceptions are not uncommon, especially in later texts where older phonotactic rules are no longer being consistently followed. -e can appear as -a after a preceding /a/ in Ur III and earlier texts, and as -ù (or -u₈) after an /u/, especially in OB, as in the OB writing lú+e > lú-ù 'by the man'. See Thomsen's discussion and examples at §172. One might speculate that -e, instead of completely disappearing after another vowel, regularly assimilates to that preceding vowel and then appears in speech as lengthening of the vowel, although the lengthening is not normally indicated in writing. Compare the phenomenon of the usual OB writing of the infinitive dù-ù-dè 'to build' with its standard Old Sumerian equivalent dù-dè, both representing underlying {dù+e+d+e}.

Contra Thomsen and some others, here we will follow the practice of writing the 3rd person possessive pronoun plus hidden loc.-term. sequences -(a)ni+e and -bi+e as -(a-)né and -bé respectively rather than -(a)ni and -bi. Similarly, we will write the plural sequences -(a)ni+ene and -bi+ene as -(a-)né-ne and -bé-ne.

DATIVE -ra (§175-179)

The dative case can only be used with personal nouns or pronouns. Impersonal objects occurring with verbs that normally take a dative object are marked instead with a locative-terminative -e. The rule is not absolute, however, at least for personal nouns, which occasionally show an -e instead of expected -ra, e.g. ir₁₁ géme ù dumu-níta dumu-munus-ni A-na-ha-né-e ba-na-gi-in 'The slave, the slave woman, and his son and daughter were certified (as belonging) to Anahani' (RTC 290:11-12 Ur III). The -e vs. -ra contrast can be neatly demonstrated by a pair of common Ur III bureaucratic expressions, a qualification of sheep (e.g. ASJ 4, 132:5) and an occupation:

    gud-e ús-sa   (sheep) that follow the oxen
    lugal-ra ús-sa (men) that follow the king

The usual citation form of the dative is -ra, the form it takes after consonants (including amissible Auslauts and the genitive -ak even when the Auslaut or /k/ is not graphically visible). When it follows a vowel, after the possessive suffixes in particular, it may also appear only as -Vr. In texts from periods earlier than the first half of the Ur III Dynasty -Vr is frequently omitted after a vowel and always in Pre-Sargonic (OS) texts at least in writing, and the presence of a dative is then graphically indicated only by a dative dimensional prefix in the verbal chain. For example, compare the following two Pre-Sargonic Lagaš passages (from VAT 4718 and DP 425 respectively):

    en-ig-gal nu-bànda ú-ú ugula e-na-šid   {ugula+ra}
    E. the overseer put it to the account of U. the foreman

en-ig-gal nu-bànda ú-ú agrig-ra e-na-šid {agrig+ra}
E. the overseer put it to the account of U. the steward

An OS example of -ra following an amissible consonant occurs in DP 59 rev. 7:

maš-da-ri-a En-èn-tar-zi-ra mu-na-de₆ {en+entar+zi(d)+ra}
The taxes were brought to (king) Enentarzi

In later stages of the language the old phonotactic rules were often dispensed with and -ra could be employed in all contexts. Thus the phrases lugal+ra 'for the king' and dumu lugal+ak+ra 'for the son of the king' were always written lugal-ra and dumu lugal-la-ra, while lugal+ani+ra 'for his king' could be written lugal-la-ni, lugal-la-ni-ir, or lugal-la-ni-ra depending upon the conventions of the period.

Perhaps the most common use of the dative case is the so-called ethical or benefactive dative, doing something "for the benefit of" someone, and in this general sense it can appear with most verbs, but in particular with verbs of giving such as:

    šúm   to give to
    ba   to allot, apportion, present to

With certain kinds of verbs, however, the dative is used (with personal nouns or pronouns) to convey directional or locational ideas, for example, verbs of:

Motion towards: du/ĝen   to come, go to
                      ku₄(r)   to enter, go in to
                      te(ĝ)   to go up to, approach
                      gurum   to bend, bow to

Position before: ĝál   to be there, be present before
                      gub   to stand before

Emotion: sa₆   to be good, pleasing to
                      gig   to be painful, hurtful to
                      ki(g) áĝ   to love (lit. 'to mete out love to')

Like the locative-terminative with impersonal nouns, personal dative -ra can mark the second member of a comparison with personal nouns or pronouns, e.g.

diĝir ir₉-ra diĝir-re-e-ne-er rib-ba {diĝir+ene+ra}
Mighty god, more outstanding than (all) the gods
(Ibbi-Suen B A 38 OB)

ᵈA-nun-na-ke₄-ne za-e šu-mu-un-ne-íl-en (ᵈanunak+ene+ra)
Thus you were lifted up higher than the Anunna-gods
(Išme-Dagan X 18 OB)

lú-ne-er an-diri = *eli annîm rabi*
He is greater than this one
(OBGT I 332, an OB bilingual grammatical text, -n- resumes -ra)

Occasionally, especially in Ur III texts, -ra, as the quintessential *personal* oblique case marker, replaces other expected postpositions, as in the following legal passage:

1 2/3 ma-na 1/2 gín kù-babbar PN-e PN₂-ra in-da-tuku-a-ke₄-eš
Because PN had (a debt of) 1 2/3 mina 1/2 shekels silver against PN₂
NSGU 117:2-5 (Ur III) (here -ra replaces expected comitative -da)

Finally, it will be seen (p. 88) that the dative can mark a second (instrumental) agent.

LOCATIVE -a (§180-186)

The locative postposition -a generally has the meaning 'in', but it may also be freely translated 'into, on, among', or the like depending upon context. Temporally it can signify 'on (a certain day)' or 'at/in/during (a certain time)'. For example, u₄+bi+a > u₄-ba 'in that day' = 'at that time, then' or uzud gúrum-ma šid-da 'goats accounted for during (the time of) the inspection'. The locative -a is a stable vowel. Unlike the /a/ of the genitive marker -ak it is apparently never elided to a preceding vowel (although nominalizing -a followed by locative -a is normally written as a single /a/ in OB verb forms). This fact has led several current scholars to propose that the locative actually features some initial consonantal sound, probably a glottal stop (so Jagersma 2010), which prevents elision to a preceding vowel: /ʔa/.

Functioning as a "locative of material" -a can indicate the substance from or with which something is made:

    é kù-ga i-ni-in-dù ⁿᵃ⁴za-gìn-na i-ni-in-gùn   {kù(g)+a, zagin+a}
    He built the temple with silver, he colored it with lapis
    (Enki's Journey 7 OB)

In Ur III texts and personal names -a occasionally takes the place of dative -ra. See Thomsen §181, H. Limet, L'Anthroponymie 87 + n. 1, Steinkeller, Sale Documents, p. 15.

Like the terminative or locative-terminative, -a can mark the second member of a comparison, e.g.

    me-bi me gal-gal me-me-a diri-ga
    Its divine power is a very great divine power, surpassing all divine powers
    (Gudea, Cyl A ix 12 Ur III)

    èš nibruᵏⁱ èš abzu-a ab-diri
    Shrine Nippur: the shrine surpassed the Abzu
    (Išme-Dagan C 1 OB)

COMITATIVE -da (§188-194)

The postposition -da is assumed to have been derived from the noun da 'side' through the process called grammaticalisation. Its meaning is '(together) with, therewith, beside, alongside', and with such general senses it can occur with many different types of verbs. It also occurs regularly to mark indirect objects with, for example:

Verbs of mutual or reciprocal activity:

    sá   to be equal with, measure up to, rival
    du₁₄ mú   to quarrel with
    a-da-man du₁₁   to compete, dispute with
    gú lá   to embrace (lit. to hang the neck with)

Certain verbs of emotion:

    húl   to be happy with, rejoice at
    saĝ-ki gíd   to frown at
    ní te/tuku   to be afraid of, fear
    su zi   to get (fearful) gooseflesh at

The comitative can express simple conjunction. Often combined with the suffix -bi it can link two nouns in a nominal phrase, and so some refer to the "conjunction" -bi-da 'and'. (The free-standing conjunction ù 'and', by contrast, is a loan from Akkadian used also to link clauses.) The sequence -bi-da is frequently shortened to -bi in this use,

and so one must keep in mind that a suffix -bi can signify conjunctive 'and' as well as
'that' (demonstrative pronoun) or 'its, their' (possessive pronoun). Examples:

    lú lú-da   man with man   =   man and man, both men
    áb amar-bi-da   cow with its calf   =   cow and calf
    nita munus-bi   male with female   =   male and female

Note the position of -bi-da before a genitive -ak in the following: maš-da-ri-a ki-a-naĝ en-èn-tar-zi du-du saĝa-bi-da-kam 'It is (-am) the m.-tax for the libation places of both Enentarzi and Dudu the administrator' (Nik I 195 1:4-2:3 OS). An Old Sumerian variant of -bi-da is -bi-ta, e.g. šu-níĝin 158 udu sila₄-bi-ta 'total 158 sheep and lambs' (VAT 4444 2:3), either an orthographic variant of -da to be transliterated as -dá, a pronunciation variant, or possibly an actual instrumental -ta postposition with comitative force.

In an <u>abilitative</u> function, the comitative case also provides the only way in Sumerian to convey the notion 'to be able'. This meaning is indicated only in the verb by a comitative dimensional infix. See CAD L 152 *le'û* lexical section for bilingual paradigms from the Old Babylonian and Neo-Babylonian grammatical texts. To illustrate:

    é in-da-an-dù   He built (-n-dù) the house with/by him(self) (in-da-) =
                           He was able to build the house

ABLATIVE-INSTRUMENTAL -ta (§203-212)

As its name indicates, the ablative-instrumental postposition -ta has two different functions. In its <u>ablative</u> use its basic meaning is "removal or separation in space or time." Spatially it signifies "away from (a place)," "out of (an area or container)." Temporally it can be used in adverbial phrases or subordinate clauses to signify "when, since, after (the time that something happened)," especially with u₄ 'day, time':

    u₄-bi-ta   from that day, since that time, thereafter

    u₄ é ba-dù-a-ta   since the day that (-a-) the temple had been built

The ablative tends to replace the locative especially in certain stereotyped expressions such as sahar-ta tuš 'to sit down in the dust', also frequently when action is being described which occurs within a place away from that of the speaker, a usage M. Civil has characterized as "location of remote deixis" (JAOS 103 (1983) 63), as in diĝir-e é-mah-a-ni-ta nam in-tar 'The god decreed destiny from (within) his lofty temple'.

In its <u>instrumental</u> use -ta signifies 'by means of, with', as in "to cut with an ax," "to fill with water." It is also used adverbially to describe emotional states, e.g.:

    lipiš-ta   with anger > angrily
    šà-ga-ni-ta   with his/her heart > willingly
    šà-húl-a-ni-ta   with his/her happy heart > happily

In many instances it is difficult to decide whether -ta is being used in a locative or instrumental sense, for example:

    1 sila₄-ga ne-mur-ta ba-šeĝ₆
    1 suckling lamb was roasted in (with?) hot embers
    (BIN 3, 74:1-2 Ur III)

    (45 sheep and goats) gir₄-ta ba-šeĝ₆
    (45 sheep and goats) were roasted in (with, using?) an oven
    (Kang, SACT I 171:1-4 Ur III)
    (Both references apud Steinkeller, Bulletin on Sumerian Agriculture 8, 62 n. 7)

TERMINATIVE -šè (§195-202)

The usual citation form of the terminative is -šè. The sign ŠÈ, however, also has the value éš. There is evidence to show that the terminative could be pronounced /eš/ when preceded by a consonant or /š/ or /še/ when preceded by a vowel. Compare writings such as gal-le-eš vs. gal-bi-šè 'greatly' or saĝ-biš for saĝ-bi-šè 'to its fore/top'. Jagersma 2010 cites the personal name marked with a terminative lú-níĝ-lagar-e-eš (FAOS 17, 96: 3-5). Thomsen therefore introduced a hybrid form /eše/ as the basic citation form of the terminative. Compare é-me-eš-e ĝe$_{26}$-nu 'Come into our house!' (Inana-Dumuzi Y 33) to be analyzed {é+me+(e)še}. (See also immediately below for P. Attinger's separation of the traditional terminative into two related but functionally different morphemes.) Scholars normally do not attempt to apply these still uncertain rules of phonological variation and for convenience normally read the sign ŠÈ as šè in most environments. See the Summary of Pronouns Chart (p. 38) for the terminative with possessive suffixes.

The general meaning of the terminative is "motion towards and terminating at" a locus or goal. It is common not only with verbs of motion and action but also with with verbs of perceiving or attending, such as "to look at," "to listen to," "to pay attention to."

    en-en-né-ne-šè hal-ha-dam   {en-en+ene+šè)
    It is to be distributed to all the (ancestral) lords
    (DP 222 r. 5:1'-2' OS)

    ka-ta è-a lugal-ĝá-šè ĝizzal$_x$ hé-em-ši-ak
    I have paid attention to what has issued from the mouth of my master
    (Išme-Dagan A 135 OB)

    igi-zi mu-un-ši-in-bar-re-eš sipa ^{d}ur-^{d}namma-ra
    They directed a righteous eye towards him, to shepherd Ur-Namma
    (Ur-Namma B 36 Ur III)
    The personal dative postposition -ra here replaces -šè, but the terminative
    required by the verb is retained in the verbal prefix -n-ši- 'toward him'.

    DN-ra nam-ti PN-a-šè a mu-na-šè-ru
    He dedicated (the votive object) to the deity DN for the life of PN
    (Common OS dedicatory phraseology)

An important secondary use of the terminative is to form adverbial expressions like gal-le-eš "greatly, much, well," u$_4$-dè-eš "like the day," or u$_4$-ul-la-šè "unto distant days, forever." Recall that Attinger (1993, pp. 168-70; 254-5) assigns this adverb-generating function to a newly identified morpheme which he calls the <u>adverbiative</u> with a pronunciation /eš(e)/, to be distinguished from the proper terminative with a pronunciation /še/. Cf. Steible, FAOS 9/2 129, who refers to this function as Terminativ-Adverbialis, a term that calls to mind the Akkadian terminative-adverbial -iš suffix which also generates adverbs. In this function the terminative varies rather freely with the locative-terminative, as in the synonymous expressions téš-e, téš-bé, téš-bi-šè 'together, as one'. Compare the following two sets of parallel passages:

    igi-bi-šè é ba-sa$_{10}$
    Before them (the witnesses) the house was bought
    (Steinkeller, Sales Documents No. 73:18 Ur III)

    igi-bé saĝ ba-šúm
    Before them (the witnesses) the slave was given over
    (ibid., No. 68:17)

    ĝiš UR.UR-šè e-da-lá   {Vn+da+n+lá+Ø}
    He waged man-to-man combat with him
    (Ent 28, 3:10 OS)

  ĝiš UR.UR-e e-da-lá
  He waged man-to-man combat with him
  (Ean 1, 9:1 OS)

Probably related to this adverbiative function is the use of the terminative in the meaning 'as, in the role or status of, for' as in:

  ur-ᵈma-mi maškim-šè in-da-an-gi₄
  He sent back Ur-Mami with him as the commissioner
  (NSGU 121:5 Ur III)

  ᵈšu-ᵈsuen ki-áĝ ᵈnanna lugal ᵈen-líl-le šà-ga-na in-pà
  sipa kalam-ma ù an ub-da límmu-ba-šè
  Šu-Sîn, beloved of Nanna, king (whom) Enlil chose in his heart
  as the shepherd of the nation and of the four world quarters
  (Šu-Sîn No. 7, 5-11 Ur III)

Like the locative-terminative the terminative can mark the second member of a comparison on the pattern of é-gal-la-ni é-zu-šè mah-àm 'his palace is greater than your temple'. Compare the expression diri-zu-šè 'more than you' (Letter Collection B 5:6 OB) For other examples and other specialized uses of the terminative see Thomsen §198-200.

COMPOUND VERBS AND THE STANDARD RECTION OF VERBAL COMPLEMENTS

As previously mentioned, many Sumerian verbs are normally associated with or require complements (indirect objects) standing in particular adverbal cases. This is especially true of what are termed "compound verbs," verbal roots with specific nominal patients (objects) which when used together render ideas often expressed by single words in our familiar western languages. For example, the compound verb ki(g) - áĝ 'to measure out love' = 'to love' presupposes an indirect object indicating the someone (dative) or something (locative-terminative) that is loved. Thomsen's Catalogue of Verbs (pp. 295-323) supplies the typical case used to mark the indirect object for many common verbs including standard compound verbs. It is a helpful resource when one begins to analyze complete Sumerian sentences. The Elementary Sumerian Glossary which is a companion to this grammar includes many compound verbs, listed by their head nouns, and occasionally notes the case postpositions commonly occurring with particular verbs.

REMEMBER: ABSOLUTIVE   -Ø (zero mark of the subject/patient)
       ERGATIVE   -e by (whom, which)
       LOCATIVE-TERMINATIVE -e by, at, on, upon, next to, for (things)
       DATIVE   -ra to, for (persons)
       LOCATIVE   -a in, into, within, among; during
       COMITATIVE   -da together with
       ABLATIVE-INSTRUMENTAL -ta from, out of; by means of
       TERMINATIVE   -šè to, towards, for, as; (adverb formative)

    IF IN DOUBT, TRANSLATE THE LOCATIVE-TERMINATIVE FIRST AS
    'with respect to', THEN USE CONTEXT TO CLARIFY ITS MEANING!

    THE NOMINAL SUFFIX -bi HAS THREE USES:

      POSSESSIVE: its, their
      DEMONSTRATIVE: this, that, these, those
      CONJUNCTIVE: and

INTRODUCTION TO THE VERB

ERGATIVITY (§38-42; 275-278)

In an Indo-European subject/object or nominative/accusative language, an intransitive verb takes only a subject, as in "the king (subject) died." A transitive verb, on the other hand, ordinarily requires not only a nominative subject but also an accusative direct object towards which the action of the verb is "directed" or transferred (thus Latin *trans-itivus* 'gone across'), as in "the king (subject) built the house (object)."

In Sumerian, an ergative language, there is no apparent distinction between transitive and intransitive verbs, the notion of "subject" takes on a decidedly larger meaning, and the notion of "direct object" is not particularly useful at all in describing the working of the verbal system. Some scholars currently working with Sumerian as an ergative language now however follow modern linguistic practice and make a syntactic distinction between the <u>subject</u> of an intransitive verb and the <u>patient</u> (virtual direct object) of a transitive verb, even though both are marked by the same absolutive case. Here we will also follow this practice and speak of a either a subject or patient which experiences or undergoes a state, process or event, versus an <u>agent</u> (from Latin agere "to do") which causes that state or event to happen.

> The term ergative (derived from a Greek verb meaning "to work, do") is used by linguists both to label the case which marks this agent and also to distinguish the languages which feature such an ergative/absolutive contrast from those, like English, which show a nominative/accusative opposition in their basic verbal morphology.

As you begin your study of the verb, it will be very helpful to keep the following axiom in mind:

> Every regular Sumerian sentence or clause will always contain a subject (or patient). An agent, on the other hand, will always be a strictly optional addition to a sentence.

The following two sentences have precisely the same basic syntax in Sumerian:

    lú ba-úš   The man died   lú+Ø ba+√+Ø

    é ba-dù   The house was built   é+Ø ba+√+Ø

lú and é are a subject and patient respectively, both standing in the unmarked absolutive case (-Ø). They are also represented in the verbal chain by the suffix of the 3rd sg. verbal subject (also -Ø, see later in this lesson). ba- is a verbal prefix unimportant to the present discussion. Now compare the same sentences with agents added:

    lugal-e lú ba-an-úš   lugal+e lú+Ø ba+n+√+Ø

    By the king the man died =
    The king caused the man to die =
    The king killed the man

    lugal-e é ba-an-dù   lugal+e é+Ø ba+n+√+Ø

    By the king the house was built =
    The king caused the house to be built =
    The king built the house

Both sentences are again identical in structure. lú and é remain in the absolutive case. lugal 'king' is the agent, marked by the ergative case postposition -e and in the verbal chain by the 3rd sg. personal pronominal prefix -n- (see the full paradigm later in this lesson).

The root úš 'to die' would be considered intransitive in English, the root dù 'to build' transitive. Since there is, however, no meaningful intransitive/transitive distinction in Sumerian, if we wish to gain any sense at all of how Sumerian might have understood the notion "to build (something)" we have no other choice in English but to resort to a passive translation: "to cause (something) to be built." Mentally converting apparent transitive roots to passives may help initially to simplify the task of analyzing Sumerian verbal forms, e.g. dù 'to be built'.

To characterize the ergative pattern more generally in terms of our familiar subject/ direct object and transitivity contrasts:

> In an ergative language, what we would normally call the subject of an intransitive verb and the direct object of a transitive verb are both marked by the same case, in Sumerian (and in many other ergative languages) by the absolutive case, while the subject of a transitive verb is marked differently, in Sumerian by the ergative case.
>
> In a nominative/accusative system, by contrast, the subjects of both intransitive and transitive verbs are marked by the same case, typically the nominative case, while the object of a transitive verb is marked differently, typically by the accusative case.

You may note that Thomsen (§277-286) refers to a Sumerian verb featuring only a subject as having only "one participant." A verb featuring both a patient and an agent is then referred to as a "two participant construction." (Similarly, in my Orientalia 44 (Rome, [1975] article on the ergative system of Sumerian, I refer to the subject/patient and agent as the "first" and "second participant" respectively.) A sentence may also feature additional "participants," i.e. a variety of indirect objects such as dative or locative phrases. Since it is technically possible for a sentence to contain two kinds of participants which are not a patient and agent, a patient and a dative indirect object for example, this terminology is useful only in carefully defined circumstances, and it will be avoided in this introduction.

Lastly, observe how the suffix -Ø and infix -n- in the examples above <u>resume</u> in the verbal chain information already supplied in the nominal chains of the sentences. The underlying purpose for such incorporation of nominal information in the verb is to provide a means of pronominalizing that information. If all the nominal chains of the four preceding examples were deleted, the remaining verbal forms would still be complete Sumerian sentences, but with pronominal, rather than nominal, subjects and agents:

        ba-úš   He died.   ba-an-úš   He killed him.
        ba-dù   It was built.   ba-an-dù   He built it.

TENSE AND ASPECT (§235-241)

While English and other modern European languages show aspectual characteristics, their verbal systems are predominately tense oriented (the major exceptions are the Slavic languages, in which tense and aspect are central and grammatically distinct features). Sumerian, on the other hand, is a predominately aspectual language, in which verbal events are viewed in the simplest terms as either "completed" or "non-completed, ongoing." A perfective verbal form will usually refer to an event which has taken place in the past, but it can also refer to a event which the speaker believes will definitely take place sometime in the future. An imperfective verbal form will usually refer to an event which is happening in the present or will be happening in the future, but it can also refer to action that was on-going in the past. The Sumerian perfective can theoretically therefore be translated by English definite past or future forms ("did, will certainly do"), while the imperfective can be translated by English past, present or future tense forms which do not emphasize or imply completion of action. Progressive, iterative or habilitative expressions will sometimes prove helpful ("was/is/will be doing, did/will do repeatedly, used to do/always does"). Many scholars make use of the native Akkadian grammarians' terms hamṭu 'quick' and marû 'fat, slow' in reference to the Sumerian perfective and imperfective aspects, and the practice will be continued here for convenience despite some past concerns about its appropriateness (see Thomsen §231).

THE SUBJECT/PATIENT PARADIGM FOR PERFECTIVE (hamṭu) VERBS   (§279; 294-299)

A nominal chain representing the (intransitive) subject or (transitive) patient of a sentence stands in the absolutive case. This subject is also marked in the perfective verbal chain by a corresponding pronominal suffix, conjugated for person, number, and gender, placed after the root and any stem modifiers (discussed elsewhere), as follows:

```
Sg  1   -(e)n         I, me
    2   -(e)n         you
    3   -Ø            he/him, she/her, it

Pl  1   -(e)nden      we, us
    2   -(e)nzen      you
    3p  -(e)š         they, them (personal)      (also just -e in OS)
    3i  √-√           they, them (impersonal)    (reduplication)
```

The contrast in the singular between 3rd and non-3rd persons is less startling if one recalls that in the present tense of English verbs a similar, albeit reversed, contrast exists, as in I/you <u>go</u> vs. he/she/it <u>goes</u>.

For the 3rd person singular no distinction is made between personal and impersonal subjects; both are marked by -Ø. For the 3rd person plural the suffix -(e)š is used, but only for personal subjects. In Old Sumerian the final /š/ can be dropped, and the 3rd pl. suffix becomes just -e. This sometimes happens even within the same text as in Nik I 7 or Nik I 14 which show both ba-ug₇-ge-éš and ba-ug₇-ge 'they died' in different lines. Whether the apparently optional deletion of /š/ is a matter of phonology (a difference of dialect or idiolect?) or of orthography is not clear.

Reduplication of the verbal root (represented above as √-√) could serve to indicate plurality of 3rd person impersonal (and occasionally personal) subjects, especially in the older stages of the language. For example:

    máš-gán máš-gán-bi ba-bir-bir
    All its settlements were scattered apart
    (Uruk Lament 5:9 OB)

    sahar-du₆-tag₄-bi eden-na ki ba-ni-ús-ús   {ki+e}
    Its many burial mounds he laid upon the ground in the steppe
    (Ent 28-29, 1:30f. OS, ni- resumes -a, ba- resumes -e}

Just as adjectives could be reduplicated to indicate either pluralization or intensification of the root idea, there is some later evidence to suggest that reduplication of the root in finite verbs could likewise convey intensification as well as pluralization, even though this practice may be a later innovation. Two contiguous lines from a scribal debate may show both uses (unless the first also illustrates pluralization):

```
    é dù-dù-a-ni mu-un-gul-gul èrim-ma-ni mu-un-bu
    nunuz ĝar-ĝar-ra-ni bí-in-gaz-gaz ab-ba im-mi-in-šú
    Her (Bird's) well-built house he (Fish) thoroughly destroyed,
       he tore up her storehouse,
    In it he smashed all her laid eggs and cast them into the sea
    (Bird and Fish 107f. OB)
```

The /e/ vowel of the subject pronouns, shown in parentheses, is, in my view, best considered an epenthetic helping vowel used, when a root ends in a consonant, to separate that consonant from the following consonantal subject suffix. As can be seen in the following examples, this helping vowel can assimilate to the vowel of the preceding verbal stem. (In the traditional Poebel-Falkenstein description the /e/ vowel is regarded instead as morphologically a part of the suffixes (-en, -eš, etc.); it is described as then elided or contracted when a preceding stem ends in a vowel.)

Examples:

ba+du+n	> ba-du-un	I/you go away
ba+gub+n	> ba-gub-bé-en (ba-gub-bu-un)	I/you stood
ba+tuš+Ø	> ba-tuš	He/she/it sat down
ba+dù+Ø	> ba-dù	It was built
ba+tu(d)+nden	> ba-tu-dè-en-dè-en	We were born
ba+ku₄(r)+nzen	> ba-ku₄-re-en-zé-en	You (pl.) entered
ba+šub+š	> ba-šub-bé-eš (ba-šub-bu-uš)	They (people) were cast down
ba+dù+dù	> ba-dù-dù	They (things) were built

THE AGENT PARADIGM FOR PERFECTIVE (hamṭu) VERBS (§280; 290-293)

A nominal chain representing the agent of a sentence stands in the ergative case, marked by the postposition -e. This agent is also marked in a perfective verbal chain by a corresponding verbal prefix conjugated as follows:

1	-Ø/ʔ	I, by me	(Jagersma 2010 posits glottal stop)
2	-e-	you, by you	(-Ø- or assimilated -V- before OB)
3p	-n-	he/she, by him/her	(-Ø- or assimilated -V- before OB)
3i	-b-	it, they, by it/them	
1	—		
2	—		
3p	-n-√-(e)š	they, by them	(-n- often unwritten until mid Ur III)

The rank order position of the ergative prefixes in the verbal prefix chain is always the last slot before the root or, put another way, the preradical position, i.e. the first prefix slot to the left of the root as we transliterate the verbal chain. See the appended Verbal Prefix Chain rank order chart.

The 1st and 2nd sg. elements are problematic in most periods. It may well be that in the earlier stages of the language the same contrast held here as in the paradigm for the verbal subject, i.e. 3rd sg. (-n- or -b-) vs. non-3rd sg. (-∅-, some vowel, or perhaps lengthening of a preceding vowel). As late as Gudea only assimilated forms of 2nd sg. -e- are attested, e.g. ba+e > ba-a-. Similarly, -n- often appears as an assimilated vowel until the end of Ur III, e.g. nu+e > nu-ù-, bí-in- > bí-ì-, etc. -e- may have been a reformulation or creation of the Akkadian scribes. Several of the Old Babylonian grammatical texts (J. Black, Sumerian Grammar in Babylonian Theory [1984]) show what is certainly an artificial distinction: 1st sg. -a- versus 2nd sg. -e-.

In this agent paradigm the distinction personal vs. impersonal is preserved only in the 3rd person pronouns. The 3rd pl. sequence -n-√-(e)š is used only for personal nouns, and the prefix -b-, like the corresponding possessive suffix -bi, is normally used only for impersonal nouns or collective groups of persons. Exceptionally, however, -b- can be used to "objectify" or refer dismissively to persons, especially slaves, as in Inana's Descent 310: ᵈinana iri-zu-šè ĝen-ba e-ne ga-ba-ab-túm-mu-dè-en "Inana, go off to your city, let us take away THAT one (-b-)!" (in cohortative ga- forms preradical -n/b- mark direct objects). -b- instead of -n- can also be found in poorly written OB texts.

1st or 2nd person pl. agent prefixes are not attested and presumably never existed. The 3rd pl. personal prefix is <u>discontinuous</u>, that is, it is composed of a prefix -n- and a suffix -(e)š (an /e/ or an assimilated /V/ appears following a consonant) placed before and after the root respectively. The shape of this affix can give rise to ambiguous verbal forms, since the the prefixed -n- and suffixed -(e)š can each have separate different uses. Compare the following:

lú ba-zi	The man rose	{ba+zi(g)+∅}
lú-ne ba-zi-ge-eš	The men rose	{ba+zi(g)+š}
lugal-e lú ba-an-zi	The king caused the man to rise	{ba+n+zi(g)+∅}
lugal-e lú-ne ba-an-zi-ge-eš	The king caused the men to rise	{ba+n+zi(g)+š}
lugal-e-ne lú ba-an-zi-ge-eš	The kings caused the man to rise	{ba+n+zi(g)+š}

The last two verbal forms are identical in form but not in function. The first includes a 3rd sg. agent marker -n- and a 3rd pl. subject marker -(e)š. The second features the discontinuous 3rd pl. agent marker -n-√-(e)š. If the subject and agent were understood and marked only by pronominal elements in the verbal chain, the bare verbal chain ba-an-zi-ge-eš would be ambiguous, and only the context could determine which meaning was intended. Note further that when the pl. marker -n-√-(e)š is used, the -(e)š suffix displaces any suffixed subject marker. The minimal verbal sentence ba-an-zi-ge-eš could thus actually represent either 'He/she (-n-) caused them (-š) to rise' or 'They (-n-√-(e)š) caused me/you/him/her/it/them to rise'! The verb in the following context passage is ambiguous and could also be translated 'they made him (etc.) return':

ki-ni-šè bí-in-gur-ru-uš   {b+n+gur+š}
He (-n-) made them (-š) return to his place
(Puzur-Šulgi letter to Ibbi-Sin 40 OB, bí- resumes -šè)

-n-√-(e)š is no doubt an early innovation, a 3rd sg. -n- prefix made plural by an added 3rd pl. subject suffix -(e)š. Compare the imperative which can be made plural using a 2nd pl. subject suffix -nzen. -n-√-(e)š is rare though not unknown in Old Sumerian (e.g. ba-ĝar-éš in Nik I 155 4:5), but particularly in economic texts singular verbal forms are regularly used for plurals, e.g. šub-lugal-ke₄-ne e-dab₅ 'the king's underlings took it' (DP 641 8:8). An explicitly plural agent marker on the verb was probably felt not to be necessary when the nominal chain already conveyed this information. On the other hand, in Ur III economic texts it is not uncommon for personal agents marked with the explicit plural element -(e)ne to be resumed in the verb by a collective -b- element rather than -n-√-(e)š, for example:

5 1/3 (bùr) aša₅ sig₅ àga-ús *Tab-ba-ì-lí*-ke₄-ne íb-dab₅
5 1/3 bùr of good field were taken by the guards of Tabba-ili
(Contenau, Umma No. 100 2:1-4 Ur III)

130 gú 7 ma-na siki sig₁₇ ki Lú-ᵈnin-ĝír-su dumu Ir₁₁-ĝu₁₀-ta dam-gàr-ne šu ba-ab-ti
130 talents 7 minas of yellow wool was received by the merchants from L. son of I.
(HSS 4, 156:1-5 Ur III)

THE SO-CALLED CONJUGATIONAL PREFIX i- (§305-321)

When one of the above ergative pronominal prefixes stands as the only element in a verbal prefix chain, i.e. when it is initial in a chain with no other prefix preceding, then — in the view of this grammar — the language employs a prosthetic vowel, usually /i/, sometimes /e/ or /a/, to render certain forms pronounceable:

```
Ø+dù+Ø    >  ì-dù       I built it              {agent Ø/ʔ + √ + 3rd sg. patient}
e+dù+Ø    >  e-dù       You built it                 (no helping vowel needed)
n+dù+Ø    >  in-dù      He/she built it
b+dù+Ø    >  ib-dù      They (collective) built it
n+dù+š    >  in-dù-uš   They (personal) built it
```

When, on the other hand, a preradical pronoun is preceded by another prefix ending in a vowel (nearly all other possible prefixes), no helping vowel is needed. Following are examples featuring four common prefixed preformatives by way of illustration (refer to the appended Verbal Prefix Chain chart), as well as two context passages:

```
ga+b+su    >  ga-ab-dù        I will replace it (-b-)       (cohortative ga-)
hé+n+dù+Ø  >  hé-en-dù        He did indeed build it        (precative hé-)
nu+n+dù+š  >  nu-un-dù-uš     They did not build it         (negative nu-)
u+b+dù+Ø   >  ub-dù           When they (coll.) had built it (prospective ù-)
```

tukum še ì-ĝál ... tukum nu-ĝál ...
If there is barley ... (but) if there is not any (barley) ...
(TCS 1, 367 rev. 2'/4' Ur III)

1 ama-áb 2 gir mu-1 zà ì-šu₄ 1 gir sig zà nu-šu₄
1 mother cow 2 1-year old heifers branded; 1 weak (thin) heifer, not branded
(Erm 14338 i 1-5 OS)

Lastly, if a sentence does not feature an agent, and no other morpheme is marked by a prefixed element, this prosthetic vowel can be prefixed merely to show that the verbal form is finite, since by definition, barring certain technical exceptions, a verb must feature some prefix to be considered finite (cf. Thomsen §273). For example:

    lú ĝen+Ø > lú V+ĝen+Ø > lú ì-ĝen   The man went

In texts earlier than the middle of the Ur III period the prefix -n- is mostly not indicated in writing, although its occasional appearance indicates that it was known or felt to be present morphologically. Since the 1st sg. element is unmarked (-Ø- or -'-), and the 2nd sg. agent is also often unmarked until later in the Ur III period, the unfortunate result of these orthographic practices is that in early texts a sentence such as é ì-dù can be translated as 'I, you, or he/she built the house', or conceivably even as an agentless sentence 'the house was built', dependent entirely upon context.

C. Wilcke observed (AfO 25 (1974-77) 85 n. 8) that in Old Sumerian texts from Nippur and Šuruppak at the northern border of Sumer, the initial prosthetic vowel is only ì-, while in texts from Umma in the middle of Sumer it is only e-. The variation between ì- and e- is manifested in other contexts besides the regular verbal prefix chain. For example, in the literary school text Scribe and His Perverse Son 132 the Nippur duplicates write ì-ne-éš 'now', while the duplicate from Ur in the south of Sumer writes e-ne-éš.

Finally, texts of early Lagaš, near Umma, show a not entirely consistent system of i/e vowel harmony, both in prosthetic and epenthetic vowels, dependent upon the vowel of the root or to some extent that of preceding dimensional prefixes: /i/ before /i/ and /u/ sounds, /e/ before /e/ and /a/ sounds, e.g. ì-šúm vs. e-ĝar. See Thomsen §7. Further:

>   gag-bi é-gar₈-ra bí-dù ì-bi zà-ge bé-a₅   {bi+n+dù+Ø} {bi+n+ak+Ø}
>   Its peg-document he inserted into the wall,
>   its oil he applied to the edge
>   (Edzard, SRU 31 6:16-18 = OS property sale formula)

In Sargonic and earlier texts the vowel a- frequently replaces ì- in agentless "passive" verbs especially before dative -na- (see Å. Westenholz, Early Cuneiform Texts in Jena [1975] 8). P. Steinkeller notes that a- is "characteristic of Fara, Pre-Sargonic and, though to a lesser extent, Sargonic texts," and that "a- appears in sentences where the agent is implied but not spelled out," differing in function from the ba- prefix in truly agentless sentences (Third-Millennium Legal and Administrative Texts [1992] 35). In Pre-Sargonic Lagaš texts a- is common in the forms ab-√ or an-√, where -b- or -n- indicate a locus rather than an agent. This is by no means a rigid system, however; a- appears in other contexts, as well as in other times and places, functionally indistinguishable, to our eyes at least, from ì-, possibly a dialectal feature. It is significant, however, that a- is also a component of the Stative Prefix al- (see below).

One may speculate that the ultimate origin of the prefix ì- (var. e-) in minimal ì+√ forms was a preradical /n/ used either with ergative or locative meaning. In the Pre-Sargonic Lagaš economic corpus, for example, where preradical /n/ is normally not pronounced, ì/e-√ forms are usually found in association with agentive or locative nominal chains which in later periods would be marked in the verb with a preradical /n/. (By contrast, minimal agentless verbs usually take the form ba-√ in that corpus.) This phenomenon would help to explain why this prefixed /i/ sound came to be written with the sign whose other main reading is /ni/, the other verbal locative prefix (see later).

The foregoing interpretation of the uses of the verbal prefix element /i/ contrasts strongly with the traditional Poebel-Falkenstein explanation of the Conjugation Prefix ì-, continued and amplified by Thomsen and others. It is in my view an elegant solution to a perennial problem of Sumerian grammar, but only a few aspects of this interpretation are gradually gaining wider acceptance. In any case the term Conjugation Prefix, referring to the prefixes mu-, bí- and ba- as well as ì-, should now be abandoned as a useless misnomer (cf. D. Edzard, ZA 78, 114 n. 13).

THE STATIVE PREFIX al-   (Thomsen §353-358)

Because some prefix is required to make a verb finite, in simple agentless verbs one often encounters verbal prefixes which do not seem to be strictly required by the meaning or syntax and which are consequently difficult to translate. The prefix ba- often serves as such a finite formative (especially the so-called "passive" use of ba-), and in such contexts it must usually be left untranslated.

The language actually has a special prefix al- for use in such situations. Since al- always occurs in agentless sentences, Akkadian translations of verbal forms featuring al- sometimes take the form of agentless Akkadian statives (conjugated verbal adjectives, often passive in sense, e.g. *paris* 'it was cut'). Thus al- has come to be referred to as the Sumerian stative prefix.

Since its primary function is to make finite a verbal form lacking any other prefix, al- should properly stand alone in a verbal form. There are, however, a few attestations of its co-occurring with a preformative, thereby defeating its original purpose by rendering it unnecessary. These very rare exceptions include a negated form nu-al-√ or nu-ul-√ and prospective forms ul-√ or ù-ul-√. The latter elided forms suggest that al- should probably be analyzed as an element /l/ plus a prosthetic vowel /a/ (see above). Since /n/ and /l/ alternate in certain contexts — compare the allomorphs la- and li- of the negative preformative nu- or the obsolete nominal formative nu- < lú 'person' — it is possible the stative prefix al- goes back to an early preradical locative prefix n+√ > an-√ which served merely to locate a minimal verb existentially "here" in space and so to render it finite. That the al- prefix adds little or no information to the verbal form can be seen from the following three parallel entries from Ur III economic texts, where a relativized finite verb featuring a stative al- varies with simple non-finite past participles:

    50 ^{urudu}ha-bù-da dúb-ba   (UET 3, 311:1)   {dúb+a}
    46 ^{urudu}ha-bù-da dúb-ba   (UET 3, 312:1)
   180 ^{urudu}ha-bù-da al-dúb-ba (UET 3, 396:1)   {al+dúb+Ø+a}
   n copper hoes, (which were) beaten?

A few other examples:

   1/18 (bùr) 20 (sar) kiri$_6$ gú pa$_5$-PAD al-ĝál
   (acreage) of orchard existing on the bank of the PAD-ditch
   (MVN 3, 13 OS)

   inim-bi igi-ne-ne-ta al-til
   This matter was concluded in front of them
   (Edzard, SRU 20:32-33 Sargonic)

   1(bán) ku$_6$ al-šeĝ$_6$-ĝá   {al+šeĝ+Ø+a}
   1 *ban* of fish which has been cooked
   (Limet, Textes No. 93:9 Ur III)

   diĝir-ama diĝir-a-a ul-su$_8$-ge-eš-a-ta   {ù+(a)l+su$_8$(g)+eš+a+ta}
   When the mother-gods and father-gods stood by
   (Lugalbanda in Hurrum 160 OB)

BASIC SENTENCE SYNTAX

Sumerian is basically a Subject-Object-Verb (SOV) language. In a verbless nominal sentence the subject normally precedes the predicate. In a verbal sentence or clause the most reliable rule is that the verb stands in final position, although poetic license in literary contexts permits exceptions. In an intransitive sentence, featuring only a subject, the word order is Subject - Verb (SV). In a transitive sentence, featuring a patient and an agent, the usual word order is Agent - Patient - Verb (SOV), although the patient can be topicalized by placing it before the agent. Indirect objects and adverbial phrases typically stand between an initial subject or agent nominal chain, if present, and the verb, although once again such phrases can be topicalized by placing them earlier in the sentence.

REMEMBER WHEN ANALYZING ANY SENTENCE:

   EVERY SUMERIAN VERBAL SENTENCE OR CLAUSE <u>ALWAYS</u> CONTAINS A SUBJECT OR
   PATIENT. IDENTIFY THE SUBJECT OR PATIENT <u>BEFORE</u> PROCEEDING FURTHER!

   A SENTENCE <u>MAY</u> CONTAIN AN AGENT. DETERMINE WHETHER AN AGENT IS PRESENT
   ONLY AFTER <u>YOU</u> HAVE IDENTIFIED THE SUBJECT OR PATIENT!

   TRANSLATE PUTATIVE TRANSITIVE VERBS PASSIVELY TO HELP LOCATE THE SUBJECT!

DIMENSIONAL PREFIXES I: INTRODUCTION

The subject (or patient) of a sentence, standing in the absolutive case, is marked in the perfective verbal chain by a suffix, a pronominal element standing after the verbal root. Nominal chains standing in any of the remaining adverbal cases can be resumed in the verbal chain by a prefix, an element standing before the verbal root. The relative position of each prefix present in the chain is fixed: dative always comes before ablative, ablative always comes before ergative, etc. See the appended Verbal Prefix Chain chart (p. 150) for a schematic representation of the rank order of prefixes.

Since the Falkenstein school of grammar maintained that the dimensional prefixes cannot begin a verbal form but must always be preceded by one of a number of Conjugation Prefixes (a term and analysis not employed in this grammar), these prefixes have also therefore been referred to broadly as dimensional infixes rather than dimensional prefixes. Edzard's 2003 Sumerian Grammar avoids the problem by instead using the neutral term "indicator."

In its fullest form, a verbal dimensional prefix consists of a pronominal element and a case element which correspond to the antecedent head noun and case postposition of a particular nominal chain. This pattern holds for the dative, comitative, ablative-instrumental and terminative prefixes, and these prefixes therefore comprise one subset which henceforth will be referred to together as the dimensional prefixes. The prefixes which resume locative, ergative, and locative-terminative nominal chains consist theoretically of pronominal elements only, in my view, and represent a second subset of prefixes which henceforth will be referred to as the core prefixes (following Jacobsen), whose description is more problematic and which will consequently be treated separately.

DIMENSIONAL PREFIX PRONOUNS (§428-430)

The pronominal elements which can occur in dimensional prefixes are similar to the prefixes of the hamṭu agent, at least in the singular:

Sg	1	mu/m	(Jagersma 2010 posits also a glottal stop in some contexts)
	2	Ø/e/r	(unassimilated -e- is not attested before OB)
	3p	n	
	3i	b	
Pl	1	?	(me is predicted)
	2	?	(e-ne is predicted)
	3p	ne	

The several forms of the 1st and 2nd sg. elements alternate according to period and the prefixed case markers with which they occur; this alternation will be discussed in detail apropos of the locative-terminative core prefixes. Like the ergative pronominal elements, certain of the above elements will, according to the phonotactic scheme followed in this grammar, require a preposed prosthetic vowel to render them pronounceable when they stand initially in a verbal prefix chain, viz.:

```
mu+da+tuš+Ø     >  mu-da-tuš       He sat with me
e+da+ti(l)+Ø    >  e-da-ti         He lived with you
n+da+ti(l)+Ø    >  in-da-ti        He lived with him/her
b+da+gub+Ø      >  ib-da-gub       He stood with it
ne+da+ĝen+Ø     >  ì-ne-da-ĝen     He came with them
```

SYNTAX OF THE DIMENSIONAL PREFIXES (§423-427)

Dimensional prefixes theoretically resume or repeat in the verbal chain information already present in one or more nominal chains of a sentence. A pronominal element and following case element refer back to an antecedant head noun (with any modifiers) and the final case postposition respectively of a particular nominal chain, for example:

        nin lugal-da in-da-tuš   The queen sat with the king

        naĝar iri-šè ib-ši-ĝen   The carpenter went to the city

A sentence may contain a number of nominal chains, but there are restrictions on the number and kind that can be resumed by full dimensional prefixes (pronominal element plus case marker). A verbal chain can (theoretically) contain a maximum of one ergative prefix, one locative-terminative prefix, one dative prefix, and one other dimensional prefix. It might also feature a preceding secondary ba- prefix. A verbal chain may not contain two prefixes from the subset of comitative, ablative-instrumental, terminative. See the appended Prefix Chain Chart for restrictions. Thus, sentence (a) is grammatical but sentence (b) is not. Sentence (b) would have to be rendered either by (c) or (d) (although a prefix -ni- could substitute for the missing second prefix, see presently):

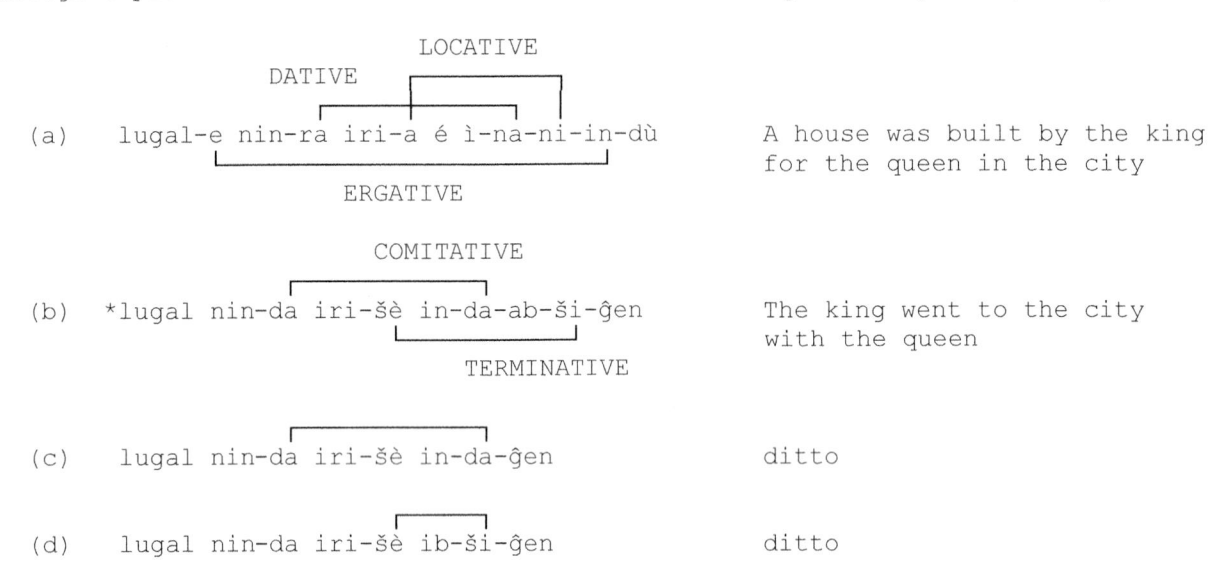

                            LOCATIVE
                DATIVE

(a)   lugal-e nin-ra iri-a é ì-na-ni-in-dù   A house was built by the king
                                        for the queen in the city
                   ERGATIVE

                   COMITATIVE

(b)   *lugal nin-da iri-šè in-da-ab-ši-ĝen   The king went to the city
                                      with the queen
                     TERMINATIVE

(c)   lugal nin-da iri-šè in-da-ĝen   ditto

(d)   lugal nin-da iri-šè ib-ši-ĝen   ditto

The above restrictions do not always apply when a comitative, ablative-instrumental or terminative case element is used without a pronominal element to lend a directional nuance to the meaning of the verb. Such instances used to be explained as deletions of specific "understood" pronominal objects, as shown below in example (b). But compare form (c) from a Gudea royal inscription, where three allomorphs of the ablative prefix are employed in sequence to give an overwhelming ablative sense to the verbal idea:

    (a)   im-è   It came out hither (-m-)   {m+√+∅}

    (b)   im-ta-è   It came out <from it> hither   {m+<b>+ta+√+∅}

    (c)   ma-da-ra-ta-è   It came out-out-out for me!   {ma+*ta+*ta+ta+√+∅}

The last form is unusual and may represent a playful stretching of the resources of the language, but it is apparently still good Sumerian and represents a good indication that the da/ta/ši case elements in particular may be used independently to add more amorphous directional ideas to a verbal form without reference to any specific goal or object.

There is not always a clear one-to-one correspondence between the nominal chains of a sentence and the markers in the verb. A prefix may, for example, pronominalize an understood nominal chain, especially one present in an earlier sentence or clause. For example, assume that sentence (b) below directly follows sentence (a) in a narrative. lugal 'king' would then be the understood subject of (b), marked only by the zero verbal subject pronoun (-Ø), and the dimensional prefix -b-ši- would refer pronominally to an understood nominal chain iri-šè 'to the city':

    (a)   lugal iri-bi-ta ib-ta-è   The king had left that city   {b+ta+√+Ø}

    (b)   a-na-aš ib-ši-gi₄   Why did he return to it?   {b+ši+√+Ø}

Further, the 3rd sg. locative-terminative prefix -ni- (discussed in a later lesson) had a broad and quite general referential use, and it often resumes non-locative nominal chains. In the following illustrations it resumes dative and terminative objects:

    kur-gal-e sipa ᵈur-ᵈnamma-ra nam gal mu-ni-in-tar
    The Great Mountain (= Enlil) decided a great fate for the shepherd Ur-Namma
    (Ur-Namma Hymn B 37 OB)

    e-bi i₇-nun-ta gú-eden-na-šè íb-ta-ni-è
    That levee he extended from Princely Canal to Desert's Edge
    (Ent 28 ii 1-3 OS)

Finally, since the marking of the same idea in both a nominal and verbal complex is redundant, either a case postposition or a dimensional prefix can be omitted for stylistic or other reasons without significant loss of information:

    lugal dumu-ni-da in-da-gub   The king stood with his son (full form)

    (a) lugal dumu-ni-da ì-gub   (shortened alternatives)
    (b) lugal dumu-ni in-da-gub

In OS Lagash economic texts, for example, omission of the nominal postposition, as well as prefixed pronominal elements, is especially common, e.g.

    lá-a-ne-ne nu-ta-zi   {lá+a+(a)nene+(ta)}
    It was not deducted from their surplus
    (Nik I 271 4:1 OS)

    dub daĝal nu-ta-zi
    It was not deducted from the wide tablet
    (Nik I 210 4:1 OS)

Alternative marking can even be found within the same text, e.g.

    PNN PN₂ e-da-sig₇
    PNN lived with PN₂
    (CT 50, 36 11:2-3 OS)

    PNN PN₂ kurušda-da e-da-sig₇
    PNN lived with PN₂ the animal fattener
    (CT 50, 36 14:1-3)

One may suggest as a general principle that the marking in the verb of any information already present in the nominal parts of a sentence, or vice versa, is basically optional and at the discretion of a particular speaker. As a result, dimensional prefixes are rarer in verbal forms in earlier texts when Sumerian was a living language. Only later, especially after Sumerian died out, did extensive resuming of nominal information in the

verb become the norm, and verbs in literary texts from the Old Babylonian schools show
the most elaborate, and often fanciful, dimensional prefix sequences. To give only one
minor example, one can encounter OB verbs featuring core prefixes that resume both a
locative and a locative-terminative as in Šulgi R 66: ^{d}nin-líl-da ki ĝíšbun-na-ka zà-ge
mu-dì-ni-íb-si-éš 'With Ninlil {mu+n+da} they filled the *sides* (-e = -b-) in the place of
the feast (-a = -ni-)'.

VOCABULARY NOTE 1

Auxiliary Verbs

Many Sumerian compound verbs were formed using a head noun and one of the two auxiliary
verbs du$_{11}$(g) 'to do' or a$_5$(k) 'to do, perform, make'. This was a highly productive method
of new word formation and many such compound verbs exist. For full listings of occurring
forms and detailed discussions of morphology and syntax see P. Attinger, Eléments de
linguistique sumérienne (Fribourg, 1993), especially pp. 319-764 for "du$_{11}$/e/di et ses
composés," and "A propos de AK 'faire' I-II," Zeitschrift für Assyriologie 95 (2005)
46-64, 208-275. For an analysis of this use of ak see also J. Ebeling in Analyzing
Literary Sumerian (London, 2007) 144ff., and note that M. Civil accepts a meaning 'to do'
for du$_{11}$ in these constructions (RAI 53 [2010] 524 n. 3). Some common examples include:

al - du$_{11}$	to desire
inim - du$_{11}$	to do words, speak (often with elliptical patient <inim>)
in - du$_{11}$	to insult
kaš$_4$ - du$_{11}$	to perform running, run
mí - du$_{11}$	to act/treat gently, take care of, nurture
silim(-ma) - du$_{11}$	to perform a greeting, greet
še-er-ka-an - du$_{11}$	to do decoration, decorate
šu - du$_{11}$	to use the hand, exert oneself, act
šùd - du$_{11}$	to do a prayer, pray
u$_6$ - du$_{11}$	to wonder at, marvel at
$^{(ĝiš)}$al - a$_5$	to work with the pickax/hoe
en-nu-ùĝ - a$_5$	to perform the watch
kíĝ - a$_5$	to do work
si-im(-si-im) - a$_5$	to do sniffing, sniff, smell

Periphrastic Verbs

The auxiliary verbs du$_{11}$(g) and a$_5$(k) are also used with ordinary compound verbs to form
new periphrastic verbs whose meanings rarely seem to differ except stylistically from
the simpler expressions. The verb of the base expression takes the form of a hamṭu
participle (explained later). Examples:

á - dúb	to flap the wings"	á-dúb - a$_5$	to perform wing-flapping
bar - tam	to choose	bar-tam - a$_5$	to do a choosing
ir - si-im	to sniff a scent	ir-si-im - a$_5$	to do a scent-sniffing > smell
ki - su-ub	to rub the earth > prostrate onself	ki-su-ub - a$_5$	to do an earth-rubbing > perform a prostration
pa - è	to make respendent	pa-è - a$_5$	to do a making-resplendent
šu - luh	to clean the hands	šu-luh - a$_5$	to perform a cleaning (of canals)
šu - tag	to touch with the hand	šu-tag - du$_{11}$	to do a hand-touching > adorn

REMEMBER: FULLY MARKED DIMENSIONAL PREFIX SEQUENCES RESUME
                EXPLICIT OR UNDERSTOOD ADVERBAL NOMINAL CHAINS.

                SOME DIMENSIONAL PREFIX CASE ELEMENTS ALONE CAN
                ADD NON-SPECIFIC DIRECTIONAL IDEAS TO THE VERB.

DIMENSIONAL PREFIXES II: DATIVE

THE DATIVE PREFIX PARADIGM (§431-437)

```
sg.  1    ma-      to me
     2    -ra-     to you
     3p   -na-     to him, her
     3i   ba-      to it, them (impersonal)

pl.  1    me-      to us              (attested in OB only)
     2    -e-ne-   to you             (attested in OB only)
     3p   -ne-     to them (personal)
```

In the singular, the dative prefix consists of a pronominal element /m/, /r/, /n/, or /b/ bound to a case element /a/, identical in form and possibly in origin with the locative postposition -a. In the 1st and 3rd person plural, it is apparently formed with the pronominal elements /m/ and /n/ bound to a case element /e/, probably identical in origin to the locative-terminative postposition -e. These dative prefixes are always written as bound open syllables, as units; the pronominal and case elements are never written separately. Of the plural prefixes, -ne- is well attested in all periods; me- is found only in a few OB texts and might have been an innovation, created by analogy with 1st sg. ma- and 3rd pl. -ne-; and -e-ne- may likewise have been an artificial creation based on the 2nd sg. pronominal element -e-. Edzard 2003, 12.8.1.5, cites at least one instance of a 3rd pl. -ne-a- instead of usual -ne-. The 1st and 2nd plural prefixes are on the whole quite rare.

When one of the prefixes -ra-, -na- or -ne- stands initially in the prefix chain, it must be preceded by the prosthetic vowel /i/ (in some contexts or dialects /a/ or /e/). By contrast, the prefixes ma-, me- and ba- may initiate a chain without the help of this vowel. No prosthetic vowel is needed when a dative prefix is preceded by another prefix ending in a vowel. Compare the following forms with and without a preceding negative preformative nu- 'not':

ma-an-šúm	nu-ma-an-šúm	He gave it (not) to me	
ì-ra-an-šúm	nu-ra-an-šúm	He gave it (not) to you	
ì-na-an-šúm	nu-na-an-šúm	He gave it (not) to him/her	
ba-an-šúm	la-ba-an-šúm	He gave it (not) to them	(nu+ba > la-ba-)
*me-en-šúm	*nu-me-en-šúm	He gave it (not) to us	(hypothetical)
ì-ne-en-šúm	nu-ne-en-sum	He gave it (not) to them	

In most periods it is common for the /n/ of -na- or -ne-, also of the locative-terminative prefix -ni- to be doubled, especially in initial position, e.g. in-na-an-du$_{11}$, in-ne-gub-ba-a, an-ne-šúm, ba-an-na-šúm, ki an-na-áĝ-ĝá-ni, na-an-ni-in-è, etc. This is an orthographic feature with no morphological significance (in the view of most scholars) which should be discounted when analyzing verbs. It is seen elsewhere in the grammar, again in connection with /n/ sounds, but also with /m/ or even /b/. Cf. inim-ma-an-ni (AuOr 14, 163 1:2' Ur III) for inim-ma-ni 'his word', šu-du$_8$-an-ni (BibMes 1, 20 rev. 3' OAkk) 'his guarantee' for šu-du$_8$-a-ni, hé-na-lá-en-ne (TCS 1, 30:6 Ur III) for hé-na-lá-e-ne 'Let them pay him!', íb-bé regularly instead of íb-e 'he says', or the frequent initial prefix sequence nam-mu- for na-mu-.

SYNTAX OF THE DATIVE (§438-440)

The dative is a personal case exclusively; it can be used only with personal referents. A dative object is marked in a nominal chain by the postposition -ra (or -r or -Ø after vowels), and in the verbal chain by a corresponding prefix. If there is no nominal chain present, the dimensional prefix represents a pronominal object. Examples:

lugal-e engar-ra še ì-na-an-šúm	The king gave barley to the farmer
énsi-ke₄ lú-ne-er níĝ-ba ì-ne-en-šúm	The governor gave gifts to the men
diĝir-ĝu₁₀ nam-lugal ma-an-šúm	My god gave kingship to me
nam-ti sù ì-ra-an-šúm	To you he gave long life

If an otherwise dative object is impersonal, it is marked in a nominal chain not by dative -ra but by the locative-terminative postposition -e and in the verbal chain by the 3rd sg. prefix ba-. While this is a generally applicable rule, note that nouns construed as collectives fall into the impersonal gender category, and it is entirely permissible for an ordinarily personal noun to be used as a collective and thus be marked by -e and resumed in the verbal chain by "impersonal dative" ba-, for example:

> um-ma-bé ad gi₄-gi₄ ba-an-šúm ab-ba-bé inim-inim-ma ba-an-šúm
> To its old women he gave advising, to its old men he gave consulting
> (Curse of Agade 29-30 OB)

There has been speculation that historically -e was regularly used with personal nouns as well, resumed in the verb by the prefix -ni-, and that the nominal postposition -ra and the personal dative pronoun series in the verbal chain were secondary innovations. See the comments and examples of T. Jacobsen in JAOS 103 (1983) 195 note j.

Many verbs of motion which we would not necessarily associate with the idea of a dative goal show this personal/dative vs. impersonal/locative-terminative contrast, as in "to approach" or "to come/go to" a person (dative) or a place or thing (loc.-term.). Thus the dative is basically a directional element, like the locative-terminative; its ethical dative or benefactive use ("to do something for the benefit of someone") may have been a secondary development. It might well turn out that dative and locative-terminative will ultimately best be explained as merely the personal and impersonal forms of the same basic case, the same species of rection or direction of motion (see now G. Zólyomi, Orientalia 68 (1999) 251-3). Following are several artificial illustrations of parallel personal vs. impersonal forms:

lugal-e érin-e še ba-an-šúm	The king gave barley to the troops
šagina-ne-er kù-babbar ì-ne-en-šúm	To the generals he gave silver
inim diĝir-ra an-e ba-te	The word of the god approached heaven
lugal-ra ì-na-te	It approached the king

OTHER USES OF THE PREFIX BA- (Thomsen §337, 341-351; Edzard 2003, 12.8.1.3)

While the marking of locative-terminative goals, especially impersonal datives, was probably the original function of the prefix ba-, over time it came to acquire additional uses.

It often serves as a kind of non-specific ablative marker ("away from, out of"), frequently co-occurring with the proper ablative dimensional case elements (-ta- and -ra-) to form the the emphatic ablative prefix sequences ba-ta-, ba-ra- and ba-da- (< ba-ta-) discussed later. One wonders whether these ablative sequences were originally derived from the adverbial expressions bar-ra or bar-ta 'outside', which became attached, in an abbreviated and reinterpreted form, to the head of the verbal chain in the manner of the prospective preformative ù-, which was almost certainly derived from the noun u₄ 'day, time', or the dimensional prefix -da- which derives from the noun da 'side'. See discussion in Falkenstein, ZA 45 (1939) 180f. Ablative ba- is often seen with verbs of actual or figurative taking away, destroying, or other forms of spatial or temporal removal from the area of the speech situation. For example, it occurs commonly with (agentless) forms of the verb úš 'to die', as in ba-úš 'he died'. With the verb de₆/túm 'to bring' it varies regularly with the ventive prefix mu- 'hither' to add opposing directional nuances: mu-un-de₆ 'he brought it in' vs. ba-an-de₆ 'he took it away'.

ba- may also function with a less obviously directional meaning as a substitute for the prefixed prosthetic vowel /i/. This use is common in verbal forms with no agents, as in é ba-dù 'the house was built', or ba-gub 'he stood', and many scholars now describe this ba- as an indicator of passive or middle voice. For such a view see the early work of C. Wilcke, Archiv für Orientforschung 25 (1974/77) 85 + n. 6, the arguments of C. Woods in his The Grammar of Perspective. The Sumerian Conjugation Prefixes as a System of Voice (Leiden, 2008), and now the description of the "middle marker" ba- in Jagersma 2010 §21.

Finally, it should be noted that in the collection of bilingual Old Babylonian Grammatical Texts (OBGT) ba- is consistently equated with the Akkadian verbal infix -t- which has four different meanings depending upon grammatical context, three direction-altering uses and one tense-related use: the separative (i.e. ablative), passive, reflexive, and perfect. Since Sumerian and Akkadian existed intimately together for a very long time in a linguistic area (German Sprachbund), it is not unthinkable that Akkadian speaking scribes may sometimes have employed the apparently at least partially corresponding Sumerian element ba- in ways similar to their Akk. -t- infix, particularly in the OB schools which were responsible for creating or preserving most of the extant Sumerian literary texts upon which we in turn base much of our grammatical description.

At some stage in the history of the language the rank order of ba- in the prefix chain must have changed, reflecting its expanded new range of uses. While it had the same origin and so, presumably, originally the same rank as the other dative prefixes, it eventually became capable of co-occurring with the 2nd and 3rd person personal dative prefixes: ba-ra-, ba-na-, ba-ne-. It does not co-occur with itself, *ba-ba-, and does not occur with 1st person prefixes in proper Sumerian contexts, i.e. *ba-ma- or *ba-me-, although the du/ĝen paradigm of the Old Babylonian Grammatical Texts does employ several ba-me- forms, with unusual and probably artificial Akkadian translations (OBGT VII 207-208, 219-229). In any event, despite its "dative" origin, ba- must be assigned a rank order slot immediately preceding that of the other dative prefixes; see the appended Verbal Prefix Chain chart for a schematic view of its rank and occurrence restrictions.

Thomsen, following Falkenstein, classes ba- among the "Conjugation Prefixes," a category of prefix which, in my view, reflects an inadequate overall analysis of the verbal prefix system. Her extended discussion of this traditional descriptive category can be found in §341-351.

PASSAGES ILLUSTRATING THE PREFIX BA-

ba- used to resume locative-terminative goals

    a na₈-na₈ nu-na-šúm-mu anše a na₈-na₈ nu-ba-šúm-mu   {anše+e}
    He used not to give him (-na-) drinking water,
    he used not to give the donkeys (-e) drinking water
    (Ukg 6 2:6'-9' OS)

anše sur_x(ÉREN)-ra-ke₄ ba-su₈-ge-éš   {ba+su₈(g)+(e)š}
They (the men) were stationed by the team-donkeys
(Genouillac, TSA 13 5:4 OS)

PN-e nu-èš sagi ir₁₁ géme é-e ba-šúm   {ba+n+šúm+Ø}
PN gave a nu'eš-priest, a cup-bearer, and male and
female slaves to the temple
(Biga, Fs. J. Klein 30 2:9-12 OAkk)

alaĝ-na-ni mu-tu nam-šita-e ba-gub   {m+n+tu(d)+Ø, ba+n+gub+Ø}
He created his stone figure and set it up for prayer
(Gudea Statue M 2:7-3:2 Ur III)

énsi-ke₄ diĝir iri-na-ke₄ rá-zu im-ma-bé   {m+ba+b+e+Ø}
The governor performs a prayer (-b-) to the god of his city
(Gudea, Cyl B 1:15 Ur III)

anzu^mušen-gin₇ gù dúb-da-zu-dè igi-zu-ù a-ba ba-gub   {igi+zu+e}
At your making (your) voice quaver like the Anzu bird,
who could stand before you?
(Šulgi X 113 Ur III)

im siki-ba-ke₄ gù ba-dé   {ba- resumes -e}
The wool-ration tablet has been called for
(TCS 1, 149:3-4 Ur III letter order)

30 gú ésir àh ésir àh tár-kul-la-ke₄ ba-ab-dah-e
He shall add 30 talents of dry bitumen to the dry bitumen of the mooring posts
(Sollberger, TCS 1, 355:1-4 Ur III)

ur-^dig-alim-ra ù-na-du₁₁
4 dumu-dab₅-ba 1/5 še <gur> lugal-ta hé-ne-šúm-mu
gur hé-ne-gi-né še hé-ne-tag-tag-ge ù 8 še gur-lugal-àm
dumu-dab₅-ba bala sun-na-ke₄ ha-ba-ab-šúm-mu
Say to Ur-Igalima:
Let 1/5 royal gur of barley each be given to the 4 'seized citizens'!
Let the gur be verified and all the barley be set aside(?) for them!
Further, 8 gur, royal gur, of barley let him give to the
'seized citizens' of the old term!
(MVN VII 398:1-9 Ur III letter order, note alternation of -ne- and ba-)

ká-silim-ma-bi ^giš al-e bí-in-ra   {bí- resumes -e}
kur-kur-re silim-silim-bi ba-kúr   {ba- resumes -e}
He struck its Gate of Well-Being with a pickax,
and for all the lands all their well-beings turned hostile
(Curse of Agade 125-126 OB)

Ablative ba-

PN-e nam-érim-bi un-ku₅ ìr ba-an-túm-mu   {ba+n+túm+e+Ø}
When (u-) PN has sworn an oath regarding
this, he shall take away the slave
(Falkenstein, NSGU 212:14 Ur III, -n- marks the object here in the imperfective)

Agentless Verbs with ba-

mu lugal-la ba-pà   A royal oath was sworn
mu lugal-la in-pà   A royal oath he swore
                         (legal phrases, cf. Steinkeller, Sales Documents p. 57)

udu ba-ur₄	The sheep were plucked	
udu nu-ur₄	The sheep were not plucked	
	(standard Ur III administrative terminology)	
mu é ba-dù	Year the temple was built	
mu lugal-e é mu-dù	Year the king built the temple	{mu+n+dù+Ø}
	(standard Ur III year-formula terminology)	

10,8.0.0 še gur-saĝ+ĝál é-a ba-si
en-ig-gal nu-bànda é-é-bar-ᵈbìl-àga-mes-šè-dù-a ì-si   {in+si+Ø}
608 s.-gur of barley were stored in the house;
Eniggal the overseer put it into the E.-storehouse
(Nik I 83 1:1-2 & 5:4-7 OS)

REMEMBER: WITH THE EXCEPTION OF ba-, DATIVE PREFIXES RESUME ONLY PERSONAL
            DATIVE OBJECTS, i.e. NOMINAL CHAINS MARKED BY THE POSTPOSITION -ra

            ba- RESUMES "IMPERSONAL DATIVES," NOMINAL CHAINS MARKED BY THE
            LOCATIVE-TERMINATIVE POSTPOSITION -e

            NON-DATIVE ba- CAN FUNCTION ALSO AS AN ABLATIVE MARKER OR
            AS AN UNTRANSLATABLE SUBSTITUTE FOR A PROSTHETIC /i/ PREFIX,
            PARTICULARLY IN AGENTLESS "PASSIVE" (OR MIDDLE) VERBAL FORMS

DIMENSIONAL PREFIXES III: COMITATIVE, TERMINATIVE AND ABLATIVE-INSTRUMENTAL

The comitative, terminative and ablative-instrumental prefixes exhibit few phonological difficulties and can be treated together as a unit. See the Verbal Prefix Chain chart for the relative rank ordering of these prefixes within the chain. The case elements -da-, -ta- and -ši- frequently occur together with a preceding pronominal element which represents the object of the case element, usually the head noun of an antecedent nominal chain. Each can, however, also be used without a pronominal element to add an adverbial, directional, <u>dimensional</u> nuance to a verbal idea. As will be seen, the ablative prefix -ra- (and -ri-) is a development from ablative-instrumental -ta- which is used only adverbially, never with pronominal elements. For more on the functions or meanings of these cases see the earlier lesson on the adverbal case postpositions.

PRONOMINAL ELEMENT PARADIGM (§290-293)

The pronominal elements which can occur with -da-, -ta- and -ši- include:

sg.	1	mu-/-ʔ-
	2	-e-/-Ø-
	3p	-n-
	3i	-b-
pl.	1	?
	2	?
	3p	-ne-

(Jagersma 2010 §16.2.5 posits glottal stop)
(-e- assimilates to preceding vowels before OB)
(-n- often unwritten before OB)

(me- is predicted)
(-e-ne- has been suggested)

The 1st sg. pronoun is the <u>ventive element</u>, to be dealt with in greater detail both in a separate lesson and under the discussion of the ergative and locative-terminative prefixes in the next two lessons. As expected, the pronominal elements -Ø-, -n-, -b- and -ne- require a preposed prosthetic vowel to render them pronounceable when they stand initially. Thus:

mu-da-ĝen	{mu+da+√+Ø}	He went with me	(no prosthesis)
e-da-ĝen-en	{e+da+√+(e)n}	I (-en) went with you	(no prosthesis)
ì-da-ĝen	{Ø+da+√+Ø}	He went with you	(prosthesis)
ib-da-ĝen	{b+da+√+Ø}	He went with it	(prosthesis)
nu-un-da-ĝen	{nu+n+da+√+Ø}	He did not go with him	(no prosthesis)

COMITATIVE (§441-450)

The usual form of the comitative prefix is -da-. In earlier texts it can also occur bound to a following -b- in the writing -dab₆(URUDU)-. In OS the 3rd pl. personal prefix -ne-da- 'with them' is regularly written with a single sign -neda(PI)-. See Yıldız, Or 50, 92 + n. 17 for the variant dam neda(PI)-ni for dam nitadam-a-ni in Ur-Namma Code §9, and perhaps compare the value /nigida/ for the PI sign. Assimilated forms of -da- include -di- or -dì(TI)-, especially before loc.-term. -ni-; and -dè-, either before or after the 2nd sg. pronoun -e- or before a verb containing an /e/ vowel as in an-dè-e₁₁ (= an-da-e₁₁) in Edzard, SRU 98 2:2 = 99 4:15 (Sargonic).

Most instances of the prefix sequence ba-da- are to be analyzed as the prefix ba-, probably with ablative meaning, plus an ablative-instrumental prefix -ta- whose /t/

has become voiced because of its position between two vowels: ba-da- < *ba-ta-. See below and Thomsen §449.

The infix -da- '(together) with, beside' is certainly to be derived by <u>grammaticalization</u> of the noun da 'side'. Compare the syntax of the noun and infix in the following:

    dub énsi-ka-bi da lú-gi-na-ka ì-ĝál
    The governor's tablet concerning this (-bi) is with Lugina (lit. at his side)
    (Sollberger, TCS 1, 303:6-7 Ur III)

    dub ba-ba-ti 720 še gur ur-mes-ra in-da-ĝál-la
    The tablet of Babati (concerning) 720 gur barley which is with Ur-mes
    (TCS 1, 60:3)
    The personal dative -ra here replaces expected -da on Urmes.

Examples of standard comitative uses:

    ki šà húl-la ᵈnin-líl-lá-šè
    ᵈen-líl ᵈnin-líl-da mu-dì-ni-in-u₅   {mu+n+da+n+n+u₅+∅}
    To the place that gladdens the heart of Ninlil
    he made Enlil ride together with Ninlil
    (Šu-Suen royal inscription, Civil JCS 21, 34 12:9-11 Ur III)

    ᵈnin-ĝír-sú-ke₄ iri-ka-gi-na-da e-da-du₁₁-ga-a šu nu-dì-ni-bal-e
    Ninĝirsu shall not overturn what he spoke about with (king) Irikagina.
    (Ukg. 34:1 OS)

    šitim in-da-ĝál [ha]-ab-da-an-sar-re
    The builders (who) are with him: have him write about them!
    (TCS 1, 197:7-8 Ur III)

    u₄ ᵈen-líl-le gù zi e-na-dé-a nam-en nam-lugal-da e-na-da-tab-ba-a
    When Enlil called faithfully to him and linked en-ship with kingship for him
    (Lugalkinedudu of Uruk 2:4-8 OS)

    ᵈa-nun-na diĝir šeš-zu-ne hé-me-da-húl-húl-le-eš   {hé+mu+e+da+húl-húl+e+š}
    May the Anuna, your brother gods, rejoice greatly over you!
    (Ur-Ninurta B 46 OB)

    ᵈnin-líl-da ki ĝíšbun-na-ka zà-ge mu-dì-ni-íb-si-éš
    With Ninlil they filled the feasting-place to the limits
    (Šulgi R 66 Ur III)

In its <u>abilitative</u> function (Thomsen §448) -da- expresses the idea 'to be able':

    sahar ᵍᶦšdupšik-e nu-mu-e-da-an-si-si
    You cannot fill earth into (-e) work baskets
    (Hoe and Plow 12 OB)

    eden ama ugu-ĝu₁₀ inim mu-e-dè-zu-un
    O desert, you can inform my mother who bore me
    (Dumuzi's Dream 13 OB)

TERMINATIVE (§451-459)

The terminative case prefix is normally written -ši-. In OS Lagaš texts it is subject to an old system of vowel harmony (Thomsen §309) in which /ši/ becomes /še/, written with the ŠÈ sign like the terminative postposition, before verbal roots featuring the vowels /e/ or /a/. This vowel harmony also affects an initial prosthetic vowel, i.e.

-šè- preceding roots in /e/ or /a/:   e-šè-ĝen, e-šè-ĝar
-ši- preceding roots in /i/ or /u/:   ì-ši-šid, ì-ši-gub

The basic meaning of -ši- is 'motion to, toward' an end-point:

    ĝe₂₆-e ᵈnin-hur-saĝ-ĝá mu-e-ši-túm-mu-un a-na níĝ-ba-ĝu₁₀
    If I bring Ninhursaĝa to you, what will be my reward?
    (Enki and Ninhursaĝ 224 OB)

    tukumₓ-bi mu-bé šu uru₁₂-dè ĝèštu hé-em-ši-gub   (ur₃+e+d+e, -ši- resumes -e)
    If he has set (his) mind to erasing these lines
    (Gudea Statue B 9:12-16 Ur III)

ABLATIVE-INSTRUMENTAL AND ABLATIVE (§460-469)

ABLATIVE-INTSTRUMENTAL -ta

In its ablative use the basic meaning of -ta- is 'removal or separation in space or time'. Spatially it signifies 'away from (a place)', 'out of (an area or container)'. Temporally it signifies 'when, since, after (the time that something happened)'. In its instrumental use it signifies 'by means of, with'.

    itu-ta u₄ 24 ba-ta-zal
    From the month day 24 has passed <u>away</u>
    (ArOr 27, 369 No. 17:7 Ur III - a standard dating formula)

    1 gu₄-ĝiš á gúb-bì ab-ta-ku₅
    1 yoke-ox whose (-bi) left horn has been cut off <u>from</u> it
    (Westenholz, OSP 1, 101 1:1-3 Sargonic)

    10 anše apin 2 kù gín-kam du₆-gíd-da ì-ta-uru₄
    He had Long Hill plowed <u>with</u> 10 plow-donkeys
    (at a cost) of 2 shekels of silver
    (M. Lambert, RA 73, 12-14 7:26-29 OS Nippur)

The ablative-instrumental prefix is normally -ta-. It can assimilate as -ti- before -ni- as early as the Pre-Sargonic period, and an allomorph -te- is also attested. For example:

    ki-sur-ra iri-na-ka íb-te-bal
    (If) she passed out from the boundary territory of her city
    (Code of Ur-Namma §17 Ur III)

ABLATIVE -ra-

-ta- frequently takes the shape -da-, especially following the prefix ba- as mentioned above. By the time of Gudea -ta- may also change to -ra-, although this is not obligatory, when preceded by a dative prefix ending in an /a/ vowel, including ba-, e.g.:

    ma-*ta-an-šúm   >   ma-ra-an-šúm   He gave it away to me
    ì-ra-*ta-an-šúm > ì-ra-ra-an-šúm   He gave it away to you
    ì-na-*ta-an-šúm > ì-na-ra-an-šúm   He gave it away to her
    ba-*ta-an-šúm   >   ba-ra-an-šúm   He gave it away to them

Examples:

    ᵘnúmun ma-ra-zi-zi ᵘnúmun ma-ra-mú-mú
    Rushes were rising up away from me, rushes were growing up away from me
    (Dumuzi's Dream 27 OB)

    gu₄ ú-gu dé-a-zu gú-mu-ra-ra-ba-al   {ga+mu+ra+*ta+ba-al}
    Your lost ox I will recover for you
    (NSGU 132:4-5)

    itu-ta u₄ NUMERAL ba-ra-zal (var. ba-ta-zal)
    From the month day NUMERAL has passed away
    (a standard date formula)

    u₄ 2 u₄ 3 nu-ma-da-ab-zal   {nu+m+ba+*ta+b+zal+Ø}
    They did not let 2 or 3 days pass
    Gudea Cyl A 23:2 Ur III

In such forms -ra- never takes an associated pronominal element but functions only to add an ablative — but not instrumental — idea to the meaning of the verb. It is in this sense that -ra- can be referred to as the ablative prefix, as distinct from the ablative-instrumental. -ra- can co-occur with -ta- (as well as with a -da- derived from -ta-) to emphasize the ablative idea, and in a half dozen attestations all three forms were used together for extraordinary emphasis. Compare the additive progression of ablatives in the following Gudea passages:

    u₄ ki-šár-ra ma-ta-è   {ma+ta+è+Ø}
    Daylight came out on the horizon for me
    (Cyl A 4:22 Ur III)

    u₄ ki-šár-ra ma-ra-ta-è-a diĝir-zu ᵈnin-ĝiš-zi-da   {mu+ra+ta+è+Ø+a}
    u₄-gin₇ ki-šár-ra ma-ra-da-ra-ta-è   {mu+ra+*ta+*ta+ta+è+Ø}
    The daylight that came out on the horizon for you was your god
    Ninĝišzida; like daylight he came out-out-out on the horizon for you
    (Cyl A 5:19-20)

A final variation appears in OB literary texts, when -ra- > -re/ri- (cf. Thomsen §468) almost always in conjunction with the root bal as in the form im-me-re-bal-bal 'He crossed over them all (the mountains)'. The root should probably be read /bel/ instead of /bal/ in order to account for the unusual assimilation pattern: {m+ba+*ta+bel+bel} > *im-ma-ra-bel-bel > im-me-re-bel-bel. Compare hur-saĝ 7-kam bé-re-bal 'he crossed over the 7th mountain' (var. im-te-bal) (Gilgameš and Huwawa version A 61), which morphologically can hardly represent anything other than {ba+ra+bal}. Compare also the imperative zú bur₅ᵐᵘšᵉⁿ-ra bal-e-eb (vars. bal-a-[..], bal-e-bí-ib) 'Turn away the teeth of the locusts (or birds)!' (Farmer's Instructions 66 OB); and ki-sur-ra iri-na-ka íb-te-bal '(If) she passed over the boundary of her city' (Code of Ur-Namma §17).

Ablative -re/ri- must be distinguished from the 2nd sg. locative-terminative prefix -ri- (see next lesson).

Ablative(-instrumental) prefixes used with non-specific, adverbial meaning, in particular the more emphatic sequences ba-ta-, ba-ra- or ba-da- (< ba-ta-) 'away from, out of', are especially common with verbs of destroying, smashing, killing, finishing and the like. In such contexts we may suppose that the use of the ablative adds some notion like 'completely, thoroughly, totally' to the verbal idea.

As the Verbal Prefix Chain chart shows, the terminative and the ablative-instrumental (or ablative) prefixes are mutually exclusive; they may not co-occur in a chain. A sentence can certainly feature two nominal chains marked by terminative and ablative-instrumental postpositions, but only one of them can be resumed in the verbal chain, for example: lugal-e ugnim eden-ta iri-ni-šè ib-ši-in-túm 'The king brought the army from the desert to his city'.

Several grammars have stated that ablative -ta, and terminative -šè, occur only with impersonal nouns. But occurrences with personal nouns while rare are indeed attested.

VOCABULARY NOTE 2

Plural Verbs

A few verbs show complementary stems depending upon whether their subjects (patients) are singular or plural. These verbs are usually referred to as plural verbs. These include:

1) ti(l) 'to live, dwell'

    sg. ti(l)
    pl. sig₇ (= se₁₂ or si₁₂)

See P. Steinkeller, SEL 1 (1984) 5, also for lu₅(g) or lu₅(k) 'to live' said of animals, with the same plural stem sig₇

2) gub 'to stand'

    sg. gub(DU)
    pl. su₈(g)(DU&DU), šu₄(g) (Gudea) (& indicates one sign written above another)

3) tuš 'to sit, reside'

    sg. tuš
    pl. durun(TUŠ), dúr-ru-un, durunₓ(TUŠ.TUŠ)(OS), dú(TU)-ru-n(a) (Gudea)

Four additional verbs show complementary marû (imperfective) and hamṭu (perfective) as well as plural stems. See pages 118f. in the lesson on imperfective finite verbs for their paradigms. Note that the standard grammars treat the verb tuš as one of this second group of verbs, offering the following paradigm:

	hamṭu	marû
sg.	tuš	dúr (so Edzard, Thomsen reads durun)
pl.	durun	durun

See Edzard 2003, 78 and Thomsen § 270, both following P. Steinkeller, Orientalia 48 (1979) 55f. n. 6, who bases his view on Presargonic and Sargonic forms of the type previously read ì-dúr-rá-a but which are now being read ì-tuš-ša₄-a, as well as on the textual evidence assembled by E. Gordon in Journal of Cuneiform Studies 12 (1958) 48, not all of which is completely convincing. While there may indeed exist some evidence for the Edzard/Thomsen paradigm in later periods, writings which lack a following /r/ that expicitly indicate a value /dur/, for example -tuš-ù-ne or tuš-ù-bi rather than -dúr-ru-ne or dúr-ru-bi, would at least suggest that in certain instances the stem tuš was used for singular marû as well as hamṭu forms. See now P. Attinger, NABU 2010 p. 75-77 for further discussion. Attinger also suggests (p. 76) that the sg. marû form might be /su(š)/.

REMEMBER: THE COMITATIVE, ABLATIVE-INSTRUMENTAL AND TERMINATIVE
                     PREFIXES CAN BE USED WITH OR WITHOUT PRONOMINAL ELEMENTS:

                              ib-ta-ĝen 'He went from it'
                              ba-ta-ĝen 'He went away'

                     ABLATIVE -ra- CAN APPEAR ONLY AFTER ONE OF THE DATIVE
                     PREFIXES ma-, -ra-, -na- OR ba-

                     THE PREFIX SEQUENCES ba-ta, ba-ra- AND ba-da- LEND AN
                     EMPHATIC ABLATIVE SENSE TO THE MEANING OF THE VERB

CORE PREFIXES: ERGATIVE & LOCATIVE-TERMINATIVE

The locative-terminative prefixes occupy the next to the last rank slot before the verbal root. The perfective (ḫamṭu) ergative prefixes occupy the rank slot immediately before the root. See the Verbal Prefix Chain chart for an overview of their forms and associated occurrence restrictions.

The locative-terminative prefixes generally resume either locative-terminative or locative nominal chains, but in the view of this grammar they are formally related to the ergative prefixes and thus have related functions. The ergative and loc.-term. prefixes consist fundamentally, again in the view of this grammar, of pronominal elements only, and so represent a subset of prefixes rather different in form from the dative, comitative, ablative-instrumental and terminative prefixes, which usually consist of both pronominal and case elements. Since they can convey locational, directional or "dimensional" ideas, they can be broadly classed with the latter as dimensional prefixes, but since they also serve to mark essential core syntactic relations, they will be henceforth referred to as the subset of core prefixes following the terminology convention established by T. Jacobsen (Zeitschrift für Assyriologie 78 (1988) 161-220).

The descriptions of the morphology and uses of the locative-terminative prefixes have been many and varied, and Thomsen's restatements have done little to bring order out of chaos. The following exposition represents a personal reinterpretation of the evidence and is offered here more as an argument than as a proven statement of fact.

THE FORM OF THE ERGATIVE/LOCATIVE-TERMINATIVE PREFIXES

Compare the paradigms of pronominal elements which mark the perfective agent, the object of the case elements da/ta/ši and dative *a (and *e), and the locative-terminative prefixes, respectively:

		ergative	da/ta/ši	dative	loc.-term.
Sg	1	∅/?	mu	ma	mu
	2	∅/e[1]	∅/e[1]	ra	ri
	3p	n[2]	n[2]	na	ni
	3i	b	b	ba	bi
Pl	1	—	?	me	?
	2	—	?	?	?
	3p	n-√-š	ne[3]	ne[3]	ne[3]

[1] -e- in OB, assimilated -V- in Ur III, -∅- earlier
[2] -n- in OB, often an assimilated -V- or vocalic allophone /y/ especially Ur III (nu-ù-, bí-ì-, ba-a-, ba-e-) and usually -∅- earlier
[3] the same element

In the singular, the four paradigms resolve into two basic patterns, one which occurs before the root (ergative) and dimensional case elements which begin with consonants (da/ta/ši), and another which occurs before the vowels /a/, /u/ and /i/. (The plural forms, several of which are possibly secondary, are omitted from the present discussion.) The vowel in the case of the dative may be the locative marker /a/, seen in the locative postposition, historically reinterpreted and reused within the verb as the case element of the personal dative. What, however, is the origin and signification of the vowels /u/ and /i/ in the locative-terminative series?

Several interpretations have been advanced. The traditional Falkenstein model explains the vowel /i/ as a form of the loc.-term. postposition -e, while mu- is a not further analyzable Conjugation Prefix. T. Jacobsen maintains that both /u/ and /i/ are case elements, the former an archaic element particularly associated with 1st and 2nd person morphemes. There is a simpler and much more interesting explanation. It does, unfortunately, depend heavily upon historical speculation and so must remain merely an hypothesis, but it does help to unify some otherwise isolated features of verbal morphology and syntax.

Just as the ergative and loc.-term. cases are marked by the same postposition, -e, I suggest that the loc.-term. prefixes are, historically, merely the ergative prefixes used a second time in the prefix chain. The loc.-term. series is thus originally identical with the ergative series, except that the consonants /m/ and /r/ replace the glottal stop or zero morph of the 1st person and the (problematic and possibly secondary) /e/ of the 2nd person. /u/ and /i/, then, originated historically, most clearly in 3rd person forms, as anaptyctic vowels, serving to separate contiguous consonantal elements. It is easier to accept that the loc.-term. prefixes are essentially consonants when one recalls that the ergative prefixes, most visibly the stable /n/ and /b/ elements, carry a load of not just three but four morphemes: person, gender, number *and case*.

The following represent all possible sequential combinations of locative-terminative and ergative elements. All are theoretically possible and most are commonly occurring, although a few are unlikely owing to their semantic improbability (i.e. co-occurrence of two 1st or 2nd person markers: "I with regard to me," "you with respect to you").

```
m+Ø > mu-          r+Ø > -ri-           n+Ø > -ni-           b+Ø > bí-
m+e > mu-e (me-)   r+e > -ri- (-re-?)   n+e > -ni- (-né-?)   b+e > bí-
m+n > mu-un-       r+n > -ri-in-        n+n > -ni-in-        b+n > bí-in-
m+b > mu-ub-       r+b > -ri-ib-        n+b > -ni-ib-        b+b > bí-ib-
```

Like the dative prefixes -ra-, -na-, and -ne-, the loc.-term. prefixes -ri-, -ni-, and -ne- (= dative -ne-) cannot start a verbal form without an initial prosthetic vowel, e.g.:

```
r+n+√  > ì-ri-in-√      BUT      nu+r+n+√  > nu-ri-in-√
n+b+√  > ì-ni-ib-√               nu+n+b+√  > nu-ni-ib-√
ne+n+√ > ì-ne-en-√               nu+ne+n+√ > nu-ne-en-√
```

Why the epenthetic vowel associated with /m/ was /u/ rather than /i/ remains unclear. /u/ occasionally appears as a helping vowel instead of more common /a/ again in connection with /m/ in ventive imperatives, e.g. de₆+m > de₆-um 'Bring it here!'. Compare also the (similarly unexplained) contrast of /u/ and /i/ in the possessive pronoun suffix paradigm: 1st sg. -ĝu₁₀ and 2nd sg. -zu contrasting with 3rd sg. -(a)ni and -bi.

The view that /u/ and /i/ originated as non-morphemic helping vowels in the locative-terminative prefix paradigm is reinforced by the vowel deletion pattern of the same possessive suffixes. Just as prosthetic /u/ and /i/ are not required before the vocalic case element *a in the dative prefix paradigm (e.g. m+a > ma-, not *mu-a-), so too the final /u/ and /i/ of the singular possessives does not appear when a vocalic grammatical marker immediately follows. Compare the singular possessive pronouns followed by the locative postposition with the corresponding singular dative prefixes:

POSSESSIVE plus LOCATIVE   DATIVE

1	-ĝu₁₀	+ a	>	-ĝá	ma-
2	-zu	+ a	>	-za	-ra-
3p	-(a)ni	+ a	>	-(a)-na	-na-
3i	-bi	+ a	>	-ba	ba-

This deletion phenomenon suggests that /u/ and /i/ also serve an anaptyctic function in connection with the possessives, permitting the purely consonantal carriers of information, /ĝ/, /z/, /n/ and /b/ to be pronounced when standing before the consonantal case postpositions -da, -ta, -šè or at the end of a nominal chain.

Of course one is led inevitably to ask whether the possessive suffixes were originally identical with the ergative and locative-terminative prefixes in form and basic function, despite their several phonological differences. I believe that this is indeed the case. /ĝ/ and /m/ regularly alternate in the two major Sumerian dialects, Emegir and Emesal, and /s/ or /z/ have historically changed to /r/ (have become rhotacized) in other languages. Furthermore, a structural parallel is provided by the Mayan language group. Like Sumerian, the Mayan languages are all basically ergative in nature, and in all Mayan languages the ergative verbal affixes which mark the agent also serve, with some phonological changes, as possessive pronouns when prefixed to nouns. A relationship between the possessive pronouns and the loc.-term. prefixes might be illustrated by such passages as

    ki-en-gi ki-uri gú bí-i-zi   {bi+e+zi+Ø}
    With respect to (-*e = bí-) Sumer and Akkad you 'raised the neck'
    (Iddin-Dagan B 29 OB)

    ĝuruš-me-en sila-šè um-è-en šà mu-un-sìg
    I, a young man, when I went out to the street
    the heart pounded there with respect to me (mu-)
    (Man and His God 34 OB)

where the underlying ideas could as well have been rendered by a construction involving a possessive pronoun: gú-bi e-zi '(Of Sumer and Akkad) you raised their neck'; or šà-ĝu$_{10}$ in-sìg 'my heart pounded there'. Conversely, compare the following uses of the possessive pronoun with a non-possessive, more general referential force:

    nam-ti-il níĝ-gig-ga-né hé-na   {hé+n+a$_5$+Ø}
    May life be made into his painful thing (i.e. a thing painful to him)
    (Ur-Namma 28 2:13-14 Ur III)

    usar ér-ĝu$_{10}$ nu-še$_8$-še$_8$
    The neighbor does not cry my tears (i.e., tears with respect to me)
    (Lugalbanda and Hurrum 155 OB)

IMPLICATIONS

Apart from the simplicity it brings to the description of the morphology of the loc.-term. prefixes, the theory advanced here is especially productive of new, albeit admittedly speculative, insights into the historical development of the components of the verbal prefix chain and the fundamental relationship and functions of the "two" ergative and locative-terminative cases, both marked by the same postposition -e.

Above all, it helps to explain why a loc.-term. prefix always seems to co-occur with a following ergative prefix, and, moreover, why it always immediately precedes it (most obvious in OB and later when -n- (and -e-) as well as -b- are regularly written). If, historically speaking, the loc.-term. prefixes are merely the ergative prefixes used a second time in the same verbal chain, then it is no wonder that the two series of elements should always appear to occur together and have neighboring rank order slots in the prefix chain.

If the above is correct, as a corollary we suddenly find ourselves in possession of a powerful new analytical tool. If the presence of a loc.-term. element always presupposes the presence of a following ergative element, then in those periods of the language in which only the 3rd impersonal sg. ergative element -b- regularly appears in writing — virtually all pre-OB stages — the presence of a loc.-term. prefix becomes in itself an indication of the presence of some personal agent in the verbal form, although the form makes no distinction among 1st, 2nd or 3rd persons. Thus bí-dù might represent 'I built it there' {b+∅+√}, 'You built it there' {b+*e+√} or 'He/she built it there' {b+*n+√}.

Once the use of the consonants /m/ and /r/ as 1st and 2nd sg. pronominal elements had been established, the way was opened to adopt them as well in the development of the dative prefixes ma-, -ra- (and me-). One is tempted to suggest that the 2nd sg. dative prefix -ra- was then re-employed as a new dative postposition -ra. This is highly speculative, but after all the dative is an exclusively personal case, and if an essential notion conveyed by the dative is "(to do something) for the benefit of some person", the recognized primacy of the 1st-2nd person "I - thou" orientation of spoken interchange might have influenced the choice of the 2nd sg. prefix -ra- as a new all-person dative postposition -ra.

Lastly, the use of the 1st sg. loc.-term. marker mu- must have been the inspiration for the use of mu- also as the 1st sg. object of the dimensional prefixes da/ta/ši, as well as for its subsequent development as a purely directional ventive element (treated in the next lesson) with a primary meaning 'in my direction, hither, to me'.

THE SO-CALLED LOCATIVE PREFIX -ni-

Most current scholars speak of a locative prefix -ni- which is not related formally or functionally to the prefixes mu-, -ri- and, according to some, to bí-. This school of thought in fact posits two prefixes, the genderless locative -ni- which is not further analyzable and the 3rd sg. personal locative-terminative -ni- which is analyzable as /n/ plus a loc.-term. /*I/ infixed case marker. Edzard, for example, now calls the former prefix the "locative 2" and the latter the "directive" following J. Krecher; see Edzard 2003, §12.8.21-26, for his arguments.

In this view, locative -ni- resumes the locative postposition -a, while loc.-term. -ni- performs the non-locative core prefix functions that will be described below. Both of these homophonous prefixes are capable of "reducing" to a homophonous -n- before the root, just as the core prefix bí- "reduces" to -b- before the root, though the conditioning factors responsible for such reductions are not always clear.

Further, past scholars have been reluctant to identify bí-, which in practice often resumes locative nominal chains, as merely the impersonal 3rd sg. counterpart of -ni-, perhaps in view of the tradition of assigning bí- to the Poebel-Falkenstein category of Conjugation Prefixes. In addition, Chicago Sumerologists some time ago voiced the theory that bí- is actually derived from a sequence *ba+I, i.e. a dative prefix plus a locative-terminative case element. The prefix -ri- was likewise to be derived from a parallel sequence *ra+I. In this view, bí- and -ri- do not therefore function strictly parallel to loc.-term. mu- and -ni- as part of the core prefix subsysterm.

Part of the problem lies in an important co-occurrence restriction on the use of bí-. A verbal chain which features a bí- prefix may never feature a dative, comitative, ablative-instrumental or terminative dimensional prefix. There is no such restriction on the use of -ni-. Thus a form like ì-na-ni-in-dù 'He built it there for him' is grammatical, but *ì-na-bí-in-dù is not. Why this restriction exists (or how it came about) is a perpetual problem for those interested in Sumerian grammar. I prefer to take it as a given feature, a product of earlier stages in the pre-literate historical development of the prefix chain about which we will never know. At any rate, if a speaker wished to include both a 3rd sg. loc.-term. prefix and, for example, a dative prefix in a verbal chain, the only permitted choice for the former was the 3rd sg. personal prefix -ni-. Thus, -ni- may resume both personal and impersonal nouns. Since locative nominal chains are common in Sumerian sentences, and since the locative-terminative prefixes -ni- and bí- were both used to resume locative nominal chains (see below), past scholars came to regard -ni- as a generic, genderless, all-purpose locative prefix and to term it as such.

To recapitulate, bí- is used only to mark 3rd person impersonal nouns, and a verbal chain featuring bí- will never feature a preceding dimensional prefix. -ni- is used for 3rd singular personal or impersonal nouns, and a verbal chain featuring -ni- may feature a preceding dimensional prefix. Such an apparent violation of the rules of Sumerian gender will seem less bothersome if one maintains that the contrast between the pronominal elements -n- and -b- was fundamentally or originally one of deixis rather than the more rigid personal vs. impersonal distinction seen in the later stages of the language.

From the time of the later Ur III texts, after the pronominal element -n- begins to be written consistently, when preradical -b- and -n- are used to mark localizing ideas rather than agents one occasionally observes in certain texts a tendency for -n- to mark locative dimensional objects more often than not. This is doubtless one of the reasons many scholars have believed that the "locative prefix" -ni- reduces, through some unspecified process, to -n- before the root. On the other hand, it is occasionally possible to demonstrate a contrasting preference in particular texts for preradical -b- to resume a loc.-term nominal chain, which is in stark contrast to the actual regular use of bí- to resume locative chains. There are enough such irregularities in the uses of localizing -ni- and bí- and localizing -n- and -b- to make proving theoretical positions conclusively difficult if not impossible. I believe the alternative description presented here has the virtues of greater simplicity and linguistic elegance, but it does not represent current opinion and must be regarded for now as an unproved minority position. See additional discussion later in the lesson on imperatives.

SYNTAX AND FUNCTIONS OF THE CORE PREFIXES

In practice, the ergative prefixes generally mark the agent in perfective verbal forms, and the loc.-term. prefixes generally serve to resume both loc.-term. and locative postpositions, since the locative element /a/ was reinterpreted historically as the prefixed personal dative case marker and no other verbal element was available to resume locative ideas. Recall, however, that the formally dative prefix ba- normally resumes an "impersonal dative" object marked by a locative-terminative postposition. Thus, not all locative-terminative nominal chains are resumed in the verb by loc.-term. prefixes.

But if the ergative (-e) and loc.-term. (-e) postpositions are historically identical, as we have maintained, and if the loc.-term. prefixes are really the ergative prefixes used a second time in the verbal chain, then is it not possible that ergative prefixes could also be used to indicate locative ideas, and, conversely, that loc.-term. prefixes could indicate ergative ideas?

By the time of his last descriptions of the verb, Falkenstein had come to the conclusion that in certain instances preradical -n- or -b- markers could only represent locative ideas; the contexts in question obviously precluded the presence of an agent in the sentence. He therefore assumed that a loc.-term. -ni- or bí- could sometimes, unpredictably, lose their vowels, reduce to -n- or -b-, and so look like ergative elements. Such phonological manipulation is unnecessary if one merely takes the evidence at face value.

Just as the nominal postposition -e can mark both an agent (by whom or which an event takes place) as well as a spatial idea (by, on(to), or next to a place), why should the ergative prefixes which resume it in the verbal chain not be capable of representing spatial ideas as well? There is no doubt that they indicate agents much more often than locative ideas, but this may be due to the fact that agentless passive-like sentences are simply somewhat less common in our texts, or perhaps to a tendency to avoid using them in a spatial sense to minimize ambiguity.

A spatial use of an ergative prefix is most often to be suspected when one encounters an -n- or -b- marker in the verb in a seemingly agentless sentence, together with an otherwise unresumed locative nominal chain, for example:

    za-pa-áĝ-ĝu$_{10}$ kur-kur-ra hé-en-dul   Let my tumult cover all the foreign lands
                                                (Sumerian Letters A 2:10 OB)

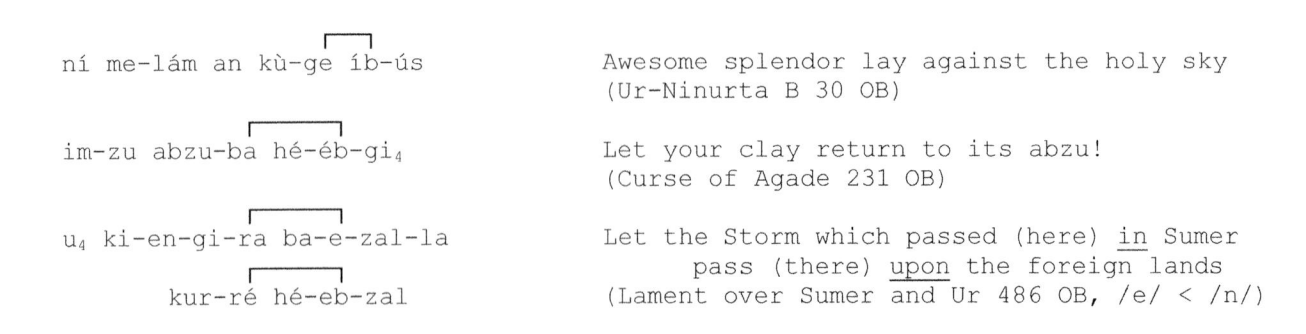

ní me-lám an kù-ge íb-ús	Awesome splendor lay against the holy sky (Ur-Ninurta B 30 OB)
im-zu abzu-ba hé-éb-gi₄	Let your clay return to its abzu! (Curse of Agade 231 OB)
u₄ ki-en-gi-ra ba-e-zal-la kur-ré hé-eb-zal	Let the Storm which passed (here) in Sumer pass (there) upon the foreign lands (Lament over Sumer and Ur 486 OB, /e/ < /n/)

Now to the converse. A locative-terminative prefix such as -ni- or bí- most often marks a locative idea 'in, at, by, on', etc. For example:

sig₄ kul-ab₄ki-a-ka ĝìri bí-in-gub	He set foot in the brickwork of Kulaba (Enmerkar and the Lord of Aratta 299 OB)
éš-dam-ma ba-ni-in-ku₄	She caused her to enter the tavern (Inana and Bilulu 98 OB)
ĝissu-zu kalam-ma bí-lá	You extended your shadow upon the country (Ninurta B Seg. D 13 OB)

It can, however, also mark an agent. But since this represents a second occurrence of an ergative element in the same verb, it follows that such a use is an indication of the presence of a second agent in the sentence, an instrumental agent by whom the primary agent causes the event to occur. The result is a causative construction. For example:

uĝ-e ú nir-ĝál bí-gu₇	Princely food was eaten by me (-Ø-) {b+Ø+√+Ø} by the people (bí-) = I caused princely food to be eaten by the people = I caused the people to eat princely food (Genouillac TCL XV 12:75 OB)
ga nam-šul-la mu-ri-in-gu₇	She (-n-) caused milk of nobility to be drunk by you (-ri-) (Lipit-Ištar D 6 OB)
ù-mu-ni-gu₇ ù-mu-ni-naĝ	When (ù-) I (-Ø-) have had him (-ni-) eat it, when I have had him drink it (elliptical patients <ú> 'food' and <a> 'water' or the like) (Dumuzi and Enkimdu 61 OB)

The existence of instrumental agents had not been generally recognized in part because Sumerian normally substitutes the dative postposition for the loc.-term. with personal nouns. For example, substituting lú 'man, person' for the impersonal collective noun uĝ in the first sentence above, the theoretical personal equivalent would be:

lú-ra ú nir-ĝál ì-ni-gu₇	Princely food was eaten by me for the man = I caused the man to eat princely food

The dative alone can indicate a second agent as in DP 584 vi 3-6 (OS):

énsi-ke₄ en-ig-gal nu-bànda mu-na-gíd	The ruler had it (the field) measured by (nu-bànda-*ra = -na-) Eniggal the overseer.

Plural intrumental agents are nicely illustrated by the following two Old Sumerian passages. In the first, the text lists individual workers by name and the length of canal built by each, and the summary of irrigation work performed features a verb containing the 3rd pl. personal dative marker -ne-. In the second, the texts lists impersonal gangs of unnamed workers by their size and foremen, and the summary of work performed features a verb containing the 3rd collective impersonal dative marker ba-:

    šu-níĝin 2 éš 2 gi e aša₅ ambar-ra šul-me nu-bànda e-ne-dù   {V+ne+n+dù+Ø}
    Total 2 cords 2 rods of ditch, Field of the Marsh,
    Šulme the overseer caused to be constructed by them (-ne-)
    (DP 657 5:1-4; cf. 617 8:5, 622 10:3, etc.)

    šu-níĝin 30 nindan 2 gi e aša₅ gàr-mud en-ig-gal nu-bànda
    šeš-tuš-a e-ma-dù   {Vm+ba+n+dù+Ø}
    Total 30 nindan 2 rods of ditch, Garmud Field, Eniggal   (ba- resumes -*e}
    the overseer caused to be constructed by (-*e) the š.-gangs
    (DP 652 5:1ff.)

Some additional examples of the locative-terminative in context:

    ma-a-ra ĝiš ma-an-du₁₁ ne mu-un-su-ub
    (My spouse) had intercourse with me, rubbed (his) lips upon me (mu-)
    (Inana and An B 17 OB, Emesal ma-a-ra = Emegir ĝá-a-ra)

    á zi-da-za ᵈutu iri-è   {V+ri+Ø+è+Ø}
    I will make Utu (the sun) come forth upon you (-ri-) at your right side
    (Eannatum 1 7:6-8 OS)

    é kù-ga i-ni-in-dù ⁿᵃ⁴za-gìn-na i-ni-in-gùn
    gal-le-eš kù-sig₁₇-ga šu-tag ba-ni-in-du₁₁
    He built the temple with (-ni) silver, he colored it with lapis lazuli,
    greatly he did decorating to it (ba-) with (-ni) gold
    (Enki's Journey 7-8 OB, illustrating the "locative of material")

    ᵈnin-hur-saĝ-ra du₁₀ zi-da-na mu-ni-tuš   {mu+n+n+tuš+Ø}
    She (Inanna) made Ninhursaĝ seat him on her steadfast knees
    (Ean 1 iv 24-26 OS)

    šu ha-mu-ne-bar-re   {ha+mu+ne+bar+e+Ø}
    Let him (-Ø-) release them!
    (TCS 1, 240:9 Ur III, šu - bar takes a loc.-term. indirect object, here -ne-)

    munus-e lú-igi-níĝin-ne ninda e-ne-gu₇
    The Lady fed the inspection personnel bread (i.e. had them eat)
    (DP 166 3:6-4:1 OS)

GENERAL CONCLUSIONS

One could speculate that the ergative/locative-terminative was a primitive and highly generic case marker, the first historically to be incorporated into the verbal prefix chain to judge from its position directly before the root. The relative positions of the remaining verbal prefix subsets may illustrate a history of progressive incorporation into the prefix chain: the farther out toward the beginning of the chain, the more recent the time of incorporation and the less "core" or syntactically vital the nature of the information conveyed. As the next earliest prefixed adverbal marker employed in the verb, the locative-terminative became a general indirect case marker par excellence, a "less marked" case linguistically speaking, and as such it is no wonder that the locative-terminative subset can actually resume any other adverbal postposition and often does, although in the later stages of the language it mainly marks locative ideas.

THE VENTIVE ELEMENT

Following the preformatives, but before any other prefix, comes the rank order position of the ventive element, shown in the Prefix Chain Chart (p. 150) as an upper case M. In the view of this grammar the basic form of this element is /m/, and it is identical with the pronominal element /m/ of the 1st sg. and pl. dative prefixes ma- and me-, the 1st sg. loc.-term. element mu-, and the mu- which serves as the 1st sg. object pronoun of the case markers -da-, -ta- and -ši- as in mu-da-gub 'He stood with me'. Since it is identical with the aforementioned m- and mu- elements, it cannot co-occur with them; it can, however co-occur with all other verbal dimensional or core prefixes.

In keeping with its use as a 1st person element, its basic meaning is "direction towards the speaker," "hither, to me." It also has a more general meaning, something on the order of "up, forth, out into view," and in this sense its use is usually so idiomatic and its contribution to the meaning of a sentence so indeterminate that the modern reader is normally forced to leave it untranslated.

While this is disputed by several contemporary Semitists, it is difficult to avoid suggesting that the Sumerian ventive was loaned into Akkadian as the ventive suffix -(a)m/ -(ni)m, which likewise has explicit 1st sg. reference "to me" (1st sg. dative), a more general meaning "here, up, forth," and, finally, in most cases idiomatic usages which again are typically untranslatable. It should also be compared with the formative suffix /m/ which appears on the other Akkadian dative suffixes (e.g. -šum 'to him' vs. accusative -šu 'him'), though once again the possibility of such a morphological loan into Akkadian is generally disputed.

FORM OF THE VENTIVE ELEMENT

The Sumerian ventive element has two allomorphs: /m/ and /mu/. It appears as /m/ directly before the root, before the prefixes ba- and bi- (i.e. before the pronominal element /b/ followed by a vowel), and directly before the dimensional prefix elements da/ta/ši, i.e. when these function only abverbially without preceding pronominal elements. In the contexts where it appears only as the consonant /m/ it cannot stand at the head of a verbal form without an initial prosthetic vowel to render it pronounceable. Additionally, when preceded by /m/ ba- and bi- assimilate as -ma- and -mi- respectively (this analysis differs substantially from earlier views, for which cf. Thomsen §337-338). Examples:

```
          m+ĝen+Ø       > im-ĝen         He came here

          m+ta+ĝen+Ø    > im-ta-ĝen      He came away

          m+ba+ĝen+Ø    > im-ma-ĝen      He came away

          m+b+n+ĝar+Ø   > im-mi-in-ĝar   He set up it there(in)

    but:  nu+m+ĝen+Ø    > nu-um-ĝen      He did not come here
```

In all other cases, the allomorph /mu/ appears. Additionally, mu- can assimilate as mi- when it precedes a loc.-term. -ni- or -ri- (again Thomsen follows an older analysis, see §336 & 338), and to ma- when it precedes a dative -ra- or -na-. Examples:

```
          m+Ø+ĝar+Ø    > mu-ĝar           I (-Ø-) set it (-Ø) up

          m+e+ĝar+Ø    > mu-e-ĝar or      You set it up
                         me-ĝar (OB)
```

m+n+ĝar+∅ >	mu-un-ĝar	He set it up
m+n+n+ĝar+∅ >	mu-ni-in-ĝar or mi-ni-in-ĝar	He set it up therein (-ni-)
m+n+da+ĝen+∅ >	mu-un-da-ĝen	He came here with her
m+ra+n+šúm+∅ >	mu-ra-an-šúm or ma-ra-an-šúm	He gave it to you
m+r+n+šúm+∅ >	mu-ri-in-šúm or mi-ri-in-šúm	He gave it by means of you
m+ne+n+šúm+∅ >	mu-ne-en-šúm	He gave it to them

Substantially the same rules hold in the imperative transformation, where the chain of prefixes is switched as a whole to suffixed position.

The phonotactic rules can be tabulated as follows:

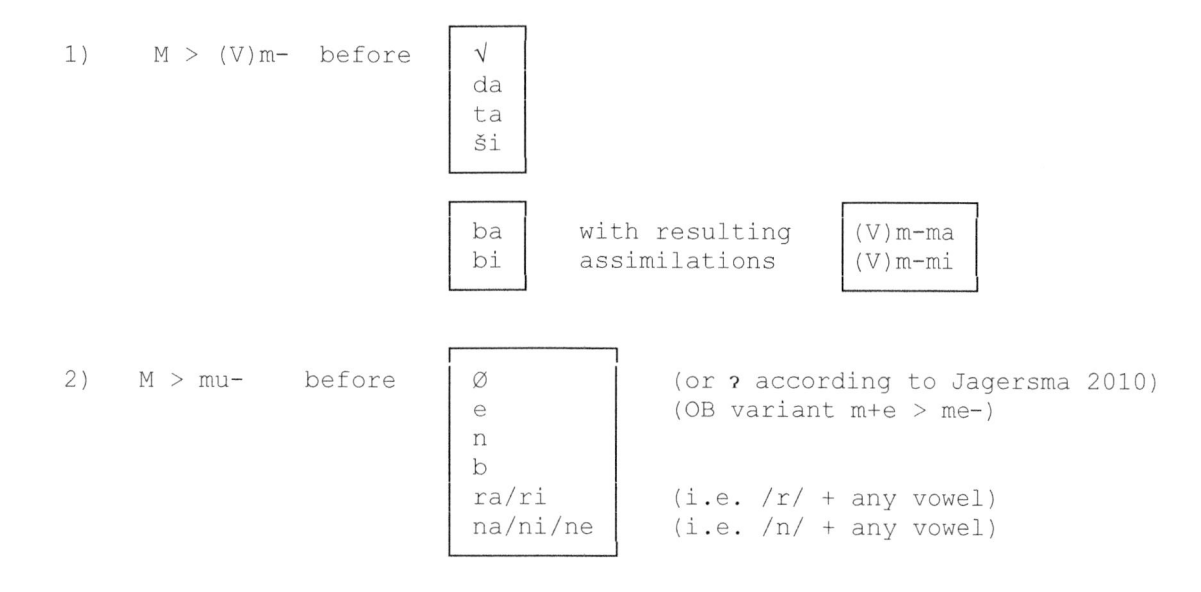

1) M > (V)m- before
   √
   da
   ta
   ši

   ba   with resulting   (V)m-ma
   bi   assimilations   (V)m-mi

2) M > mu- before
   ∅   (or ʔ according to Jagersma 2010)
   e   (OB variant m+e > me-)
   n
   b
   ra/ri   (i.e. /r/ + any vowel)
   na/ni/ne (i.e. /n/ + any vowel)

The preceding analysis, based in part on earlier suggestions of Thorkild Jacobsen in Materials for the Sumerian Lexicon IV (Rome, 1956), was elaborated in the early 1970's by D. Foxvog and W. J. Heimpel at the University of California at Berkeley. This particular analysis of the forms of the ventive has only in part become more generally accepted. Many scholars, Thomsen for example, still speak of two separate elements, -m- and mu-, and some believe that im-ma- is a not further analyzable prefix. See the pertinent descriptions in Attinger 1993 and Edzard 2003, also the earlier substantial article on ventive phenomena by J. Krecher in Orientalia 54 (1985) 133-181.

NOTES ON ORTHOGRAPHY AND USAGE

1) The sequence mu-ub-, whether before the root or one of the dimensional prefixes da/ta/ši, is rare, though not unattested. See Šulgi A 47: uĝ saĝ-gíg-ga u₈-gin₇ lu-a u₆ du₁₀ hu-mu-ub-du₈ (with var. -du, for -du₁₁) "The Black-Headed Folk, numerous as ewes, sent pleased admiration in my direction'. There are also cases in which (V)m- occurs before the root or a dimensional prefix where an expected resumptive -b- is missing from the verbal chain. This phenomenon has lead some scholars to question whether

some, though not all, such (V)m- writings conceal a hidden assimilated /b/, e.g. m+b+√ > mm+√ > im-√. See Attinger 1993, §178a for discussion, earlier views, and counter-arguments. This is a seductive analysis, but as an argument from silence it is difficult to prove, and it has the theoretical disadvantage of hypothesizing two forms of M with the same phonological shape, unless we posit a long-consonant phonological realization, i.e. im:-√ vs. ordinary im-√, which is not reflected in the writing. Note in passing that unlike mu-√ forms im-√ verbal forms are apparently nonexistent in Lagash I Pre-Sargonic texts and begin to appear regularly only in the time of the Gudea inscriptions. Perhaps the /mu/ allomorph served the same purpose as /(V)m/ in Old Sumerian.

2) It is common in older texts for the double /mm/ of the assimilation m+bi > Vm-mi or m+ba > Vm-ma- to be written with just a single /m/. Compare the following three sets of parallel passages from Šulgi Hymn D 219/335 (Ur III) and Gudea Cyl A 6:23/7:23 & Cyl A 6:16/7:13-14 (Ur III):

a) níĝ ki-en-gi-ra ba-a-gu-la kur-ra ga-àm-mi-íb-gu-ul   {ba+n+gul+Ø+a}
   That which has been destroyed here in Sumer I will destroy in the foreign land

   níĝ ki-en-gi-ra ba-a-gu-la kur-ra ì-mi-in-gu-ul   (= im-mi-)
   That which had been destroyed here in Sumer he destroyed in the foreign land

b) šu-nir ki-áĝ-ni ù-mu-na-dím mu-zu ù-mi-sar   (= um-mi-)
   When you have fashioned his beloved standard for him and written your name on it

   šu-nir ki-áĝ-ni mu-na-dím mu-ni im-mi-sar
   He fashioned his beloved standard for him and wrote his name on it

c) é-níĝ-GA-<ra>-za kišib ù-mi-kúr ĝiš ù-ma-ta-ĝar   (= um-mi-, um-ma-)
   When you have altered the seals in your storehouse and set out wood from it

   é-níĝ-GA-ra-na kišib bí-kúr ĝiš im-ma-ta-ĝar
   He altered the seals in his storehouse and set out wood from it

3) The assimilation mu- > ma- before dative -ra- or -na- is optional and unpredictable. Compare the variation in the verbal prefixes of Gudea Cyl A 12:3-7:

   sig-ta ĝišha-lu-úb ĝišNE-ha-an mu-ra-ta-è-dè   {m+ra+ta+è(d)+e+Ø}
   igi-nim-ta ĝišeren ĝiššu-úr-me ĝišza-ba-lum ní-bi-a ma-ra-an-tùmu   {m+ra+n+tùm+e+Ø}
   kur ĝišesig-a-ka ĝišesig ma-ra-ni-tùmu   {m+ra+n+n+tùm+e+Ø}
   From above halub and nehan wood will come forth for you,
       from below cedar, cypress, and juniper will bring themselves in for you,
       from within the mountain of ebony ebony will be brought in for you

4) Some have proposed that the prefix sequence mi-ni-, attested first in the Gudea inscriptions, is not merely an assimilated (allomorphic) form of mu-ni-, parallel to OB mu-ri- > mi-ri- and mu-ra- > ma-ra-, but is to be analyzed in some different fashion. But P. Delnero, in Fs. P. Attinger (OBO 256, 2012) 139ff., has shown them to be identical. See Attinger 1993 §177 for an exposition of the previous alternative explanations.

5) Since the 2nd person agent marker -e- seems to have developed secondarily during the Ur III period, perhaps by analogy with the fuller paradigms of Akkadian subject pronouns, it is reasonable to assume the that the ventive allomorph mu- which occurs before it came into use by analogy with the mu- occurring before the elements -n- and -b-. Further, many passages which show the OB 2nd sg. variant me- < m(u)-e- also offer the standard writing in a duplicate text, e.g. Lugalbanda 106: inim ga-mu-e-da-ab-du$_{11}$ 'I will say a word regarding you' with var. ga-me-da-ab-du$_{11}$.

6) In reading Sumerian one will encounter a variety of exceptions, neologisms, or pure oddities in verbal prefix sequences in forms featuring the ventive element, not only in

literary texts, which are mostly the products of the OB scribal schools, but also in Ur III economic and administrative documents at a time when new orthographic conventions are being established.

FUNCTIONS OF THE VENTIVE ELEMENT

In only a few clearly defined contexts is it possible state that the ventive is definitely or most likely functioning with 1st person reference. Elsewhere its meaning is more or less problematic. The following observations can be made:

1) In the dative prefixes ma- and me- it ALWAYS marks 1st person:

```
ma+n+šúm+Ø  >  ma-an-šúm      He gave it to me
šúm+me+b    >  šúm-me-eb      Give it to us!    (OB imperative)
```

Care must be taken to distinguish these true dative prefixes from (a) the -ma- infix in the assimilated sequence m+ba > -m-ma- often written with only one /m/ in earlier texts, e.g. ì-ma-, nu-ma-, hé-ma- for im-ma-, nu-um-ma-, hé-em-ma-, etc.; and (b) the me- prefix which contains the 2nd sg. element -e- (a variant of mu-e-), e.g. mu-e-ĝar or me-ĝar 'you set it up'. Only a few attestations of 1st pl. dative me- are known, including the above imperative found in the myth Inana's Descent, while the me- that is a variant for mu-e- is well attested in OB.

2) When it appears immediately before a dimensional case element da/ta/ši or an ergative prefix it MAY represent a 1st sg. pronominal object or loc.-term. prefix, but most often it doesn't:

```
m+da+gub+Ø  >  mu-da-gub      He stood with me

m+n+šúm+Ø   >  mu-un-šúm      He had me give it    (unusual)
                              He gave it here      (usual)
```

3) When it appears before a dimensional prefix featuring an explicit pronominal object it NEVER has explicit 1st person reference:

```
m+ra+n+šúm+Ø    >  mu-ra-an-šúm    He gave it (up) to you
m+e+da+Ø+dù+Ø   >  mu-e-da-dù      I built it (up) with you
```

4) With certain motion verbs it OFTEN conveys the notion "hither, here," frequently contrasting with the prefix ba- in its ablative use:

```
m+ĝen+Ø       >  im-ĝen         He came here        (ventive)
ba+ĝen+Ø      >  ba-ĝen         He went away        (ablative)
m+ba+ĝen+Ø    >  im-ma-ĝen      He came away        (ventive + ablative)

m+n+de₆+Ø     >  mu-un-de₆      He brought it in
ba+n+de₆+Ø    >  ba-an-de₆      He took it away
```

5) Verbs of motion or action are in general more likely to show the ventive than verbs of state, consistent with its fundamental directional character.

6) Verbs of state can be given a directional nuance with the addition of a ventive, e.g. ĝál 'to exist', ĝál + ventive 'to produce'; zu 'to know', zu + ventive 'to recognize' or 'to (make) learn'.

7) In the succinct language of Ur III administrative texts, verbs featuring an agent are more likely to show a ventive, while agentless verbs tend to show a "passive" ba- or a neutral ì- prefix. Compare the standard contrast in Ur III year formulas between plus-agent mu-dù {m+n+dù+Ø} 'he built it' vs. agentless ba-dù 'it was built'.

8) Personal dative prefixes seem to attract the ventive, i.e. mu-ra-, mu-na-, mu-ne-, likewise with the Akkadian ventive, e.g. *iddinaššum < iddin-am-šum* 'he gave to him'.

9) The ventive may add a kind of telic nuance, "up to the required or final point, to the point of completion," as, possibly, in the following:

    ur-lum-ma énsi umma^(ki) en-an-na-túm-me e ki-sur-ra ^(d)nin-ĝír-su-ka-šè mu-gaz   {m+n+gaz+Ø}
    Enanatum pounded Urlumma, the governor of Umma,
    all the way up to the boundary ditch of Ninĝirsu
    (En I 29 10:6-11:2 OS)

10) When a prefix chain begins with an element which requires a preceding prosthetic vowel, the ventive may perhaps be chosen instead to add a little directional color in place of the neutral, meaningless vowel /i/:

    mu-na-an-šúm   He gave it out to him   rather than   ì-na-an-šúm
    mu-ni-in-ĝar   He set it up there   rather than   ì-ni-in-ĝar

11) In many other cases the ventive is an added stylistic feature too nuanced for confident translation. Compare the following two passages involving the verb <inim> du₁₁ 'to say' where the ventive is untranslatable:

    e ki-sur-ra ^(d)nin-ĝír-su-ka e ki-sur-ra ^(d)nanše ĝá-kam ì-mi-du₁₁   {Vm+b+n+du₁₁+Ø}
    "The boundary levee of Ninĝirsu and the boundry levee of Nanše
    are mine!" he declared
    (Ent 28-29 4:24-28 OS)

    an-ta-sur-ra ĝá-kam ki-sur-ra-ĝu₁₀ bí-du₁₁   {b+n+du₁₁+Ø}
    "The Antasurra is mine, it's my border territory!" he declared
    (Ukg 6 4:7'-9' OS)

In the following hymnic passage, the second verb repeats the first with the addition of a ventive adding a nuance that is, again, untranslatable:

    lugal nam gi₄-rí-íb-tar^(ar) nam-du₁₀ gú-mu-rí-íb-tar^(ar)   {ga+(mu+)r+b+tar}
    O king, I will decree destiny regarding you,
    I will decree a good destiny regarding you
    (Šulgi D 384 Ur III)

12) Finally, many sets of parallel passages could be adduced to suggest that the ventive adds a mild directional nuance to a verbal form, although confident translation remains difficult. Compare the following earlier and later lines from a continuous narrative:

    á mu-gur le-um za-gìn šu im-mi-du₈   {Vm+b+n+du₈+Ø}
    He (the warrior) bent out (his) arm and held out a lapis writing-board
    (Gudea Cyl A 5:3 Ur III)

    á mu-gur le-um za-gìn šu bí-du₈-a   {b+n+du₈+Ø+a}
    (The warrior) who bent out (his) arm and held a lapis writing-board
    (Gudea Cyl A 6:3f.)

REMEMBER: THE VENTIVE ELEMENT HAS TWO MAIN CONTEXT-DEPENDENT USES:

        - 1ST PERSON PRONOMINAL OBJECT OF DIMENSIONAL/CORE PREFIXES
        - DIRECTIONAL PARTICLE MEANING 'HITHER' or 'UP, OUT, FORTH'

RELATIVE CLAUSES: THE NOMINALIZING SUFFIX -a

The verbal suffix -a is known by several names which describe its apparent functions: the "nominalizing," participializing," or "relativizing" particle. Thomsen refers to it as the Subordination Suffix (§483-491; 512-518). Edzard 2003 recognizes several different homophonous -a suffixes depending upon grammatical context. Current scholarship now generally refers to it as the nominalizing suffix. Quite simply, -a in most cases generates finite or non-finite relative clauses.

ORTHOGRAPHY

In certain periods the writing system often fails to show this -a suffix clearly. For example, in Gudea the participle ki áĝ+a 'beloved' will often be written simply ki áĝ, while the OB scribes will consistently write ki áĝ-ĝá or ki áĝ-a. In reaction to this phenomenon earlier scholars have employed sign values which include a final /a/, e.g., áĝa for áĝ, aka for ak, etc. This theory of an "overhanging vowel" (überhängender Vokal) has a basis in fact for a number of signs: such longer forms are actually attested in Akkadian signlists. Whether one uses these longer values is a matter of individual taste or current convention, but they are better avoided unless needed specifically to help clarify meaning. The problem is orthographic rather than grammatical and goes hand in hand with the tendency of earlier texts not to write, for example, the /a/ vowel of the 3rd sg. possessive suffix -(a)ni or of the genitive postposition -ak, e.g., lugal-ni 'his king' or é lagaš^{ki}-ka 'in the temple of Lagash'.

The presence of a following locative postposition -a is often obscured in later orthography by the suffix -a. For example, the temporal clause {u₄ é Vn+dù+Ø+a+a} 'on the day he built the house' might be written u₄ é in-dù-a, rather than plene ("fully") as u₄ é in-dù-a-a. In such abbreviated writings it is difficult to decide whether the locative -a has elided to relativizing -a or if the combination of the two markers was perhaps pronounced as a long vowel whose length was not regularly indicated in writing.

Finally, when analyzing forms one must be careful not to misconstrue instances of a nominalizing -a followed by the possessive suffix -(a)ni. The /a/ of the possessive normally appears only after consonants. Thus in the phrase é dù-a-ni 'his built house' {é dù+a+(a)ni}, the vowel /a/ should be understood as the nominalizing suffix, rather than the helping vowel associated with the possessive.

GENERAL SYNTAX

The suffix -a occupies the last rank order position after any verbal stem modifiers including the modal suffix -(e)d- and any subject or imperfective agent pronominal suffixes. A single -a is occasionally seen at the end of a series of parallel clauses, marking the subordination of the entire series rather than individual verbs within the series. Thomsen may be correct in stating (§483) that -a is a syntactic particle rather than the mark of a morpheme. One basic function is to transform an underlying finite declarative sentence into a relative or subordinate clause, either finite:

   lugal-e é in-dù   > lugal lú é in-dù-a
   The king built the house The king, the man who built the house,

or non-finite (in which verbal prefixes are for the most part deleted):

   é ba-dù   > é dù-a
   The house was built The house that was built

A relative clause stands in apposition to a noun, occupying a place in an expanded nominal chain between the head noun (and any adjectives) and following possessive/demonstrative, personal plural and case markers. Put another way, a relative clause is embedded in a nominal chain as a kind of secondary adjective. In the following illustration, (a) representing the sentence underlying the relative clause is embedded in the nominal chain (b) to produce the expanded nominal chain (c):

    (a)   lugal-e é mah in-dù   The king built the lofty temple

    (b)   é mah-bi-ta   From that lofty temple

    (c)   é mah | lugal-e <é mah> dù-a | -bi-ta > é mah lugal-e dù-a-bi-ta
                                                                      From that lofty temple built by the king

Note here that the patient of the sentence underlying the relative clause is deleted to avoid redundancy. (As will be seen later, when the head noun of the expanded chain represents the agent of the relative clause, a relative pronoun is substituted for the nominal agent of the clause.)

In more complex sentences the head noun of the extended nominal chain in question may be difficult to identify immediately, or may even be deleted in certain standard idiomatic contexts, but the basic syntax will always be the same.

A sentence can contain nominal chains representing a subject, an agent, and indirect objects or adverbial phrases, and each type of chain can be modified by a relative clause. In a sentence containing several coordinate relative clauses, -a commonly appears only on the last verb, e.g. á mu-gur le-um za-gìn šu bí-du$_8$-a 'He who bent out (his) arm and held a lapis writing board' (Gudea Cyl A 6:3f. Ur III). The verb in a relative clause can be finite, with prefixes and suffixes intact, or non-finite, in which most prefixes and suffixes are deleted, the verb becoming essentially a participle.

NON-FINITE RELATIVE CLAUSES

Clauses Modifying a Subject or Patient

1) In its simplest use -a is suffixed to non-finite verbal stems to produce short relative clauses which can often be translated as adjectival past (passive) participles, for example:

    é šub-ba   the house that collapsed > the collapsed house
    é dù-a   the house that was built > the built house
    inim du$_{11}$-ga   the word that was spoken > the spoken word   {du$_{11}$(g)+a}

A subset of such simple participles are those adjectives which sometimes or regularly take an -a suffix like kal(a)g+a > kal-ga, 'mighty', du$_{10}$(g)+a > du$_{10}$-ga 'good', or sa$_6$(g)+a > sa$_6$-ga 'pleasing'. The difference between a simplex adjective and one featuring a suffixed -a is normally a nuance which escapes us. J. Krecher (see Thomsen §80) has argued that an adjective with a suffixed -a is more "determined" than one without, e.g., lú du$_{10}$-ga 'the man who is good', i.e. the good man (about whom we're speaking)', as opposed to lú du$_{10}$ 'a good man (in general)'.

2) Non-finite verbal forms can, by definition, feature no prefix other than the negative preformative nu- 'not', and so simple participles cannot themselves be marked for the presence of an agent. The relative clause can, however, include a nominal chain which does indicate the agent:

    lú-e é in-dù   >   é lú-e dù-a
    The man built the house   The house built by the man

This very common pattern is called the MESANEPADA CONSTRUCTION after the name of an early ruler which illustrates it:

    mes an+e pà(d)+a   >   Mes-an-né-pà-da   The noble youth chosen by An

In passing, compare at this point an idiomatic circumlocution, common in Gudea and earlier Lagash royal inscriptions typically read by the beginning student, which often alternates with the Mesanepada Construction in strings of royal epithets. Here a dependent genitive signals an implicit agent (cf. Thomsen §14):

    énsi á šúm-ma ᵈnin-ĝír-su-ka   The governor who was given strength
                                         of (and, by implication, by) Ninĝirsu

3) The Mesanepada Construction refers to an nonfinite clause that contains an explicitly marked agent. Relative clauses can also feature nominal chains which supply other sorts of information:

    é iri-a dù-a   the house built in the city
    lú úriᵏⁱ-šè ĝen-na   the man who went to Ur
    níĝ šu-ta šub-ba   a thing fallen from the hand
    é ur₅-gin₇ dím-ma   a house fashioned like this

4) Non-finite imperfective verbal stems featuring the modal suffix -(e)d- (participial forms loosely referred to as infinitives) can be relativized:

    kù-babbar šúm-mu-dè   {√+e+d+e}   >   kù-babbar šúm-mu-da   {√+e+d+a}
    to (-e) give the silver   the silver that is to be given

The resulting relative construction can then feature a final copula:

    kù-babbar-bi kù-babbar šúm-mu-dam   {√+e+d+a+m}
    That silver is silver that is to be given

which, with deletion of the redundant head noun of the relative clause, can become:

    kù-babbar-bi šúm-mu-dam
    That silver is to be given

Clauses Modifying an Agent or Indirect Object
----

1) Clauses modifying an agent tend to be finite, but non-finite examples do exist (cf. Thomsen §515, 517d), for example:

    en-e a huš in-gi₄   >   en a huš gi₄-a
    The lord turned back   The lord who turned back the raging waters
    the raging waters   (Gudea Cyl A 8:15 Ur III)

2) Note the deletion of the agentive marker with the preceding resulting relative clause. In all types of clauses featuring ergatives or dimensional indirect objects the adverbal case marker associated with the underlying source sentence is suppressed. Compare a clause featuring a personal dative object in its underlying declarative form:

    lú-ra kù-babbar ba-na-šúm   >   lú kù-babbar šúm-ma
    Silver was given to the man   The man (to whom was) given silver

3) A possessive suffix can be used with the implication that the "possessor" is the agent of the clause. For example:

```
lú-ra kù-babbar ì-na-an-šúm    >    lú kù-babbar šúm-ma-ni
He gave silver to the man           His man (to whom) silver was given =
                                    The man to whom he gave silver
```

Compare the possibly related idiomatic use of the genitive in the following phrases from the Gudea cylinders, which occur in contexts that recommend a translation in which the "possessor" is the implied agent:

```
lú é dù-a-ke₄      By the man of the built house =         {dù+a+ak+e}
(Cyl A 20:24)      By the man who built the house

lú é dù-a-ra       For the man of the built house =        {dù+a+ak+ra}
(Cyl A 15:13)      For the man who built the house
```

FINITE CLAUSES

In finite clauses verbal affixes are not deleted, and the resulting nominal chains are somewhat more complex, convey more explicit information, and have broader uses than the simpler non-finite constructions. See most recently F. Karahashi, "Relative Clauses in Sumerian Revisited," AV Black (2011) 167-171.

Simple Restrictive Clauses

A finite relative clause is typically used when two declarative sentences having the same subjects or agents are merely to be linked as main and restrictive relative clauses. In such cases a virtual relative pronoun, usually lú 'man, person' for personal nouns, níĝ 'thing' for impersonals, is used in the relative clause to avoid repetition of the head noun representing the subject or agent of the new nominal chain. Assume the following two source sentences:

```
(1) lugal úri^ki-šè ì-ĝen      The king went to Ur
(2) lugal-e é in-dù            The king built the temple
```

Either sentence can be embedded in the other as a restrictive clause, resulting in one of two new sentences:

```
(a) lugal | lú é in-dù-a | úri^ki-šè ì-ĝen      The king who built the temple
                                                went to Ur

(b) lugal | lú úri^ki-šè ì-ĝen-na | é in-dù     The king who went to Ur
                                                built the temple
```

In both new sentences new nominal chains have been generated, each containing a relative clause standing in apposition to the head noun lugal. Now all nominal chains must end with a case marker, and since the new expanded nominal chain in (c) represents the subject of the main verb ì-ĝen, it stands in the absolutive case:

```
(c) | lugal lú é+Ø n+dù+Ø+a | + Ø   úri^ki-šè V+ĝen+Ø
```

Since the new expanded nominal chain in (d) represents the agent of the main verb in-dù, it stands, on the other hand, in the ergative case:

```
(d) | lugal lú úri^ki+šè V+ĝen+Ø+a | + e   é+Ø n+dù+Ø
```

Note that in (a) the ergative postposition -e on lugal has been suppressed in the process of generating the relative clause, and that in (b) the ergative at the end of the new nominal chain has elided to the preceding relativizing particle -a, a normal occurrence. Note also the embedded clause of (c) can be abbreviated even further with the elimination of the relative pronoun and the ergative prefix on the verb to produce a simple past participle, e.g. lugal ᵍⁱˢmes abzu-a dù-a 'the king who planted the mes-tree in the Abzu' (Enki and the World Order 4 OB)

Temporal and Causal Subordinate Clauses (§489-491)

Finite relative constructions are commonly used with specific head nouns and case postpositions to form standard sorts of temporal or causal subordinate clauses. The structure of these subordinate clauses is slightly different from that of the nominal chains incorporating restrictive relative clauses discussed above. In such a subordinate clause an entire sentence is relativized and stands in apposition to the head noun of the newly generated clause. There is no suppression of internal case markers and no use of relative pronouns.

1) Following are standard combinations of head noun and case marker employed with relativized sentences to generate <u>temporal</u> subordinate clauses:

    u₄ SENTENCE+a+a   in/on the day (that), when
    u₄ SENTENCE+a+ta   from the day (that), after, since
    u₄ SENTENCE+a+gin₇   like the day (that), during, while
    mu SENTENCE+a+a   in the year (that)
    eger SENTENCE+a+ta   after (temporal); from the back of, behind (local)
    en-na SENTENCE+a+šè   until, as long as (temporal); up to, as far as (local)

Examples:

    PN u₄ nam-gala-šè in-ku₄-ra-a   {Vn+ku₄(r)+Ø+a+a}
    (For) PN, on the day he entered the status of gala-priest   {-n- resumes -šè}
    (Fish Cat. 412:2 Ur III)

    u₄ ᵈinanna-ke₄ igi nam-ti-la-ka-ni mu-un-ši-bar-ra-a
    When Inanna extended her eye of life out towards him
    (Gudea Statue C 2:11-13 Ur III)

    en-na ì-ĝen-na-aš   {V+ĝen+Ø+a+šè}
    Until he has come
    (Grégoire, AAS p. 36 Ur III)

Note that the head nouns u₄ 'day' and eger 'back' are VERY OFTEN idiomatically deleted, resulting in potentially confusing forms such as:

    úriᵏⁱ-šè im-ĝen-na-ta é in-dù
    After he came to Ur, he built the temple

The confusion is compounded by the tendency of the locative postposition -a to be elided in later texts, at least in writing, to a preceding relativizing -a, resulting in a form which offers no clue as to its underlying structure, for example:

    iri-šè im-ĝen-na é-gal-la-ni in-dù
    When he had come to the city, he built his palace

standing for:

    u₄ iri-šè im-ĝen-a-a é-gal-la-ni in-dù

2) The following combinations of head noun and case marker are commonly employed with a nominalized sentence standing as the rectum of a genitive construction to generate <u>causal</u> subordinate clauses:

    bar SENTENCE+a+ak+šè/a   because, for the sake of, instead of, in place of
    mu SENTENCE+a+(ak+)šè   because, instead of, about ('to the name of')
    nam SENTENCE+a+ak+šè   on the occasion of, it being so that, since

    bar lugal ᵈen-líl-le á šúm-ma ì-me-a ì-zu-a-ke₄-eš   {Vn+zu+Ø+a+ak+šè}
    Because they (the people) knew that he was a king given might by Enlil
    (Utuheĝal's Annals 54 Ur III)

    bar še-bi nu-da-sù-sù-da-ka   {nu+n+da+sud-sud+Ø+a+ak+a}
    Because he could not make this (large amount of) barley grow lushly
    (Ent 28-29 2:27 OS) (note the abilitative use of -da-)

    mu sipa zi ba-ra-ab-è-a-šè sila daĝal ki-a-ne-di ĝál-la-ba ér gig ì-še₈-še₈
    Because it (fate) had made the faithful shepherd go away, bitter tears
    were being wept in those broad streets where there was (once) dancing
    (Ur-Namma A 18-19 OB)

    nam é-kur ki-áĝ-ĝá-ni ba-hul-a-šè
    It being so that his beloved Ekur-temple had been destroyed
    (Curse of Agade 151 OB)

3) Like u₄ or eger in temporal clauses, bar, mu, or nam is often deleted, leaving only the suffixes to help indicate the causal idea. This deletion phenomenon has led to the describing of the sequence -a-ke₄-eš as an independent adverbial suffix meaning 'because'.

    ur-saĝ ug₅-ga ì-me-ša-ke₄-eš   {V+me+(e)š+a+ak+šè}
    Because they were slain heros
    (Gudea Cyl A 26:15 Ur III)

    1 2/3 ma-na 1/2 gín kù-babbar PN-e PN₂-ra in-da-tuku-a-ke₄-eš
    Because PN had (a debt of) 1 2/3 mina 1/2 shekel silver against PN₂
    (NSGU 117:2-5 Ur III)

TEMPORAL OR CAUSAL ADVERBIAL EXPRESSIONS (§184; 201; 205)

Any of the preceding combinations of head noun and adverbal case marker can be used in simple nominal chains to produce adverbial phrases. With the temporal clauses above, compare, for example, u₄-da udu e-hád siki-bi é-gal-la a-ba-de₆ 'whenever the sheep was pure, and its wool had been taken into the palace' (Ukg 6 1:18'-19' OS). In the following examples, note that a possessive pronoun can replace the rectum in constructions that require a genitive.

    u₄-da   on the day, at the time, when, whenever, if
    u₄-ba   at that time, then
    u₄-bi-ta   since that time, thereafter, afterwards

    eger é-ĝá-šè   to the rear of my house (local)

eger-ĝu₁₀-šè	after me (also in the sense "after I die")
eger-a-na	behind him
eger numun-na-šè	after the sowing (lit. seed)
en-na zú-si-šè	until the sheep-shearing (season) (TCS 1, 282:3)
bar lugal-za-ke₄-eš	because of your king
bar-ĝu₁₀-a	for my sake
bar-zu-šè	because of you
bar-bi-ta	because of this
mu-bi-šè	because of that (cf. Akk. *ana šum > aššum)
mu ur-gi₇-ra-šè	(dead animals) for (feeding) the dogs
mu ú-gu dé-a-šè	because it had gotten lost (Limet, TSU 86 Ur III)
nam-bi-šè	because of that, therefore
nam-iri-na-šè	For the Sake of His City (OS personal name)
nam é dù-da lugal-la-na-šè	for the sake of the house that was to be built of (i.e. by) his king (Gudea Cyl A 17:7)
ĝá-ke₄-éš-hé-ti	Let Him Live For My Sake! (Ur III personal name with an elliptical <nam>, MVN 11, 163:13)

For adverbs of manner and localizing adverbial expressions see also the lessons on nouns, adjectives and adverbs.

OTHER SUBORDINATION DEVICES

tukum-bi (or tukum) is the primary subordinating conjunction, with the meaning 'if'.

A rare suffix -a-ka-nam 'because of, for the sake of' can produce causal clauses:

> ku₆ ĝá-ĝar-ra-šè nu-mu-túm-a-ka-nam. šubur nu-bànda gú-ne-ne-a e-ne-ĝar
> Because they (the fishermen) had not brought in (the money) for the (amount of) fish assigned, Šubur the overseer "put it on their necks" (i.e. made them liable for it) (Bauer, AWL 183 2:2ff. OS) (again with an elliptical head noun <nam>?)

An equally rare suffix is -na-an-na 'without, except for' (= Akk. *balum*), see Falkenstein, NSGU II p. 40 ad 10', C. Wilcke, ZA 59 (1969) 83 n. 78.

> PN-na-an-na lú nu-ù-da-nú-a   {nu+n+da+nú+Ø+a}
> That except for PN no one had slept with her
> (NSGU 24:10'-11' Ur III)

In a usage called the "subjunctive" by Thomsen (§484), a subordinate clause is made dependent upon a main clause which features a verb, for example, of speaking, commanding, or knowing. Compare perhaps the use of the Akkadian subjunctive suffix -*u* in oaths.

> kù-babbar mu-na-an-šúm-a, nam-érim-bi in-ku₅
> That he had given him the silver,
> he swore that oath (i.e. an oath to that effect)

> bar lugal ᵈen-líl-le á šúm-ma ì-me-a, ì-zu-a-ke₄-eš
> Because they (the people) knew that he was a king given might by Enlil
> (Utuheĝal's Annals 54 Ur III)

REMEMBER: THE NOMINALIZING SUFFIX -a GENERATES RELATIVE CLAUSES.

A RELATIVE CLAUSE IS ALWAYS EMBEDDED IN A NOMINAL
CHAIN, MODIFYING THE HEAD NOUN. AS A KIND OF SECONDARY
ADJECTIVE, IT ANSWERS THE QUESTION: "WHAT KIND OF?"

PREFORMATIVES (MODAL PREFIXES)

The preformatives have also been called modal prefixes (Civil, Thomsen), modal profixes (Jacobsen), or modal indicators (Edzard). The latter terms refer to the uses of a subclass of this class of prefix: the idea of modality in linguistics concerns such notions as obligation, necessity, permission or ability. The older term preformative refers to the rank order of the class: a preformative must always stand as the first element in a verbal chain; no other verbal prefix may precede it. This outermost rank-order position suggests that this class of prefix was the last historically to have been incorporated into the verbal prefix chain; it is noteworthy that these prefixes do not resume nominal chain information like the core and dimensional elements. Since not all members of this rank of prefixes are, strictly speaking, modal elements, the traditional term preformative is retained here. See Thomsen §359-421 and Edzard 2003, pp. 113-127.

NEGATIVE nu- (la-, li-) 'not' (§359-365)

nu- negates both finite and non-finite verbal forms. It is written nu- everywhere except before the verbal prefixes ba- or bí- where in all but the earliest periods it usually appears as la- or li- respectively: nu+ba > la-ba-, nu+bi > li-bí-.

Thomsen describes one use of nu as the "negative counterpart to the enclitic copula" (§363), but this minimal form is perhaps better explained as a negated finite copula with a regular deletion of the final /m/, e.g. {kù nu+m+Ø} > kù *nu-um > kù nu 'It was not (made of) silver'. Compare the use of the precative (see below) with a following copula: hé-em or hé-àm 'Let it be!', which can also appear without a final /m/, i.e. hé-a or even just hé. In OB nu- is occasionally employed as a verbal root meaning 'not to be' as in in-nu "he is/was not". See the lesson on the copula for more discussion.

WISH AND ASSERTION (POSITIVE AND NEGATIVE) (§366-403):

Earlier views

Recent traditional grammatical descriptions have given the following sorts of labels for this group of modal prefixes:

hé- (ha-, hu-)	Precative (or Optative) & Affirmative
ga- (gi$_4$-, gú-)	Cohortative & Affirmative
na-	Prohibitive (or Negative Precative)
na-	Affirmative (or Volitive or Negative Question)
ba-ra-	Vetitive & Categorical Negative

hé- and ha- are (apparently free) allomorphs as early as the Pre-Sargonic period, and a further allomorph hu- appears before the prefix mu- in OB (Edzard 2003 p. 116; Thomsen §394; M. Civil, RA 60 [1966] 15). Similarly, ga- occasionally takes the forms gi$_4$- before bí- and gú- before mu- in Ur III and later.

Problems have always surrounded the understanding of these prefixes. In older descriptions, ga- is properly 1st person cohortative "let me" and assertive/affirmative "I shall", and ba-ra- is its negative counterpart. ba-ra-, however, can also occur with other persons. Likewise, hé- is properly 3rd person precative "let him" and assertive/affirmative "he will indeed", and na- is its negative counterpart. But both can also occur with other persons. Since the Emesal dialect uses a single prefix dè- (with assimilated variants da- and du$_5$) in place of precative hé- for all persons, it may be that main dialect hé- was originally used for all persons and ga- represents a later

1st person development, a phenomenon in line with the gradual historical emergence of 1st and 2nd person forms in other verbal paradigms.

It has been suggested that the meaning of these prefixes may depend in some measure upon whether they occur with marû or hamṭu stems. While there is frequent inconsistency, with marû they often seem to express wish, with hamṭu they often seem to express assertion. Since the marû/hamṭu distinction is one of aspect, this phenomenon might be explained in the following way. The notion of wish combined with that of imperfective aspect could signify that the speaker desires that some event may happen, but cannot yet visualize the completing of the event; it is not in his power to state that the event will definitely happen, and so the verbal form expresses only a wish. When the notion of wish is combined with perfective aspect, on the other hand, the speaker is stating that he both desires the event to happen and that he can visualize the certain completion of the event, whether in the past or the future. In this case, his wish is tantamount to actuality, and the resulting verbal form expresses an assertion or affirmation that the event definitely will take (or has taken) place. The following schema, borrowing features from M. Civil (1968 American Oriental Society lecture handout), summarizes the possibilities. This formulation is very hypothetical.

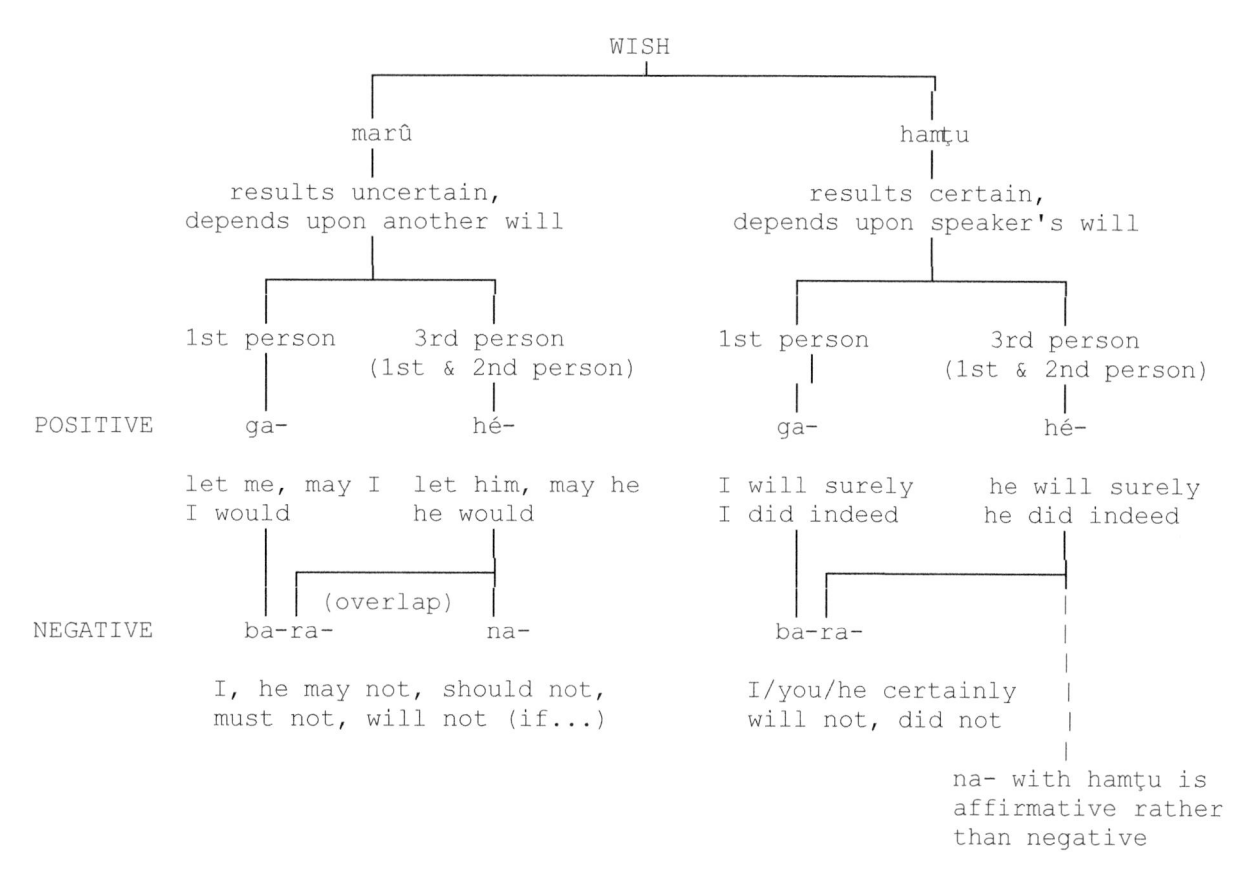

```
                                    WISH
                    ┌────────────────┴────────────────┐
                   marû                             hamṭu
            results uncertain,                 results certain,
          depends upon another will         depends upon speaker's will
            ┌──────────┴──────────┐            ┌──────────┴──────────┐
         1st person           3rd person    1st person           3rd person
                            (1st & 2nd person)                 (1st & 2nd person)
POSITIVE    ga-                  hé-            ga-                  hé-

         let me, may I     let him, may he   I will surely      he will surely
         I would           he would          I did indeed       he did indeed
            │                   │                │                    │
            │        (overlap)  │                │                    │
NEGATIVE   ba-ra-              na-            ba-ra-                  │
         I, he may not, should not,         I/you/he certainly        │
         must not, will not (if...)         will not, did not         │
                                                               na- with hamṭu is
                                                               affirmative rather
                                                               than negative
```

Newer view
──────────

M. Civil has now ("Modal Prefixes," Acta Sumerologica 22 [2000] 29-42) criticized the notion that a modal prefix "has different meanings dependent on the aspect of the verb" (so Thomsen p. 204, citing Edzard and Yoshikawa), stating that, rather, "It is modality that in a great measure governs the aspect of the verb. Thus, for instance, deontic modals naturally tend to have incompletive aspect; one can hardly ask someone to do something already completed or in the past." In his article he presents a new description of the preformatives, based on a modern two-category classification of modality, "deontic" vs. "epistemic." <u>Deontic</u> modality refers to "the necessity or possibility of an act, i.e. expresses the will of the speaker <u>about himself</u> or others." It expresses ideas such as "he has to, ought to, should go; let us go; I will go; may he; would it were; and the imperative Go! or Do not go!" Epistemic modality "expresses the knowledge, beliefs, and opinions of the speaker about his world." It expresses ideas such as "he is, may be, must be; he can; if he is, although he is." See further F.R. Palmer, *Mood and Modality* (Cambridge, 1986) 18f. and passim. Civil's categorization is incorporated in part into the following new description which also employs many of his examples:

PRECATIVE (OPTATIVE) hé-

    a) Deontic function:

        (1) expresses obligation: "one should do it"

            na-de$_5$ ab-ba níĝ kal-kal-la-àm gú-zu hé-em-ši-ĝál
            The advice of an old man is a very precious thing,
            you should submit yourself to it!
            (Instructions of Shurppak 13 OB)

        (2) expresses desires, hopes: "let/may it happen"

            gú ^{giš}má gíd-da i$_7$-da-zu ú gíd-da hé-em-mú
            On your river banks where boats are towed let long grass grow!
            (Curse of Agade 264 OB)

    b) Epistemic function: depends upon some condition expressed by adjoining clause. This use may be labeled "subjunctive": "if X be true"

        (1) hé- comes in first clause

            še nam-sukkal-e hé-du$_7$ èn-bi tar-re-dam
            Whether the barley is indeed fit for the sukkal-office,
            it is to be checked
            (Sauren, Genf No. 249:7-9 Ur III)

            nar za-pa-áĝ hé-en-du$_{10}$ e-ne-àm nam-àm
            If a musician can make his sound pleasant, he is really a musician!
            (Proverbs 2.57 OB)

            a-rá hé-bí-šid zà-bi-šè nu-e-zu
            If the multiplication table has to be recited by you,   {hé+bi+e+šd+Ø}
            you don't know it to its very end!
            (Dialogue 1, 57 OB)

        (2) hé- occurs in both clauses: the condition is counterfactual or a set of possibilities

            lú umma^{ki} hé lú kur-ra hé ^{d}en-líl-le hé-ha-lam-me
            Whether he be a man of Umma or a foreigner may Enlil destroy him!
            (Entemena 28-29 6:17-20 OS)

            lú-bi lugal hé-em énsi hé-em
            Whether that person be a king or a governor
            (Šulgi E 78 Ur III)

            lú-še lugal-ĝu$_{10}$ hé-me-a, saĝ-ki huš-a-ni hé-me-a
            Were that man my king, were that his furious brow!
            (Gilgamesh and Akka 71-72 OB)

(3) hé- comes in a following clause, describing a consequence

>
> dub-sar gal-zu ᵈnisaba-ka-me-en
> ĝéštu-ga šu hu-mu-ni-du₇-àm
> Because I am a wise scribe of Nisaba,
> I am perfect in intelligence
> (Šulgi A 19, 21 OB)

PROHIBITIVE (Civil: NEGATIVE OPTATIVE) (deontic) na- "do not, one should/must not"

> túg dan₂-dan₂-na-zu na-an-mu₄-mu₄-un
> You must not wear your well-cleaned clothes!
> (Gilgamesh and Enkidu 185 OB) (negative advice)
>
> á-ĝu₁₀ ga-sù-sù á-ĝu₁₀ na-an-gig-ge
> I want to extend my arms, may my arms not get sore!
> (Lugalbanda II 170 OB) (negative wish)

VETITIVE (Civil: NEGATIVE SUBJUNCTIVE) (epistemic) ba-ra- "cannot, shall not, must not"

> The vetitive follows a conditioning main clause and negates epistemic hé-.
>
> lugal-me-en ní ba-ra-ba-da-te su ba-ra-ba-da-zi
> Since I am king, (therefore) I cannot get afraid of it or get gooseflesh at it
> (Šulgi A 70)
>
> PN dam šà-ga-na-ke₄ ha-ba-du₁₂-du₁₂
> ba-ra-ba-dù-dè bí-du₁₁   {bara+ba+n+dù+e+d+e(n)}
> "Let PN be married by a spouse of her own desire.
> I would not hinder her," he declared
> (Edzard, SRU 85 r. 2'ff. Sargonic)
>
> mu-lugal ur-lum-ma-ra lú ba-ra-ba-dù
> King's oath, no one shall be detained for Urlumma!
> (ITT 4, 7001:3f. Ur III)

COHORTATIVE ga- "may I, I want to"

> ga- can by pluralized with the 1st pl. subject suffix -en-dè-en. Civil states
> that cohortatives normally take a perfective stem, but plurals may be imper-
> fective. Michalowski has demonstrated that the cohortative can show split-
> ergative patient marking, which can account for some, though not all, preradical
> -n- or -b- markers. Preradical -n- or -b- thus mostly indicate either (accusa-
> tive) direct objects or locative indirect objects.
>
> 1/2 gín kù-babbar é-zi-ĝu₁₀ ha-na-ab-šúm-mu   {hé+na+b+šúm+e+Ø}
> ĝá-e ù-ĝen ga-na-ab-šúm
> Let him give a half shekel of silver to Eziĝu!
> I myself, when he has come, I will give it (back) to him.
> (Sollberger, TCS 1, 269:4-7 Ur III)
> Note the contrast of marû stem with ha- but hamṭu with ga-,
> as well as split-ergative patient marking (-b-) in both forms.
>
> 30 gú ésir àh ésir àh tár-kul-la-ke₄ ba-ab-dah-e ĝá-e ga-na-ab-su
> He shall add 30 talents of dry bitumen (-b-) to (ba- = -e) the dry bitumen
> of the mooring posts, and I myself will repay it (-b-) to him.
> (TCS 3, 355:1-4 Ur III)

kur-ra ga-an-ku₄ mu-ĝu₁₀ ga-an-ĝar   {-n- resumes -a}
I want to go into the mountains, I want to establish my reputation there!
(Gilgamesh and Huwawa 5 OB)

e-ne ga-ba-ab-túm-mu-un-dè-en
We want to take that one (-b-) away!
(Inana's Descent 343 OB)

eger dub-me-ka a-na-àm ga-ab-sar-en-dè-en
What (-b-) is it we should write on the backs of our tablets?
(Dialogue 3, 1 OB)
Civil: "consultative/deliberative" function.

ga- can generate frozen nominalized verbal forms, usually of the shape ga-ab-√ (gáb-√ in OS) or ga-an-√, "used as nomina agentis for transitive and intransitive verbs, respectively" (Civil, JAOS 88, 10). The function of preradial -b- in these split-ergative forms is clear. It usually marks a 3rd person impersonal patient, e.g. ga-ab-sa₁₀ 'I would buy it!' > 'purchaser'. The function of the -n- in ga-an-√ forms is more equivocal. If ga-an-√ is properly used only with intransitive verbs, then in at least some terms the -n- may indicate a locus, e.g. ga-an-tuš 'I would live in it' > 'tenant, resident' (Akk. *waššābu*). If it indicated a patient it could only mean 'I would make him live', a less satisfactory meaning in view of the Akk. translation. The analysis is simpler in the case of ga-√ forms, e.g. ga-ti 'I would live!' > 'ex-voto (gift)'. See a full discussion and exhaustive list of examples in G. Selz, RA 87 (1993) 29-45.

AFFIRMATIVE na-   (§371-382)

Civil calls this a mark of "reported speech" and notes that this prefix is used (a) in the opening passages of mythical or epical texts; (b) in the introduction to certain types of direct speech; (c) in the letter formula ù-na-a-du₁₁ ... na-bé-a (see below). Traditional grammars have recognized two different na-preformatives: prohibitive (negative precative) "may he not" as opposed to affirmative "he will indeed." Jacobsen describes this affirmative na- as a "presumptive volitive," translating approximately "he determined, decided to." Thomsen (§374) states that na + marû = prohibitive, and na- + hamṭu = affirmative, though there are exceptions. W. Heimpel has suggested (JCS 33 [1981] 98), on the other hand, that the apparent negative and positive meanings of na- might be reconciled by regarding na- as capable of indicating a "negative rhetorical question," approximately "did he not?" or "is it not the case that?".

uru^ki na-nam uru^ki na-nam me-bi na-pà-dè
Was not the city indeed here, was not the city indeed here,
was not its divine power being revealed?
(Nanše A 1 OB)

en-e kur lú ti-la-šè ĝéštu-ga-ni na-an-gub
The lord directed his attention to the mountain of the one who is alive
(Gilgamesh and Huwawa 1 OB)

ì-ne-eš lú lú-ù-ra a-na na-an-du₁₁
Now, what did one man (decide to) say to the other man?
(Enmerkar and the Lord of Aratta 394 OB)

PROSPECTIVE ù- (a-, i-) "when, after" (§409-414)

ù- certainly developed via "grammaticalization" from the noun u₄ 'day, time' used in temporal subordinate clauses with the meaning 'when' (u₄ ...-a) or 'after' (u₄ ...-ta). When not written combined with a following consonantal prefix (un-, ub-, um-), the prospective is normally written ù- except before the verbal prefixes ba- or bí- where it may appear as assimilated a- or ì- respectively: u+ba > a-ba-, u+bi > ì-bí- (compare the similar pattern for negative nu- above). ù- always appears in a subordinate clause indicating an event which took place, or will have taken place, before an event described in a following main clause:

dumu úku-rá-ke₄ ur₅ SAĜxHA-na ù-a₅ ku₆-bi lú nu-ba-dab₆-kar-ré   (u+n+ak+Ø)
When a poor man's son has made a fish-pond loan, no one shall take away its fish!
(Ukg 6 3:6'-9' OS, -dab₆- is an OS writing for -da-ab-)

This sentence is functionally equivalent to one featuring an u₄ ...-a temporal subordinate clause: u₄ dumu úku-rá-ke₄ ur₅ SAĜxHA-na in-ak-a-a. In fact, it is not uncommon for ù- to co-occur in a sentence with a temporal adverb based on u₄. A nice older example is Ukg 6 1:11'ff.: u₄-da udu e-hád siki-bi é-gal-la a-ba-de₆ 'whenever (lit. on a day when) the sheep was pure, and (so) its wool was taken away into the palace ...' (ù- has assimilated to the following ba-).

Finally, ù- is occasionally used to generate what have been termed "polite" imperatives. This use is most commonly seen in the formula which opens letters: (PN na-bé-a) PN₂-ra ù-na-a-du₁₁ '(What PN says), do say to PN₂!' {u+na+e+du₁₁}

CONTRAPUNCTIVE ši- (ša-, šè-, šu-) "(and) so, therefore, correspondingly" (§404-408)

This preformative, which can assimilate to any following vowel, is attested quite early, but it is relatively rare and one can still only guess at its meaning from the contexts. Based on its OB occurrences it seems to indicate that an event takes place as a consequence of a preceding event:

na-rú-a mu-bi lú-a nu mu-bé ši-e
en men lum-ma nam-ti i₇-piriĝ-eden-na
The statue's name is not that of a man, <u>rather</u> its name says:
"(Ninĝirsu) the lord, the crown of Lumma, is the life of the Piriĝ-eden canal"
(Ean 1, rev. 10:23-29 OS)

ì-ge-en aratta^ki ur adda sar-gin₇ šu-ta im-ta-ri
ĝá-e u₄-ba ša-ba-na-gúr-e-dè-en
In the event that she (Inana) shall push away Aratta as
if it were a dog running to carrion,
I, on that day, shall <u>therefore</u> have to bow down to him!
(Enmerkar and the Lord of Aratta 290f. OB)

FRUSTRATIVE nu-uš- (Emesal né-eš- or ni-iš-) "if only, were it that" (§418-420)

This preformative, considered most likely to be a coalescence of the negative and contrapunctive preformatives *nu-éš > nu-uš, is poorly attested and restricted thus far to OB examples. It appears to indicate an unrealizable wish (Jacobsen) or a rhetorical interrogative like "why not?" (Civil):

nu-uš-ma-ab-bé-en   {<inim> nuš+ma+b+e+n}
If only you could tell me (or: why can't you tell me)
(Gilgamesh Enkidu and the Netherworld 246 OB)

šu-zu nu-uš-bí-in-tuku bar-zu né-eš-mi-in-ĝál   {nuš+m+b+n+ĝál}
If only I could (or: why can't I) hold your hand,
if only I could make your body be here
(Cohen, Eršemma p. 94:36f.)

CONJUNCTIVE   -n-ga- "and, also, furthermore; and then, consequently" (§322-328)

This prefix is normally classed functionally among the preformatives since, like them, it stands before all other prefixed elements and adds secondary information. It may, however, appear following a proper preformative, and so it must be described either as a secondary preformative or merely as a prefix whose rank order slot lies between the preformatives and the ventive element.

In earlier periods in which preradical /n/ is normally not written in verbal forms, -n-ga- can appear simply as -ga-, e.g. e-ga- (with vowel harmony) in OS Lagaš. In OB and later it appears as (i)n-ga- or (i)m-ga-. Like the pronominal element -n-, -n-ga- cannot start a verbal form without the help of a prosthetic vowel.

-n-ga- can serve to link two or more sentences or clauses which normally have the same agents or subjects. It can also be combined with the loaned Akkadian conjunction ù 'and' to express the notion 'either ... or' or 'neither ... nor' as in the following:

sipa-zi gù-dé-a gal mu-zu gal ì-ga-túm-mu   {V+(n)ga+túm+e+Ø}
Righteous shepherd Gudea knew great things
and also brings forth great things
(Gudea, Cyl A 7:9-10 Ur III)

alaĝ-e ù kù nu za-gìn nu-ga-àm   {nu+m+Ø} {nu+(n)ga+m+Ø}
This statue was neither (made of) silver
nor moreover was it (made of) lapis lazuli.
(Gudea, Statue B 7:49 Ur III)

REMEMBER:	NEGATIVE	nu- (la-, li-)	not
	PRECATIVE	hé- (ha-, hu-)	may he, he should, whether
	COHORTATIVE	ga- (gi₄-, gú-)	may I, I shall
	PROHIBITIVE	na-	may he not
	AFFIRMATIVE	na-	he shall (shall he not?)
	VETITIVE	ba-ra-	can not, must not
	PROSPECTIVE	ù- (a-, ì-)	when, after
	CONTRAPUNCTIVE	ši- (ša-, šu-)	so, therefore
	FRUSTRATIVE	nu-uš-	if only
	CONJUNCTIVE	(i)n-ga-	and, also, furthermore

THE IMPERATIVE

GENERAL CHARACTERISTICS (§495-498)

The imperative can be described as a <u>transformation</u> of an underlying declarative verbal form in which the elements of a verbal prefix chain are shifted as a whole from prefix to suffix position, displacing any underlying verbal suffixes. The relative rank order of the shifted prefix elements is maintained. For example: ba-an-du$_{12}$ 'He married her' > du$_{12}$-ba-an 'Marry her!'

An imperative form may not feature a preformative, including the secondary preformative -n-ga-. Since imperatives and plus-preformative verbal forms are thus mutually exclusive, the imperative transformation technically may be assigned the rank order of a preformative for descriptive purposes, as has been done in the Prefix Chain Chart. As a result of this restriction, note that an imperative cannot be negated, since negation is accomplished only by means of one of the negative preformatives. A negative command ("Do not!") must therefore be expressed instead as a negated 2nd person declarative wish form using one of the negative preformatives na- or ba-ra- "You may, must not!"

Since the imperative expresses a command, an event visualized by the speaker as one which will indeed be completed rather than a wish which may or may not be realized depending upon outside circumstances, it is always generated using a perfective verbal root. A reduplicated root in an imperative form therefore signifies plurality of a subject or patient or intensification of the verbal idea.

An imperative is an inherently 2nd person singular form; it takes no explicit 2nd person subject or agent marker. It may, however, be pluralized by adding the 2nd person plural subject marker -nzen to the end of the shifted prefix chain. This plural marker is written -zé-en, but it can also appear as -Vn-zé-en, -Vb-zé-en or -Vm-zé-en when the context requires a preceding /n/ /b/ or /m/ element. The precise morphological significance of these variants is not always immediately clear.

A then intriguingly new analysis of the subject/object phenomena in the imperative was advanced by P. Michalowski (JCS 32 (1980) 86ff.), who saw in them a manifestation of Sumerian <u>split ergativity</u>. In his view, imperatives, also cohortatives, show a nominative/accusative marking scheme like declarative marû forms, rather than the ergative patient/agent opposition found in declarative ḫamṭu forms, and the 3rd sg. pronouns -n- or -b- here thus mark (accusative) objects rather than agents, although the presence of a 2nd person agent is of course implied by the presence of an object marker. Thus in the form zi-ga-ab 'Make it rise!' -b- marks the direct object "it"; the corresponding personal form would then be zi-ga-an 'Make him rise!' This is an attractive hypothesis, but it must contend no less with inconsistencies in the choice of -n- versus -b- in occurring forms in the OB texts from which most of our examples are drawn, and it cannot as yet be considered as fully proven. See the interesting criticism of Edzard, 2003, p. 90f., who has a different interpretation of the -n/b- pronominal data and who concludes, contrary to present opinion, that "the question of 'split ergativity' does not seem to be of any question in Sumerian."

No explicit suffixed subject/patient markers are permitted in imperative forms, and the patients/objects one encounters are normally only those marked by the 3rd sg. elements -n- or -b-. The 3rd pl. element -ne- seems theoretically possible but is not attested, to my knowledge. Thus it is possible to use an imperative to say "Marry her!" but impossible to use an imperative to say "Marry me!" For non-3rd sg. person patients one must use a precative (hé-) or cohortative (ga-) construction, e.g. "Let him marry me!"

MINIMAL IMPERATIVES   (All examples to follow are drawn from actual text passages.)

The most basic, and commonest, imperative forms are very short, consisting only of a ḫamṭu root followed by a vowel, usually /a/, very rarely /e/. Since an imperative is a finite verbal form, one that is localized in time and space, one can view such a form as a transformation of a minimal declarative form which must be marked by an otherwise nonsignificant anaptyctic vocalic prefix in order to make the form finite; thus tuš-a 'Sit!' {tuš+V} corresponding formally to an agentless declarative form ì-tuš 'He sat' {V+tuš+Ø}. This final -a has been explained as an imperative marker (old), a development of the "Conjugation Prefix" ì- (more recently), or in some cases a sort of aspectual morpheme (M. Yoshikawa, ZA 69 [1979] 161ff., see Thomsen §497). Since minimal imperatives of this sort are not marked for patients (direct objects), they will generally convey intransitive ideas, e.g.:

    ĝen-na (rare: ĝen-né)   Go!
    zi-ga   Rise!   {zi(g)+a}
    silim-ma   Be well!
    šèĝ-ĝá   Rain!
    tuš-a   Sit!
    e$_{11}$-dè   Descend! (Dumuzi & Geštinana 4ff.)   {e$_{11}$(d)+e}

The choice of the final vowel in these minimal forms may to some extent be ascribed to geographical dialect. Line 19 of the Nippur version of the OB Sumerian-Akkadian bilingual du/ĝen grammatical paradigm OBGT VII (MSL IV 89-99) shows ĝen-na = *a-[lik]* 'Go!' while the Ur version (UET 7, 101+) shows ĝen-né = *a-lik*. The Ur version also omits six sections of the Nippur version featuring verbal forms beginning with the prefixes an- and al-. Nippur, the find-place of the majority of the preserved OB literary tablets, lies on the northern periphery of ancient Sumer, while Ur lies in its southern heartland. The use of /a/ as an initial prosthetic vowel is much more common in Nippur and other Akkadian-dominated northern sites, and since a large number of our source texts come from Nippur, the religious and cultural heart of Sumer and the site of a major Old Babylonian scribal school, it is no wonder that the preferred suffixed vowel of extant imperatives should likewise statistically turn out to be /a/.

Imperatives are frequently marked only for the presence of a patient (object), using one of the 3rd sg. pronominal elements -n- or -b-, and the same vowel /a/, or rarely /e/, is required to separate the root from the following consonantal elements. In the following examples /a/ appears between the root and a following final object element /b/:

    zi-ga-ab   Make it rise!   {zi(g)+b}
    zi-ra-ab   Erase it!   {zir+b}
    húl-la-ab   Make them happy!   {húl+b}
    en-nu-ùĝ ak-ab   Perform the watch!   {a$_5$(k)+b}
    bal-e-eb   Turn them away!   {bal+b}

In other cases no anaptyxis is needed, following the normal phonotactic patterns of the prefix chain as described in earlier lessons, for example:

    ĝar-bí-ib   Set it there!   {ĝar+b+b}
    sar-bí-ib   Make it run from there!   {sar+b+b}

An imperative is not always overtly marked for a patient, even though one may be syntactically present in the sentence:

    gul-a   Destroy it!   for gul-la-ab
    de$_6$-a   Bring it!   for de$_6$-ab
    du$_{11}$-ga-na   Say it to him!   for <inim> du$_{11}$-ga-na-ab
    di-ĝu$_{10}$ ku$_5$-dè   Decide my case!   for ku$_5$(d)-dè-eb (Proverbs 9 E 4)

VENTIVE IMPERATIVES

An imperative which features only a suffixed ventive element, √+m, corresponding to a declarative form m+√ > im-√, takes one of three forms: √-um (rare), √-àm (more common), or √-ù (most common). The last form, which seems merely to illustrate the common tendency for nasal consonants to drop in final position, is traditionally, but too simplistically, explained as an assimilated or variant form of an "imperative suffix" -a or -e. Several observations on the phonological shapes of these minimal forms are in order.

The use of /u/ as a anaptyctic vowel in association with the suffixed ventive element is in line with its appearance instead of epenthetic /i/ in the declarative ventive prefix form mu-, i.e. m+n+√ > mu-un-√ rather than a *mi-in-√ parallel with b+n+√ > bí-in-√. Compare also the /u/ associated with the 1st and 2nd sg. possessive pronouns -ĝu$_{10}$ and -zu rather than the /i/ of 3rd sg. -(a)ni or -bi Why the sound /u/ is preferred to /i/ in connection with an /m/ element (sound) remains an open question. (T. Jacobsen (AS 16 [1965] 71ff.) theorized that /u/ was an obsolete localizing case marker which he called the "tangentive" used in connection with 1st and 2nd person referents, a view not generally accepted.) The writing -àm instead of -um appears to be an OB convention, perhaps a neologism in which the "imperative suffix" -a takes the place of an epenthetic vowel, to be analyzed as √+a+m rather than √+Vm, possibily influenced by the phonological shape of the corresponding Akkadian ventive suffix -*am*.

In the following examples of minimal ventive imperatives note the absence of expected patient markers. One explanation for this phenomenon is that resumptive elements in the verbal chain are at bottom always optional. Another is that at least some final /m/ markers might actually stand for an assimilation of {m+b}, in line with the current suggestion of some scholars that a declarative form like im-√ can actually stand for Vm+b+√, orthographically indistinguishable from im-√ standing for simple Vm+√.

túm-ù-um	Bring him in! (ZA 97, 4:10)	expected: túm-mu-un
de₆-um	Bring it here!	expected: de₆-mu-ub
zu-àm	Learn it (completely)!	expected: zu-mu-ub
te-(e)-àm	Approach there!	
ĝen-ù	Come here!	rare writing
ĝen-nu	Come here!	rare writing
ĝe₂₆-nu	Come here!	usual writing (old reading: ĝá-nu)
ĝe₂₆-nu-um-zé-en	Come here (pl.)!	note reappearance of the /m/ before the plural suffix
gi₄-ù	Come back here!	
ù-sá kul-ù	Sleep, hurry here!	
é ĝál-lu	Open up the house!	expected: ĝál-mu-ub
i-lu ĝar-ù	Set up a wail!	expected: ĝar-mu-ub
sud-rá-áĝ zi-bu-ù	Rise up light!	Emesal for zi(g)-gu-u(m)

A form such as ur₁₁-ru 'Plough it!' (PAPS 107, 505:31) is problematic. Syntax demands a patient marker -b. Is the form a minimal ventive {ur₁₁+V+m} with deletion of /m/ or just a minimal imperative {ur₁₁+V} with assimilation of a final vowel to the vowel of the root? Cf. ^{túg}bar-dul₅ tuk₅-ù 'Weave your b.-garment!' (Winter and Summer 211). In both instances, which involve a root vowel /u/, a ventive seems semantically difficult unless it adds a telic nuance "completely, to the very end."

With the above, contrast the following ventive forms which are explicitly marked for the presence of a patient, albeit not always with the correct choice or -n- vs. -b-. Note that before the element mu-, as with ba- or bí-, any <u>Auslauts are suppressed</u>, since an amissible consonantal Auslaut never appears when another consonant follows:

túm-mu-un	Bring him in!	{túm+m+n}
túm-mu-un-zé-en	Bring (pl.) her here!	{túm+m+n+zen}
gi₄-mu-un	Make him return here!	{gi₄+m+n}

è-mu-na-ra-ab-zé-en	Make (pl.) it come out for him!	{è(d)+m+na+ra+b+zen}
šu ba-mu-u₈	Release (the hand from upon) me!	{ba(r)+m+n}
mu lugal pà-mu-ni-ib	Make him (-ni-) swear a royal oath!	{pà(d)+m+n+b}
íl-mu-ub	Lift it up! (SP 22, 183)	{íl+m+b}

In OB and later texts a superfluous vowel is sometimes written following the root even when there is no phonological justification for it, reflecting either a misunderstanding of the proper use of an epenthetic vowel or an inappropriate application of the imperative formative -a or -e used in minimal imperatives.

    húl-húl-la-mu-un-da
    Rejoice greatly over him!
    (Inana E 19 OB)
    Note the hamṭu reduplication.

    zú bur₅^{mušen}-ra bal-e-bí-ib (vars. bal-a-[ ], bal-e-eb)
    Turn away there the teeth of the locusts/birds!
    (Farmer's Instructions 66 OB)

    šubur-a-ni kur-ta e₁₁-dè-mu-na-ab
    Make his servant come up from the netherworld for him!
    (Gilgameš Enkidu and the Netherworld 240 OB)
    Cf. the minimal imperative kur-šè e₁₁-dè in Dumuzi and Geshtinana 4-10, and note the gender error -b- for -n- unless "servant" here is an impersonal noun.

In carefully written texts, however, the presence or absence of a epenthetic vowel following the root can signal a difference in meaning, primarily in connection with a following element -ma-. Just as a 1st sg. dative prefix ma- can start a declarative form without a preceding prosthetic vowel, e.g. ma-an-šúm 'he gave it to me', so too a corresponding 1st sg. dative imperative will properly show no epenthetic vowel between the root and following -ma-, and, as in the preceding section, any Auslaut is suppressed before this dative prefix. On the other hand, when a suffixed -ma- represents a shortened writing of the impersonal dative chain -Vm-ma- < m+ba, an epenthetic vowel will properly appear between the root and the chain, corresponding to the prefix sequence m+ba > im-ma-; and in this case, any Auslaut <u>will</u> appear. The following first three examples show 1st sg. dative ma-, the last three ventive plus ba-:

é-ĝu₁₀ dù-ma Build my temple for me! (Biga, Fs. Klein 30 1:12 OAkk)	{dù+ma}
10 gín kù-babbar šúm-ma-ab Give me 10 shekels of silver! (Falkenstein, NSGU 20:7 Ur III)	{šúm+ma+b}
tukum-bi šu mu-ri-bar-re mu-zu du₁₁-ma-ab If I release you, tell me your name! (Proverbs 5 D 5 OB)	{du₁₁(g)+ma+b}
ki-tuš du₁₀-ga-ma-ni-íb Make (your) domicile pleasant there! (Gudea Cyl A 3:1 Ur III)	{du₁₀(g)+Vm+ba+n+b}
im-ma-al gú i₇-da-ke₄ i-bi-zu ĝar-ra-am-ma Set your eye upon the wild cow on the riverbank (Kramer, Eretz-Israel 16, 142*:30 OB Emesal)	{ĝar+Vm+ba}
ĝen-àm-ma = at-la-kam 'Come (sg.) away!'	{ĝen+Vm+ba}
ĝen-àm-ma-zé-en = at-la-ka-nim 'Come (pl.) away!' (OBGT VII 10 & 105, Ur version)	{ĝen+Vm+ba+(n)zen}

Clear scribal errors do creep into texts. In the following literary passage, while
four textual duplicates write a correct 1st sg. dative prefix (followed by an ablative
-ra-), one writes a nearly homophonous but erroneous {m+ba} sequence:

    ní-zu ba-ma-ra (var. ba-àm-ma-ra)   {ba+ma+*ta, var. ba+Vm+ba+*ta}
    Give away to me your terror!
    (Gilgameš and Huwawa version A 144, with ablative -ra-)

With Vm+ba forms compare the following examples illustrating the use of the prefix ba-
(in its ablative function) without a preceding ventive element or helping vowel:

    dug-gin₇ gaz-ba   Be smashed to bits like a pot!   agentless verb
    é-zu de₆-ba   Take away your house!   patient not indicated
    du₁₂-ba-an   Marry her!   patient indicated
    dab₅-dab₅-ba-ab   Take them all away!   pl. reduplication + patient

LOCATIVE CONSTRUCTIONS

When one of the pronominal elements /n/ /ni/ /b/ or /bi/ is not being used in an imperative to mark a patient (direct object) or second agent, it can mark a locus, generally
but not always resuming either a locative or locative-terminative postposition.

√+b and √+bi

In the following passages the use of /b/ and /bi/ is unremarkable:

    ĝen-nu dumu-ĝu₁₀ ki-ta-ĝu₁₀-šè tuš-a-ab   {tuš+a+b}
    = *alka mārī tišab ina šapliya*
    Come here my son and sit below me!
    (Examenstext A 3 Neo-Assyrian)

    lú-kúr iri gibil-a al-dúr-ru-ne-eš ki-tuš-bi-ta sar-bí-ib   {bí- = -ta}
    Chase away from their dwellings the enemy living in the new city!
    (Letter Collection B 5:11-12 OB)

Compare however the following parallel passages. In the first a cohortative verb
features a preradical -b- that resumes a loc.-term. postposition, while in the second the
corresponding imperative features a -bi suffix that resumes a loc.-term. postposition
elided to the suffix -zu.

    šà-ge guru₇-ĝe₂₆ an-ta ga-ab-gi₄   {ga+b+gi₄}
    šà-ge guru₇-a-zu an-ta gi₄-bi   {gi₄+*b}
    Let me go down to wherever my heart desires!
    Go down to wherever your heart desires!
    (Lugalbanda II 176/193 OB)

-bi clearly serves the same purpose as the -b- prefix in the earlier line, but why is
the imperative not simply gi₄-ib as predicted by the analysis employed in this grammar?
The latter form, though rare, does exist; compare the fragmentary OB grammatical text
Ni4143, 9'-10' (Black, Studia Pohl Series Maior 12, 152):

    é gú gi₄-ib   =   *bi-ta-[am* ...]   Return the house to the riverbank! (?)
    gú ga-ab-gi₄ =   *am-ša/ta*? [...]   I will return it to the riverbank! (?)

A further question is why the writing in these forms is BI rather than the BÍ which
is the usual prefix writing in declarative verbal forms? Perhaps to avoid confusion
with the dè and ne readings of the BÍ sign? In the following line the first (causative) imperative shows a -b- marking a patient, but the second (intransitive) imperative again shows a -bi writing that resumes a locative postposition:

> u₄ gig-ga u₄ gaba-zu zi-ga-ab u₄ é-za gi₄-bi
> O bitter storm, O storm make your front rise, O storm return to your house!
> (Lamentation over Sumer and Ur 483)

Compare also line 83 of The Farmer's Instructions, the main Nippur version and the version of text C₃ (Civil, Farmer's Instructions p. 49), where the three variants of the second imperative leave its morphological analysis somewhat equivocal:

> šid-bi du₆-ul-(la-)ab zar-re-éš nú-a-ab (var. nú-bí-[ib?])
> šid-bi du₆-lá   zar-re-éš nú-bi
> Assemble a sufficient number(?) for it and lay down (the grain) in sheaves!

Perhaps the OB scribes reserved -b primarily for marking patients, while -bi was employed specifically to mark loci. It seems unlikely that -bi was employed for reasons of euphony, i.e. a more pleasing sounding /gibi/ rather than /gib/. The orthographic phenomenon incidentally appears again in the OB grammatical texts, cf. OBGT VI 56/105 (MSL IV 81-82):

> ĝar-bi = *šukun*   'Place!'
> bí-ĝar = (*taškun*) 'You placed'

More interesting are the two contiguous forms OBGT VI 56-57 (MSL IV 81):

> ĝar-bi = *šukun*   'Place!'
> ĝar-ni = (blank)

Here -bi and -ni are given no explicit Akkadian grammatical correspondences such as accusative suffixes or causative infixes. This would make sense if the OBGT compiler was aware that such minimal forms the -ni and -bi elements were properly used in this period only to mark loci, a use not capable of being expressed through Akkadian verbal morphology. Contrast the minimal imperative ĝar-ra which is given the same minimal Akkadian correspondence *šukun* 'place!' at the beginning of the paradigm (OBGT VI 1). Note also that elsewhere in the ĝar paradigm the epenthetic vowel is used correctly in imperatives. √-bi and √-ni forms are in this respect once again anomalous.

√+n and √+ni

A form like √-mu-un in which /n/ marks a patient (direct object) offers no orthographic or analytical difficulties, likewise a form like √-ni-ib in which /ni/ clearly marks a locus or a second agent. But the frequent OB minimal imperative form √-ni raises questions, as does the fact that it is difficult to find an occurring OB or earlier verbal form √-Vn in which /n/ marks a locus.

In the past √-ni has usually been read √-ì, in which the -ì was understood as the "Conjugation Prefix" ì- that has not altered to become the imperative suffix -a. See discussion and examples of A. Falkenstein, ZA 49 (1950) 132. So analyzed, √-ì is not marked for the locative.

On the other hand, in Song of the Plowing Oxen 143/144 gu₄ ĝen-a ĝen-a ᵍᶦˢšudun-a gú ĝar-ni 'Go oxen, go, put the neck in the yoke!' the editor M. Civil also read ĝar-ì, but understood -ì as a locative-terminative infix, a vocalic element symbolized by him as -*I- (see AOAT 25, 90), although he admitted that a locative -ni suffix is also possible. We are hampered in our analysis of this passage not just by the absence of an -ib suffix marking the object, but also by the lack of a predicted epenthetic vowel after the root to yield a form ĝar-ra-ni-ib which would be fully correct for this context. Civil's solution is an option, but it is undeniable that it is -n- or -ni- that regularly resumes a locative in declarative verbal chains.

Conceivably pertinent is the common phenomenon of the loss of /n/ and its replacement by -ì seen sporadically in Ur III texts. For loss of final /n/ cf. nu-ù-gi-ì for nu-un-gi-in 'he did not verify it' (NSGU 213:22,28-30); ab-gi-ì 'he verified it' (PBS 9, 86:7 apud Edzard, SRU p. 123); ìr nu-me-ì (for nu-me-en) bí-du₁₁-ga 'that he declared "I am not a slave"' (NSGU 34:11). The loss of medial /n/ is also common throughout the Ur III period. Cf. ú-gíd-da bí-ì-mú 'he made long grass grow there' (Šulgi D 338); tum-ma-al^ki-e pa bì-i-é (var. bí-in-è) 'the Tummal he made replendent' (passim in the Tummal Inscription). Initially, the prefix ì-√ for ergative in-√ is ubiquitous until late in the Ur III period. Could ĝar-ì thus be an orthographic convention for a locative form ĝar+n > /ĝarin/, perhaps with a deleted /n/ and compensatory vowel lengthening: /ĝari:/?

A better solution probably lies in identifying those rare OB passages which do write an expected epenthetic vowel between the root and the -ni suffix, viz.

>   lú še-numun ĝar-ra-za igi-zu ĝar-ni (var. ĝar-ra-ni)
>   Keep your eye on (-a) the man who sets out the barley seed
>   (Farmer's Instructions 49 OB)
>
>   ᵈšára dumu ki-áĝ ᵈinana-gin₇ ti zú-zu-a u₄-gin₇ è-ni (var. è-a-ni)
>   Like Šara the beloved son of Inana shoot forth your in barbed arrows like daylight!
>   (Lugalbanda and Enmerkar 142-143 OB)
>
>   ᵈézinu ní-za ĝéštu a₅-ni (var. ĝéštu-ga-a-ni)
>   Ezinu, pay attention to (-a) yourself!
>   (Sheep and Grain 163 OB)
>   The odd syllabically written variant /ĝéštug ani/ argues strongly
>   against a reading a₅-ì in the main text.

While not dispositive, such evidence favors a reading -ni in contexts featuring a locative indirect object, despite the uncomfortable lack of expected epenthetic vowels.

The following examples of √-ni, all OB, are all in transitive or causative contexts featuring oblique objects, and all are missing a final /b/ and an epenthetic /a/:

>   ᵈur-ᵈnin-urta ᵍⁱššudun gú-ba ĝar-ni
>   Place the yoke onto (-a) their necks, Ur-Ninurta!
>   (Ur-Ninurta A 43)
>
>   ù-na-a-du₁₁ silim-ma-ĝu₁₀ šu-ni-šè ĝar-ni
>   Place my letter of greetings into (-šè) her hand!
>   (Message of Ludingira 7)
>
>   še guru₇-e ĝar-ni
>   Place the barley upon (-e) the grain-heap!
>   (OBGT III 25, MSL IV 69)
>
>   im nam-ti-la-ke₄ du-rí-šè nu-kúr-ru mu-bi gub-ni
>   Make its name stand on (-e) the clay-tablet of life, never ever to be altered!
>   (Rim-Sin B 52 = Haya hymn)

These following two OB examples feature intransitive verbs and locative indirect objects. As in earlier examples Auslauts are suppressed:

>   igi diĝir-za-ka sa₆-ni   {sa₆(g)+ni}
>   Be pleasing in (-a) the eyes of your god!
>   (Scribe and His Perverse Son 176, cf. 181)
>
>   gaba kù-ĝá-a u₄-gin₇ è-ni   {è(d)+ni}
>   Come out like the daylight upon (-a) my holy breast!
>   (Enmerkar and the Lord of Aratta 102)

Compare the same intransitive verb è(d) with suffix -bi in a similar locative context, paired with a transitive imperative:

    nin₉ du₆-da è-bi, du₆-da igi íl-la-[ni-íb(?)]   {du₆(d)+a} {è(d)+bi}
    Sister, go out upon the hill, lift your eyes upon the hill!
    (Dumuzi's Dream 76, 78 OB)

Conclusions

Several conclusions may be drawn from the preceding discussion. First, it seems undeniable that both √-bi and √-ni mark indirect objects, mainly locatives, in OB imperatives, taking the place of rare or unattested √-b and √-n with that use. Second, it must be stressed that these phenomena seem to occur almost exclusively in OB texts, with a nearly complete absence of predicted postradical anaptyxis in √-ni forms and also with an absence of a final /n/ or /b/ element marking a patient/direct object in transitive forms, e.g. ĝar-ra-ni-ib. The probable suppression of verb Auslauts before -ni, as though -ni were functioning phonotactiically like a mu- or bí-, is also remarkable. All this suggests that √-bi and √-ni are innovations that in particular syntactic contexts would be technically ungrammatical in earlier periods of the language. One might possibly compare certain finite imperfective verbs ending in a -dè suffix (see below, pg. 125f.), in which a modal element /d/ which would otherwise be subject to deletion at the end of a verbal chain may have been written as an allomorph /de/ in order to signal explicitly its presence.

See now Attinger, NABU 2004/75, with the response of Jagersma, NABU 2006/93, for additional examples and a different basic analysis of these phenomena. Both consider these √-bi and √-ni forms which mark loci to be proof that the locative(-terminative) markers in declarative verbal forms, bí- and -ni-, also 1st sg. mu-, have as their fundamental shapes /bi/, /ni/ and /mu/, rather than /b/, /n/, and /m/ plus an epenthetic vocalic element — the position maintained in this grammar. If these are truly the fundamental shapes of these elements, then the theory that they reduce to /b/, /n/, and /m/ before the root may be correct, vindicating the earlier proposals of Falkenstein.

Their arguments are seductive but rendered less convincing by lack of evidence from earlier periods and the general lack of data owing to the relative paucity of imperative forms in all periods. The neologisms of late Ur III texts and OB school texts often skew the analysis of the earlier spoken language.

REMEMBER: AN IMPERATIVE IS A FINITE, DECLARATIVE, PERFECTIVE
                  VERBAL FORM, WHOSE PREFIX CHAIN HAS BEEN SHIFTED AS
                  A WHOLE TO A SUFFIX POSITION.

                  AN IMPERATIVE IS AN INHERENTLY 2ND PERSON SG. FORM
                  WHICH CAN BE PLURALIZED BY ADDING THE SUFFIX /(n)zen/.

                  THE IMPERATIVE, LIKE THE COHORTATIVE AND FINITE
                  IMPERFECTIVE FORMS, SHOWS A SPLIT-ERGATIVE MORPHOLOGY
                  IN WHICH A FINAL /n/ or /b/ CAN MARK AN "ACCUSATIVE"
                  DIRECT OBJECT.

                  THE SIMPLEST IMPERATIVES SHOW ONLY A SUFFIX -a
                  OR, IF VENTIVE, ONLY -u, -um OR -àm.

IMPERFECTIVE FINITE VERBS

Up to now in this introduction, discussions of the Sumerian verb have been limited to perfective verbal forms. To summarize what has been said previously about tense and aspect, a perfective verb describes an event viewed by the speaker as completed and as a whole event, and we can generally translate a Sumerian perfective form with an English past tense form, although one occasionally encounters a context where a future tense form would be appropriate and theoretically possible (e.g. Ean 1 16:24 etc.). An imperfective verb describes, on the other hand, an event viewed as uncompleted or on-going, without regard for a beginning or ending point, and we can usually translate it with an English present or future tense form, although it could just as well represent an event viewed as on-going in the past. Practically speaking, when dealing with ordinary finite verbs we will normally translate perfective forms in the past tense, while imperfectives can generally be translated in the present or future tense depending upon context (though descriptions of the /ed/ morpheme as a future tense marker can complicate this theory).

Sumerian imperfective verbs are properly distinguished from perfective verbs in two ways: by a difference in the shape of the verbal stem, and the use of different affix paradigms for the core pronominal subject (patient) and agent.

> Later Akkadian scribes described Sumerian perfective and imperfective verbal stems with the Akk. terms *hamṭu* 'quick' and *marû* 'fat' respectively. M. Civil has recently shown that the contrast was also known in Sumerian as lugud 'short' versus gíd 'long', certainly referring to the generation of literally "longer" imperfective stems by modification of perfective stems. See "The Forerunners of Marû and Hamṭu in Old Babylonian," in Riches Hidden in Secret Places (Winona Lake, 2002) 63-71 as well as Thomsen, The Sumerian Language §231. In keeping with common practice, we will freely employ the terminology hamṭu vs. marû in the following discussions.

THE IMPERFECTIVE (marû) STEM   (§212ff.)

The perfective stem is the basic, unmarked, form of the verb, the form that usually appears in glossary or vocabulary listings. The only modification seen with the perfective stem is reduplication, normally indicating plurality of an impersonal subject (patient), but also possibly repetition or some variety of intensification of the root idea. This phenomenon is referred to in grammatical studies as <u>hamṭu reduplication</u> or <u>plural reduplication</u>.

The imperfective stem is formed in one of four (or three, see below) ways, according to the analysis by M. Yoshikawa (not followed by all scholars). See the next lesson on participles for more discussion of variations and peculiarities of marû stem formation.

1) <u>Affixation Class</u> (M. Yoshikawa, J. Krecher, T. Jacobsen, this grammar). This is the commonest class of verbs. Here the marû stem is formed by suffixing an element -e, which can assimilate to a preceding vowel, to the hamṭu root. Krecher has suggested that this -e is in origin actually the marû stem of the principal Sumerian auxillary verb du$_{11}$(g) 'to do'. See Thomsen § 225-226 for a list of common verbs which follow this pattern, three examples of which are:

dù	dù-e	(or dù-ù)	to build
šúm	šúm-e	(or šúm-mu)	to give
gíd	gíd-e	(or gíd-i)	to stretch, pull

Note that Edzard, also Thomsen, Jagersma, and most others, believe that this -e is a 3rd sg. marû pronominal suffix rather than a marû stem formative element. They thus believe that this large class of verbs, which are called Regular Verbs, does not show any special marû stem. This view is a feature of the older, traditional Poebel-Falkenstein school of analysis. See Edzard 2003, p. 83f. for his last statement on this matter.

2) <u>Reduplication Class</u> This is the second most common class of verbs. Here the marû stem is formed either by simple reduplication or by what Thomsen §227, for example, calls "partial reduplication," i.e. reduplication of the ḫamṭu root with regular deletion of a final consonant. Such final consonant deletion apparently does not occur in pluralizing ḫamṭu reduplication. See Thomsen §228 for a list of common examples such as:

ĝar	ĝá-ĝá	to set, place	
gi₄	gi₄-gi₄	to return	
naĝ	na₈-na₈	to drink	(na₈ and naĝ are the same sign)
zi(g)	zi-zi	to rise	
zu	zu-zu	to know	

Deletion of the final consonant of the reduplicated ḫamṭu root, whether in ḫamṭu or marû reduplication, is not always complete; with some verbs it may be retained in either the first or second root. See Edzard 2003, 12.6.2 for examples of the phenomenon, including:

bi-iz	bi-bi-zé	to drip	{biz+biz+e}
bi-ir	bi-ib-re	to scatter	{bir+bir+e}
gùn	gú-ug-nu	to be colorful	{gùn+gùn+e}
te-en	te-en-te	to cool	{ten+ten}
hal	ha-al-ha	to apportion	{hal+hal}

A root which normally forms its marû stem by reduplication may occasionally form the marû stem instead by affixation of -e. This alternation may illustrate a tendency towards an increasing regularization of the method of marû formation.

3) <u>Alternating Class</u> Three verbs, è(d), te(ĝ)/ti, and ri(g) were originally said to comprise this class, supposedly showing a short ḫamṭu form and a longer marû form with an added final consonant which appears when a vowel (e.g. the marû suffix -e) follows. But the verb ri was confused with de₅(g) and does not belong to this class (see W. Sallaberger, AV Klein [2005] 233 n. 6), and te and ti can be harmonized, for example by reading these signs as teĝ₃ and teĝ₄ respectively (see ePSD). But cf. for example šu ba-an-ti-iš (MVN 2, 100 rev. 17 Ur III). The status of this entire class is now suspect.

4) <u>Complementary Verbs</u> This is a class of four common verbs which show an entirely different root as the marû stem, mainly in the singular. These stems can vary for both aspect and number. See also the description of the plural verb tuš/durun on p. 82.

a) Four stems: ĝen/du 'to come, go'

	ḫamṭu	marû	
sg.	ĝen	du	Both stems are written with the DU sign
pl.	re₇ /ere/	su₈(b)	Both stems are written DU&DU or DU.DU; also seen are er₁₄(DU.DU) in OS and er in Ur III

b) Three stems: de₆/túm 'to bring'

	ḫamṭu	marû	
sg.	de₆	túm/tùm	de₆ and túm are both written with the DU sign
pl.	lah₄, lah₅	lah₄, lah₅	lah₄ is written DU&DU, lah₅ is DU.DU

P. Steinkeller, AOAT 325 (2004) 557-576, now speaks of two verbs, distinguishable only in the sg.: (1) bring I = 'mit sich führen, geleiten' referring to persons or animals which can move by themselves. Forms: ḫamṭu sg. túm, marû sg. tùm, pl. lah₄/₅; and (2) bring II = 'liefern' referring to objects which must be carried. Forms: ḫamṭu sg. de₆, marû sg. tùm. In OB, the older de₆/túm distinction becomes less relevant, and the pattern becomes that of an affixation class verb: túm/tùm for ḫamṭu and túm-mu for marû. Cf. mi-ni-in-tùm-uš 'they brought it in there' (Bird and Fish 7). For the newest study see further V. Meyer-Laurin, ZA 100 (2010) 1-14, who considers the situation to be "weitaus komplexer" in OB texts, requiring further study. Note finally the existence of the Emesal roots ga(-ga) and ir (M. Jaques, AV Attinger [2012] 193ff.).

c) Two stems: du₁₁(g)/e 'to do'

    sg.   du₁₁(g)   e   The marû participle (and infinitive)
    pl.   e   e   uses the special stem di(d)

d) Two stems: úš/ug₇ 'to die'

    sg.   úš   ug₇/ug₅   úš and ug₇ are both written with the TIL sign
    pl.   ug₇/ug₅   ug₇/ug₅   By OB ug₇ is used for all contexts. (See Attinger, NABU 2011, p. 6f. for a new analysis.)

IMPERFECTIVE PRONOMINAL PARADIGMS (§294ff.)

To review the subject (patient) and agent paradigms for perfective (ḫamṭu) verbs:

A nominal chain representing the subject (patient) of a sentence stands in the absolutive case. This subject is also marked in the perfective verbal chain by a corresponding pronominal suffix, conjugated for person, number, and gender as follows:

        Perfective Subject

1	-(e)n	I, me
2	-(e)n	you
3	-∅	he/him, she/her, it
1	-(e)nden	we, us
2	-(e)nzen	you
3p	-(e)š	they, them (personal)
3i	√-√	they, them (impersonal)

A nominal chain representing the agent of a sentence stands in the ergative case, marked by the postposition -e. This agent is also marked in a perfective verbal chain by a corresponding conjugated verbal prefix as follows:

        Perfective Agent

1	-∅-	I, by me
2	-∅-/-e-	you, by you
3p	-n-	he/she, by him/her
3i	-b-	it, they, by it/them
1	--	
2	--	
3p	-n-√-(e)š	they, by them

Now, an imperfective verb which does not feature an agent will properly show the same suffixed subject (patient) paradigm that is found in perfective forms. For example:

    en-na ba-ug₅-ge-a   {ba+ug₅+e+∅+a}
    Until he shall die
    (Enki & Ninhursag 221 OB)

    níĝ igi-bi-šè ᵍᶦˢtukul la-ba-gub-bu-a   {nu+ba+gub+e+∅+a}
    A thing before which a weapon cannot stand
    (Lament over Sumer and Ur 298 OB)

```
du₆-du₆ ki a nu-e₁₁-da a ma-ra-e₁₁-dè                              nu+e₁₁(d)+Ø+a}
Among the hills, (places) where water had not come down          (mu+ra+e₁₁(d)+e+Ø)
(before), water will come down for you
(Gudea Cyl A 11:14-15 Ur III)

Kisiga^ki iri ul ki ĝar-ra-ba,                                    {nu+dab₅+e+Ø}
zi-du nu-dab₅-bé érim-du nu-dib-bé                                {nu+dib+e+Ø}
In Kisiga, their ancient well-founded city, one who walks
rightly is not seized, but one who walks evilly shall not pass
(Ibbi-Suen B Segment B 6 Ur III)
Note that the "passive" patient of dab₅ and the "intransitive"
subject of dib have exactly the same marû morphology.

u₄ im-šú-šú igi im-lá-e šà-ka-tab ì-zu-zu                         {Vm+šú-šú+Ø}
The day was becoming obscured, vision was being reduced,
starvation was being known
(Lament over Sumer and Ur 305 OB)

tùr nu-dù-e amaš nu-ĝá-ĝá                                         {nu+dù+e+Ø}
Cattle pens were not being built, sheepfolds were not being set up
(Nisaba Hymn 27 in Reisman Diss. p. 105 OB)

bar-mu-uš na-dúb-bé                                               {na+dúb+e+Ø}
It is shaken because of me
(Eršemma No. 171:21, -mu = Emesal for -ĝu₁₀)
```

An imperfective verb which features an agent, on the other hand, marks the agent by means of a suffix which is *identical to that of the perfective subject* except in the third person plural, where -(e)ne replaces -n-√-(e)š:

Imperfective Agent

1	-(e)n	I
2	-(e)n	you
3	-Ø	he, she, it
1	-(e)nden	we
2	-(e)nzen	you
3p	-(e)ne	they (personal)

/(e)/ is here understood as an epenthetic vowel which appears after roots ending in a consonant. It can assimilate to the vowel of the root.

Thus, in imperfective forms the category of "agent markers" is shifted in the verbal chain from the prefixed position seen with perfective verbs to a suffixed position after the stem. At the same, the category of "patient markers" is theoretically shifted from the suffixed position seen with perfective verbs to a prefixed position, occupying the prefix slot of the perfective agent immediately before the root. Most current scholars see in this pattern of pronoun shift a demonstration of split ergativity, in which finite imperfective verbs demonstrate a nominative/accusative orientation instead of the ergative/absolutive pattern seen in the perfective verb. The erstwhile patient of a verb is redefined as an accusative "direct object" while the agent becomes a nominative "subject." See Michalowski, Journal of Cuneiform Studies 32 (1980),86-103, Thomsen §42, Attinger 1993, 150-52, along with Edzard's objections in 2003, 12.7.5. Note that agent and patient case marking on nominal chains remains unaltered; only the imperfective verbal chain can demonstrate this split ergative marking phenomenon.

P. Attinger offered the following full paradigm for the marû patient (direct object)(see
his detailed argument in Zeitschrift für Assyriologie 75 [1985] 161-178 following on the
earlier proposal of J. van Dijk in Orientalia NS 39 [1970] 308 n. 1.):

Imperfective Object

```
1    -(e)n-    me           (realized as /e/, /V/ or /n/)
2    -(e)n-    you
3p   -n-       him, her
3i   -b-       it, them

1    --        us           (perhaps me-?)
2    --        you
3p   -ne-      them (personal)
```

In this scheme, the 1st/2nd sg. perfective suffix -(e)n is shifted to prefix position,
while the the perfective agent prefixes -n- and -b- take on the function of imperfective
direct object. According to Attinger's analysis, which is not yet fully accepted, the
1st and 2nd sg. forms can appear either as -n-, indistinguishable from 3rd sg. ergative
-n-, or as -e- or an assimilated vowel. It is difficult to demonstrate these 1st and
2nd person forms with confidence, particularly in texts from before the Old Babylonian
period. In practice one usually sees only the 3rd sg. -n- or -b- prefixes and occasionally an -e- prefix for which an alternate explanation is often possible. Further,
since in the older, native Sumerian periods -n- is normally not written before the root
even to mark the perfective agent, one normally encounters only the impersonal -b- as a
direct object marker, and that only sporadically. One must keep in mind that before the
Old Babylonian period and the death of spoken Sumerian the marking of most case relationships within the verbal chain was essentially optional. For example, the marking of
imperfective objects is inconsistent throughout the early Ur III period Gudea texts:

Object properly marked:

  an-dùl daĝal-me ĝissu-zu-šè ní ga-ma-ši-íb-te   (ga+m+ba+ši+b+te)
  You are (-me-en) a wide umbrella, unto your shade
  I will go to refresh myself
  (Cyl A 3 14-15)

  aša$_5$ gal-gal-e šu ma-ra-ab-íl-e   (mu+ra+b+íl+e+Ø)
  e pa$_5$-e gú-bi ma-ra-ab-zi-zi   (mu+ra+b+zi-zi+Ø)
  All the great fields will *raise the hand* for you,
  The levees and ditches will raise their banks for you
  (Cyl A 11:12-13)

Object not marked:

  šà-bi ha-ma-pà-dè   (hé+ma+(b)+pàd+e+Ø)
  The meaning of it may she reveal to me
  (Cyl A 2:3)

  ĝiš-hur é-a-na ma-ra-pà-pà-dè   (mu+ra+(b)+pàd-pàd+e+Ø)
  All the plans of his temple he will reveal to you
  (Cyl A 7:6)

  ^{d}nin-ĝir-su é-zu ma-ra-dù-e   (mu+ra+(b)+dù+e+n)
  Ningirsu, I will build your temple for you
  (Cyl A 8:18)

Objects inconsistently marked in continguous lines:

  é u₄-dè ma-ra-dù-e   {mu+ra+(b)+dù+e+Ø}
  ĝi₆-e ma-ra-ab-mú-mú   {mu+ra+ab+mú-mú}
  The day will build the temple for you,
  the night will make it grow up for you
  (Cyl A 12:1-2)

  ur-saĝ ma-a-du₁₁ šu zi ga-mu-ra-ab-ĝar   {ga+mu+ra+b+ĝar}
  ᴰnin-ĝir-su é-zu ga-mu-ra-dù   {ga+mu+ra+(b)+dù}
  me šu ga-mu-ra-ab-du₇   {ga+mu+ra+b+du₇}
  Hero, you have spoken to me; I will put forth
  a trusty hand for you. Ningirsu, I will build your
  temple for you. I will make the *me* perfect for you
  (Cyl A 2:13-14)

A few examples of object markings from early administrative texts:

  lú a-ga-dèᵏⁱ na-ne-gaz-e
  He must not kill men of Akkad!
  (Wilcke, JCS 29, 186:6-7 Sargonic letter-order)

  PN₁ nagar u₄ 30-šè PN₂-ra hé-na-an-šúm-mu   {hé+na+n+šúm+e+Ø}
  Let him give PN₁ the carpenter (-n-) to PN₂ for 30 days
  (TCS 1 218:3-6 Ur III)

  10.0.0 še sig₅ gur-lugal PN-ra hé-na-ab-šúm-mu   {hé+na+b+šúm+e+Ø}
  Let him give to PN 10 royal *gur* of good barley (-b-)
  (TCS 1 7:5-7 Ur III)

  mu-túm-e-a mu lugal-bi in-pà   (mu+n+túm+e+Ø+a)
  He swore by the king's name that he will bring him (-n-) in
  (MVN 7, 526:4-5 Ur III)

  PN ù PN₂ ha-mu-ne-gi₄-gi₄   (ha+mu+ne+gi₄-gi₄+Ø}
  PN and PN₂ — let him send them (-ne-) back here
  (FAOS 19, 37 Ad 1:9 letter Ur III)

Some further examples from Old Babylonian texts:

  šeš-a-ne-ne ku-li-ne-ne èn tar-re im-mi-in-kúš-ù-ne   {Vm+b+n+kúš+e+(e)ne}
  His brothers and friends exhaust him (-n-) with questioning (-bí-)
  (Lugalanda and Enmerkar 225f.)

  e-ne-ne en ĝipar-ra bí-in-huĝ-e-ne   {b+n+huĝ+e+(e)ne}
  ereš-diĝir máš-a im-mi-in-dab₅-bé-ne   Vm+b+n+dab₅+e+(e)ne}
  gudu₄ hi-li-a bí-in-gub-bu-ne   {b+n+gub+e+(e)ne}
  They install a high priest (-n-) in the Gipar (-bí-),
  they take a high priestess (-n-) though a kid-omen (-bí-),
  they have a priest (-n-) in (his) prime doing the serving there
  (Hendursaga A 73-75)

  lú mu-sar-ra-ba šu bí-íb-uru₁₂-a mu-ni bí-íb-sar-re-a   {b+b+ùr+e+Ø+a}
  Any person who shall sweep the hand over (= erase)   {b+b+sar+e+Ø+a}
  this inscription and write his (own) name upon it   (bí- resumes -a)
  (Anam 2:32-35 = RIM E4.4.6.2)

PROBLEMS AND SCRIBAL ERRORS

OB literary texts frequently feature textual variants or problematic verbal forms open

to several different interpretations, which can make secure translation difficult. For
example, does the following passage illustrate Attinger's 1st sg. imperfective object
marker in the form of mu-e(n)-, with the 1st sg. marker serving to render a 1st pl. idea?
Or is mu-e- a misunderstood writing for an actual 1st pl. me- direct object pronoun based
on the 1st sg. dative prefix me-? Or could -e- simply be a normal 2nd sg. agent marker
which indicates a second agent in the sentence that accomplishes the action?

>   me-en-dè: ᵍᶦˢnimbar-gin₇ šu nu-du₁₁-ga-me a-na-aš mu-e-gul-gul-lu-ne
>   ᵍᶦˢmá gibil-gin₇ sa-bíl-lá nu-ak-me a-na-aš mu-e-zé-er-zé-er-re-ne
>   Us - Why do you (-e-) have them (-e-ne) destroy (us) like a palm tree,
>   despite our not having laid a hand(?) upon it?
>   Why do you (-e-) have them (-e-ne) annihilate (us) like a new boat
>   despite our not having plastered(?) it (with bitumen)?
>   (Lamentation over Sumer and Ur 241-242 OB)

Compare the following passage from the same text, reconstructed from the same textual
exemplars, in which the 1st plural object is apparently written me-:

>   [gu]-ti-umᵏᶦ lú ha-lam-ma-ke₄ me-zé-er-zé-re-ne   {me+zé(r)-zé(r)+ene}
>   Gutim, the destroyers, are wiping us out!
>   (Lamentation over Sumer and Ur 230)

One must also be careful to distinguish a preradical -n- which marks an object from an
-n- which resumes a locative, especially common in OB texts, e.g.

>   kur-ra ga-an-ku₄ mu-ĝu₁₀ ga-an-ĝar   (kur+a ga+n+ku₄)
>   I would go into (-n-) the mountains and establish there (-n-) my name
>   (Gilgamesh and Huwawa 7 OB)

Finally, one will encounter many apparent errors in the choice of 3rd sg. -n- vs. -b-
object markers in OB texts. In the following, -n- is apparently an error for impersonal
-b- unless the -n- marks an unnamed locus "here":

>   za-e é-ubur-ra ma-ra-an-dù-ù-ne   {mu+ra+n+dù+e+(e)ne}
>   For you they will build a milking house (-n-)
>   (Sheep and Grain 136 OB)

On the other hand, apparent errors sometimes have logical explanations. In the following, impersonal -b- is possibly employed because the object, King Urnamma, is dead and
now an impersonal lifeless corpse:

>   ur-ᵈnamma bára gal kur-ra-ke₄ mu-ni-ib-tuš-ù-ne
>   They seat Ur-Namma on the great dais of the netherworld
>   (Urnamma A 136 OB)

In this late Ur III contract from Nippur, both marû verbs seem to be grammatically
faulty, the first showing a preradical -n- rather than -b-, the second lacking any
preradical mark:

>   10 gín kù-babbar itu mìn-èš-ta u₄-5-àm zal-la
>   Lugal-hé-ĝál <u>in-lá-e-a</u> bí-in-du₁₁
>   tukumbi nu-l[á], 20 še [gur-lugal] <u>ì-áĝ-e-a</u> mu lugal in-pà
>   Lugalheĝal declared that he will weigh out 10 shekels of silver
>   when 5 days have passed from the month Mineš.
>   He invoked the king's name that if he does not pay he will
>   measure out 20 royal *gur* of barley
>   (Grégoire, AAS 78:5-6 Ur III)

In addition to gender errors in the marû object marking system, other sorts of problems
are common in the marking of agents in OB passages. In the following two lines for

example, the first verb is nearly correct, lacking only an explicit preradical -n- to
mark the 3rd. sg. personal object. The second verb, however, shows a preradical -e-
whose interpretation is difficult. Is it a second, prefixed, 2nd sg. agent marker
repeating the suffixed agent marker -en, or perhaps an allomorph of a localizing -n-?

    ĝá-e ᵈnin-hur-saĝ-ĝá mu-e-ši-túm-mu-un a-na-àm níĝ-ba-ĝu₁₀   {m+e+ši+n+túm+en}
    za-e ᵈnin-hur-saĝ-ĝá mu-e-túm-mu-un-nam   {m+e+túm+en+am}
    I: if I bring Ninhursaĝa here to you, what will be my reward?
    You: if you indeed bring Ninhursaĝa here ...
    (Enki and Ninhursaĝa 224/226 OB)

FINITE IMPERFECTIVE VERBS WITH SUFFIXED MODAL /d/ ELEMENT

An element /d/, usually called the /ed/-morpheme, may be suffixed to the marû stem
of the verb to add what may be a modal nuance to the imperfective form, namely a notion
such as possibility (can, might be done), necessity (must, needs to be done) or
obligation (ought, should, is to be done). T. Jacobsen proposed that it can further
convey a "pre-actional" idea, referring to future situations which are "about to begin,"
while others, including Edzard, have described it as a mark of future tense. See the
following lesson on participles and infinitives for more discussion and illustrations
of the form and functions of /d/ in connection with non-finite verbal constructions.

The meaning of /d/ in OB finite verbs is sometimes not clear. The following illustra-
tive examples will therefore come mostly from earlier periods:

    tukum-bi u₄-da-ta PN ù dumu-ĝu₁₀-ne ha-ba-zàh-dè-eš   {hé+ba+zàh+e+d+eš}
    If after today PN and my children might run away
    (ITT V 9594:2-3, Falkenstein ZA 55 (1963) 68 Ur III)

    u₄ PN ba-úš-e-da-a   {ba+úš+e+d+a+a}
    Whenever (in the future) that PN may die
    (Falkenstein, NSGU 7:15 Ur III)

    dumu ù-ma-ni-ke₄-ne arad-da la-ba-gi₄-gi₄-dè-ša-a   {nu+ba+gi₄-gi₄+d+eš+a}
    That the children of Umani should not return (to court) about the slave
    (Falkenstein, NSGU 64:16'-17' Ur III)

    dub lú nu-ub-da-su-su-da-ne   {nu+b+da+su-su+d+a+(e)ne+ak+Ø}
    The tablet of the persons who don't have to repay it
    (Forde, NCT 19:52 Ur III)

    1 máš gú-na šeš-kal-la mu nu-da-su-su-da-šè šu bar-re   {nu+n+da+su-su+d+a+šè}
    1 tax-kid of Šeškalla, because he didn't have to   {bar+e+d}
    repay it, (is) to be released
    (Oppenheim, Eames Collection Bab 9:1ff. Ur III)

    mu lugal u₄ ba-zàh-dè-na-ĝá NIR-da hé-a bí-in-du₁₁   {ba+zàh+e+d+en+a+ĝu₁₀+a}
    By the king's name, on a day that I might flee may
    it be a felony, he declared
    (BE 3/1, 1:4-6 Ur III}

    u₄ temen-ĝu₁₀ ma-si-gi₄-na é-ĝu₁₀ u₄ šu-zi ma-ši-tùmu-da   {ma+ši+tùm+e+d+Ø+a}
    The day you shall sink my foundation (pegs) for me,
    the day when a righteous hand is to be brought to my house for me
    (Gudea Cylinder A 11:18-19 Ur III)

    á-áĝ-ĝá lugal-ĝá-ke₄ ì-gub-bé-en nu-tuš-ù-dè-en   {nu-tuš+e+d+en}
    (As) I am serving at the instructions of my king, I must not sit
    (Letter of Aradmu to Šulgi No. 1, 25 OB)

    ĝá-e u₄-ba ša-ba-gúr-e-dè-en
    And indeed I, on that day, will consequently (ša-) have to bow down to him
    (Enmerkar and the Lord of Aratta 291)

    alaĝ-gin₇ kùš-kùš-a dé-a-meš ì-sè-ge-dè-en-dè-en   {V+sè(g)+e+d+enden}
    Are we to be made like statues which are poured into moulds?
    (Lamentation of Sumer and Ur 229)

FINITE IMPERFECTIVE VERBS ENDING IN /de/

An old problem in Sumerian grammar has been the analysis of finite imperfective verbs ending in the suffix -dè. With non-finite verbal forms this suffix is easily understood as the modal element /d/ plus locative-terminative -e, since non-finite forms follow the rules of nominal chain formation and so regularly end with a case marker (or the copula). But unless they are made into relative clauses by means of the nominalizing suffix -a, finite verbs are not nominal chain constructions. What then is the final /e/ element in such forms?

In particular cases one can identify a reasonable origin for an unorthodox form. Compare the following non-contestation formula from an Old Babylonian sales contract:

    u₄-kúr-šè lú lú-ù nu-un-gi₄-gi₄-dè mu lugal-bi in-pà-dè-eš
    That in the future one person shall not return (to court)
    against the other, a royal oath to that effect they swore
    (JCS 20, 44:20-22 Nippur, Rim-Sin 25)

Here nu-un-gi₄-gi₄-dè incorrectly conflates two commonly occurring variant forms: a negated infinitive nu-gi₄-gi₄-dè 'to not return' with a locative-terminative -e loosely dependent upon a verb of speaking, and a nominalized finite verb nu-un-gi₄-gi₄-da 'that one would not return against him' which anticipates the -bi pronoun in the main clause. Other cases however are not so easily explained.

The simplest answer may lie with the phonotactics of the /d/ element. When /d/ is not followed by some vocalic element such as a subject pronoun, that is, when it stands as the last element in the finite verbal chain, /d/ is thought to be regularly deleted (see the full description /d/ in the lesson on participles and infinitives). Thus, in finite imperfective verbs with a 3rd person sg. subject or agent marked by a final zero suffix (-Ø), the immediately preceding /d/ element would be deleted and there would be no explicit way to indicate the presence of this modal morpheme in the verb. An obvious solution lay at hand. By analogy with ubiquitous infinitives of the shape ĝá-ĝá-dè 'to place', the suffix -dè was occasionally placed at the end of finite verbal chains as a kind of allomorph of the /d/ element. While the final /e/ is in origin the locative-terminative case postposition, which cannot occur by definition on non-nominalized finite verbal chains, it has no syntactic function in such aberrant forms. Thus, previous attempts to assign a special morphological function to this final /e/ are unnecessary. It has no meaning per se; it only functions in this specific environment to make the /d/ element evident. This phenomenon is probably an OB innovation.

Compare the following lines from the OB Homocide Trial (Jacobsen, Analecta Biblica 12, 130ff.). In line 41 the verb should read al-gaz-e unless the form is a conflation of finite al-gaz-e and an infinitive gaz-e-dè. In the two parallel forms the final 3rd person pl. subject marker /(e)š/ renders the /d/ pronounceable:

    munus-e a-na bí-in-ak-e al-gaz-e-d[è] bí-in-eš   {al+gaz+e+d+Ø}
    "The woman, what was she doing (that) she is to be killed,"
    they declared (lines 40-41)

    nita 3-a-bi ù munus-bi igi ᵍⁱˢgu-za PN-šè ì-gaz-e-dè-eš   {V+gaz+e+d+(e)š}
        bí-in-e-eš
    "Those three men and that woman should be killed
    before PN's chair" they declared (lines 32-34)

    PNN al-gaz-e-dè-eš   {al+gaz+e+d+(e)š}
    PNN are to be killed (lines 55-59)

Additional examples:

    kù mu-[un]-na-ba-e šu nu-um-ma-gíd-i-dè   {nu+m+ba+gíd+e+d+∅}
    (The god Numušda) offers him silver, but he would not accept it
    (Marriage of Mardu 77 OB)

    iz-zi im-ma-ab-kal-la-ge-dè   {Vm+ba+b+kalag+e+d+∅}
    He has to strengthen the wall (of the rented house)
    (Chiera, PBS 8/1, 102 r 8f. OB)

    mu nu-sar-dè in-na-ab-sar   {nu+sar+e+d+∅}
    A name which should not be written that one has written for him
    (Laws of Ur-Namma epilogue g10a, OB copy)

Excluded from this discussion are those Ur III or earlier verbs which often drop the
final /n/ of the 1st or 2nd sg. subject/agent suffix -en, e.g. Šulgi X 137 na-ba-an-kúš-
ù-dè-e 'may you not grow weary of this', for which a parallel in Šulgi D 393 offers nam-
ba-kúš-ù-dè-en. Another example:

    PN dam šà-ga-na-ke₄ ha-ba-du₁₂-du₁₂
    ba-ra-ba-dù-dè bí-du₁₁   {bara+ba+n+dù+e+d+e(n)}
    "Let PN be married by a spouse of her own desire.
    I would not hinder her," he declared
    (Edzard, SRU 85 r. 2'ff. Sargonic)

    REMEMBER: IMPERFECTIVE STEMS ARE FORMED IN FOUR WAYS:

                               - AFFIXATION OF -e
                               - REDUPLICATION (WITH LOSS OF AMISSIBLE AUSLAUTS)
                               - (USE OF AN ALTERNATE STEM WITH ADDED FINAL COUNSONANT - uncertain)
                               - SUBSTITUTION OF A DIFFERENT, COMPLEMENTARY ROOT

                           TRANSITIVE AND CAUSATIVE IMPERFECTIVE FINITE VERBS, ALSO
                           IMPERATIVES AND COHORTATIVE FORMS, DEMONSTRATE "SPLIT
                           ERGATIVITY" IN THEIR SUBJECT-OBJECT PRONOUN PATTERNS.
                           THE AGENT (NOW THE NOMINATIVE SUBJECT) APPEARS AFTER THE
                           ROOT, AND THE PATIENT (NOW THE ACCUSATIVE OBJECT) APPEARS
                           IN THE PRERADICAL POSITION. CORRESPONDING ERGATIVE AND
                           ABSOLUTIVE CASE MARKERS ON NOMINAL CHAINS ARE UNAFFECTED.

PARTICIPLES AND THE INFINITIVE

THEORETICAL CONSIDERATIONS

The following first two sections were originally part of a position paper presented to the 1992 meeting of the Sumerian Grammar Discussion Group held in Oxford, England.

Basic Structure of Participles and the So-called Infinitive

1) The non-finite verbal forms of Sumerian are, generally speaking, distinguished from finite forms by the absence of verbal prefixes, although participles can be negated by means of the negative preformative nu-. This distinction is not absolute, however, since the verbal root begins the form also in the case of the imperative transformation and the rare OB so-called prefixless-finite construction.

2) Participles (verbal adjectives) and the "infinitive" are structurally related. Their interrelationship may be described in terms of differences of aspect and presence or absence of the modal suffix /d/ and the nominalizing suffix -a. Compare the non-finite forms of the root ba 'to allot, distribute', here with a dummy patient níĝ 'thing', that will be used paradigmatically in the following presentation (ba-e represents any marû stem, including those formed by reduplication or root alternation):

Form	- /a/	+ /a/	Meaning
hamṭu participle	níĝ ba	níĝ ba-a	allot a thing
marû participle	níĝ ba-e	níĝ ba-e-a	allotting a thing
marû participle + /d/	níĝ ba-e-d	níĝ ba-e-d-a	a thing having to be allotted

níĝ ba   Describes a thing done without concern for or emphasis on the on-going process of doing it, implying the constancy, regularity or permanance of an event, or a process with an inherent end-point (a telic event). This form is the basis of nominal compounds such as níĝ-ba 'alloted thing > portion, gift', ki-ùr 'leveled place > terrace', sa-pàr 'cord spreader > net', an-dùl 'sky coverer > canopy', or of such occupational terms as dub-sar 'tablet writer > scribe', za-dím 'stone fashioner > lapidary', má-gíd 'boat tower', or of such attributive forms as á-tuku 'having strength > powerful', níĝ-tuku 'having things > rich', níĝ-nu-tuku 'not having things > poor', nir-ĝál 'being lordly > authoritative'. Cf. Gudea Cyl A 6:26 ur-saĝ níĝ-ba-e ki áĝ-ra 'for the hero who loves gifts', i.e. for whom the loving of gifts is perhaps an unchanging, constant feature of his character. With the addition of a nominalizing -a suffix this form becomes what is usually described as a past (active or passive) participle: ki áĝ-a '(that which is) loved'.

níĝ ba-e   The doing of a thing with concern for the process, duration, repetition or potentiality of the event, a process without an inherent end-point (an atelic event). This imperfective form may be the basis of such occupational terms as ad-gi₄-gi₄ 'one who returns the voice > advisor' or maš-šu-gíd-gíd 'one who reaches the hand into the kid > diviner'. Cf. attributives such as gal-di 'one who does things in a great manner', nin₉ mul-mul 'the ever radiant sister', or u₄ iri gul-gul 'the storm (which goes about) destroying cities'. This form can could be described as a present participle. An added -a suffix may make the participle more definite or merely relativize the form.

níĝ ba-e-d /d/ may add a modal idea to the participle, chiefly necessity (must, needs to be done) or obligation (ought, is to be done), also purpose (in order to, for the purpose of doing). It might possibly add an irrealis, conditional nuance. Jacobsen observed that it can also convey a "preactional" idea, referring to future situations which are "about to begin." Edzard (1967) described it as a Tempuszeichen par excellence," and in his last statement (2003, p. 82) he again takes it as a future indicator, at least with intransitive finite verbs. But if it conveys a future tense idea it probably developed that use secondarily, and since the marû stem already connotes present or future action, such a use of /d/ would seem to be redundant. Frequently the meaning of /d/, especially in OB finite verbs, is unclear (see later on imperfective finite verbs.) A ba-e-d form with a loc.-term. case marker, ba+e+d+e, is generally referred to as the Sumerian infinitive, and it can seem to have that kind of use, but in closer analysis one should always keep in mind that it is basically a marû participle with some modal meaning. The term "infinitive" will be used here for convenience only, as a way of referring to non-finite forms with suffixed /d/ in certain contexts.

3) It is a fundamental axiom of Sumerian grammar that a proper Sumerian verbal sentence or clause must feature on a basic level a subject (patient) and a verb. An infinitive construction is actually a kind of verbal clause, consisting of a subject (patient) and a modifying participial verbal complex √(marû)+d, standing in the positions of a head noun and adjective in a nominal chain, though sometimes the two parts are separated by modifiers of the head noun and or adverbial expressions. The verbal complex must always end with a case marker (or a case-masking copula), unless the chain is embedded within another chain either as an attributive adjectival clause or as the regens of a genitive construction. The case normally seen with a simple infinitive is loc.-term. -e. Note in passing that when analyzing infinitive constructions in this ergative language, giving verbal roots passive translations in "transitive" contexts can sometimes be helpful.

4) In addition to applying to non-finite forms, whether described as participle or infinitive, the rules of nominal chain formation, one should keep in mind the basic *relativizing* function of the nominalizing suffix -a. -a generates attributive relative phrases or clauses which then occupy the rank order slot of a primary or secondary adjective in new, expanded nominal chains. If the finite verb in the sentence é in-dù 'he built the house' is relativized, the resulting clause é in-dù-a can be used as the head noun and attributive of a new nominal chain, for example {é in-dù-a}-bi-šè 'towards that house which he built'. Substituting a non-finite past participle or present participle plus modal /d/ in the last phrase yields: {é dù-a}-bi-šè 'towards that house which was built' or {é dù-e-da}-bi-šè 'towards that house which is/was to be built'.

5) To help simplify the analysis of "infinitives" one may identify two basic types of infinitive constructions, those with and those without a relativizing -a suffix. For example:

    (a) kù šúm-mu-dè   to (-e) have to give silver   {šúm+e+d+e}

    (b) kù šúm-mu-da   silver which has to be given   {šúm+e+d+a}

In (a) the infinitive šúm+e+d functions as an attributive modifier, often a kind of gerundive, i.e. a present participle with a modal nuance, approximately 'the ought to be given silver'. The final -e is the locative-terminative case marker which links the infinitive construction with the rest of the sentence, whether as a loose indirect object of a verb of speaking, for example, or as a more independent adverbial expression. This -e often functions in form and meaning like the "to" used with English infinitives.

In (b) šúm+e+d is relativized, the form in which it occurs, for example, with possessive pronouns in the imperfective Pronominal Conjugation (see below) or in a copular sentence such as kù-bi (kù) šúm-mu-dam 'that silver is (silver which is) to be given'.

The difference in meaning between a participle or infinitive with and without a nominalizing -a is sometimes difficult to appreciate. Perhaps the problem is comparable in some cases to the distinction between simple adjectives with and without an -a suffix, e.g. lú-du$_{10}$-ga vs. simple lú-du$_{10}$, studied by J. Krecher (1978) and discussed in this grammar in the early lesson on nouns and adjectives.

Phonotaxis of the Element /d/

1) The most recent comprehensive description of the modal /d/ element is that of Edzard 2003 p. 132, who speaks as follows of four allomorphs of what has traditionally been called the /ed/ morpheme:

   a) [ed] after a C and before a V
   b) [(e)d] after a V and before a V
   c) [e(d)] after a C "in final position"
   d) [(e)(d)] after a V "in final position" in a form such as gi$_4$-gi$_4$.

Note that Edzard's analysis of the /d/ element differs from that of this grammar in that Edzard, following Falkenstein, has not accepted the existence of Yoshikawa's marû stem-forming suffix -e. Instead, in his view the [e] seen in association with the /d/ element is a component of an /ed/ morpheme. This older analysis in part has led earlier scholars to conclude that there is a large class of verbal roots, called Regular Verbs or *Normalform* Verbs, which do not differentiate marû stems. For such roots it is the presence of the /ed/ element which generates a marû participle or an infinitive. With this view of /ed/ compare the Poebel-Falkenstein-Edzard analysis of imperfective finite verbs like ib-šúm-e 'he will give it', where the final -e suffix represents a coalescence of three morphemes: Vb+šúm+e {3rd sg. + agent + future}. The Yoshikawa system, followed by this grammar, would analyze instead Vb+šúm+e+Ø, in which the /Ø/ represents two morphemes {3rd sg. + agent} and the -e only one {marû}.

2) The preceding phonotactic scheme looks somewhat like that of the genitive case marker /ak/. The [k] is deleted before a) a consonant (the possessive pronouns and the CV case markers); b) at a word boundary (#), e.g. at the end of an anticipatory genitive chain; and c) before the absolutive case marker -Ø, which functions phonotactically like a word boundary. It is retained before a vowel. One can make the analogy complete by theorizing that /d/ is also deleted before CV possessive pronouns but not -(a)ni or -(a)nene; and before CV case markers. As an attributive phrase within a nominal chain, the participle is, after all, capable of being followed by a possessive/demonstrative pronoun and a case marker. Edzard's analysis presupposes an epenthetic vowel [e] in certain contexts, parallel to the [a] of the genitive /ak/. For the present, however, this grammar assumes the existence of Yoshikawa's /e/ marû stem formative and that the modal element is properly just /d/. Compare an infinitive such as the Old Sumerian hal-hal-dè (Westenholz, OSP 2, 44 2:2), which on its face argues against the presence of any such epenthetic vowel between the final consonant of the root and the /d/ element. For a more detailed traditionalist discussion of this matter compare for example G. Steiner in Journal of Near Eastern Studies 40 (1981) 21-41 with M. Yoshikawa's differing views in Journal of Near Eastern Studies 27 (1968) 251-261.

3) If, for the sake of discussion, one holds both with the above full phonolgical deletion scheme for /d/ and also Yoshikawa's marû formative -e, one is left with the uncomfortable result that a number of Sumerian "infinitives" will not show the /d/ element, i.e. any actual explicit phonological mark of an infinitive (cf. Edzard's allomorph (d) above). Granted, the language permits a parallel total deletion also in the case of genitive forms like ama dumu 'the mother of the child' {ama dumu+ak+Ø}. On the other hand, those scholars who hold with Edzard's view that the base element is /ed/ must likewise hold that marû participles based on marû stems formed using Yoshikawa's -e suffix which are distinct from "infinitives" featuring modal /ed/ do not exist. In other words, all marû participles taking the form ba-e are instead to be analyzed as ba+e(d). This view would raise the question of how one would translate all these /ed/ forms with any

consistency. This is possibly why Edzard opted for a general meaning of "future tense" rather than any modal meaning in his descriptions of the /ed/ morpheme.

The following summarizes a collection of actually occurring forms that illustrate the above proposed full deletion scheme in conjunction with the application to marû participles (infinitives) of nominal chain rules and the nominalizing suffix -a.
ba-e-d before a possessive pronoun and a case marker

1 sg.	+ abs.	ba+e+d+ĝu₁₀+Ø	>	ba-e-ĝu₁₀
2 sg.	+ loc.	ba+e+d+zu+a	>	ba-e-za
3 sg. per.	+ loc.	ba+e+d+(a)ni+a	>	ba-e-da-na
3 sg. imp.	+ loc.	ba+e+d+bi+a	>	ba-e-ba

ba-e-d before a case marker or the 3. sg. copula

absolutive	ba+e+d+Ø	>	ba-e	
ergative/loc.term.	ba+e+d+e	>	ba-e-dè	
locative	ba+e+d+a	>	ba-e-da	
comitative	ba+e+d+da	>	ba-e-da	
terminative	ba+e+d+šè	>	ba-e-šè	
genitive	ba+e+d+ak	>	ba-e-da	(anticipatory genitive)
3rd sg. copula	ba+e+d+Vm	>	ba-e-dam	

ba-e-d plus nominalizing -a and nominal chain elements

word boundary	ba+e+d+a+#	>	ba-e-da	(regens of a genitive)
locative	ba+e+d+a+a	>	ba-e-da(-a)	(locative often elided)
3rd sg. copula	ba+e+d+a+m	>	ba-e-dam	
pronoun + case	ba+e+d+a+(a)ni+e	>	ba-e-da-né	(pron. conjugation)

Notice the two different possible sources for the copular sequence ba-e-dam. Note further the number of different possible underlying morphemic origins for the sequence ba-e-da which can result from the deletion scheme, restated together here:

locative	ba+e+d+a	>	ba-e-da	
comitative	ba+e+d+da	>	ba-e-da	
genitive	ba+e+d+ak	>	ba-e-da	(anticipatory genitive)
-a + word boundary	ba+e+d+a+#	>	ba-e-da	(regens of a genitive)
-a + locative	ba+e+d+a+a	>	ba-e-da	(locative often elided)

Some of the old problem of determining the functions of infinitival /ede/ vs. /eda/ forms may stem in part from such multiple possible origins of the /ba-e-da/ sequence.

In the example sets to follow, textual references for verbal forms which could feature a phonotactically concealed /d/ will be avoided to lessen confusion in the basic presentation of data. At the end of this lesson, however, a selection of passages has been assembled which could reasonably be adduced to illustrate a concealed final /d/.

ORTHOGRAPHIC PECULIARITIES ASSOCIATED WITH THE INFINITIVE OR PARTICIPLE

It is not uncommon for an infinitive showing the /d/ suffix to feature a verb which does not look like a proper marû stem as currently understood. Compare the following:

    ᵏᵘšе-sír é-ba-an 2-a kéš-re₆-dè   {kéš(e)dr+e+d+e}
    To tie sandles into two pairs
    (PDT 361:4-5 Ur III)

    60 sa gi ki PN-ta a-šà kéš-e-dè maš-maš-e šu ba-ti
    Mašmaš received 60 bundles of reed from PN to tie up a field
    (Nik II 182:1-4 Ur III)

324 sa gi ka i₇-da i₇ ᵈamar-ᵈsuen é ĝá-ra ké\u0161-dè   {ĝar+a+∅}
324 bundles of reed at Ka'ida, the river of Amar-Suen, to tie up
an established house
(Kang, SACT II 161:1-4 Ur III)

The first reference shows a plene (full) form of the infinitive; the second shows a
slightly simplified plene writing; the last shows an abbreviated writing. Compare the
writing dù-dè generally found in texts from before Ur III, as in the Gudea inscriptions,
with the plene writing dù-ù-dè which is standard in later texts. Other roots, especially those featuring an /u/ vowel, show the same tendency to abbreviated, non-plene
writing of the marû stem particularly in earlier texts. For example, 'to feed (animals)'
is normally written gu₇-dè in OS or Ur III texts, e.g. še-numun še anše gu₇-dè 'seed
barley and barley to feed the donkeys' (Bauer, AWL 21:2 OS); or gu₄-ĝu₁₀ gu₇-dè hé-na-
ab-šúm-mu 'let him give my ox to him to be fed' (Sollberger, TCS 1, 3330 rev. 1'-3'
Ur III). One might conjecture that the spoken language in such cases supplied the
lengthened vowel needed to indicate a marû stem generated by an assimilated -e suffix.
In the written language the presence of a following /d/ element may have been felt to
be a sufficient indicator of the presence of a marû stem. As M. Powell suggested (Fs.
Diakonoff (1982) 317): "Verb roots with vowels in final position are rarely written
plene in the infinitive because it is not necessary to do this to avoid confusion."

In some cases native sign lists justify our choosing a sign value that shows a homorga-
nic final vowel (überhängender Vokal) to produce a desired lengthened marû stem where
needed. An example can be seen in the writing of the infinitive as uru₁₂-dè 'to level';
the hamṭu stem is simply the same sign read ùr. Many roots containing a /u/ vowel
show this property, e.g. kúr/kúru 'to alter', ku₅/kudr/kur₅/kuru₅ 'to cut', tuk/tuku
'to have', or ur₁₁/uru₄ 'to plow'. In other cases no such native justification exists,
but the same phenomenon may be at work. Cf. Gilgameš and Aga 58: dím-ma-ni hé-sùh(u)
galga-ni hé-bir-re 'so that his reasoning will become confused, his judgment disarrayed'.

More problematic is the very common writing AK-dè 'to do, make', for which M. Powell in
his study of this verb (loc. cit.) posits for infinitives the allomorph kè(AK) before
modal /d/. P. Attinger, a student of Edzard, proposes in his later study in Zeitschrift
für Assyriologie 95, 46ff. & 208ff. the alternate analysis of an allomorph /k/ before
modal /ed/. Such interpretations argue for the analysis {AK+e+d+e} > kè-dè, a form
showing a proper marû stem plus /d/ and the locative-terminative. Note that the value kè
for the AK sign is attested in the OB Proto-Ea sign-list and, further, that a variant
syllabic writing ke₄-dè is found in texts from Garšana (see Jagersma 2010 §28.7).

Finally, cases exist where no simple orthographic explanation can easily be found for
infinitives apparently built on hamṭu stems. In earlier texts at least one can suppose
that abbreviated, "morphographemic," or "mnemonic" writing is possibly at work in such
cases, in which a hamṭu root is written but the corresponding marû stem is supplied by
the reader. Compare two finite forms from royal inscriptions of Šu-Sîn and Utuheĝal:

    lú mu-sar-ra-ba šu bí-íb-ùr-ùr-a mu-ni bí-íb-sar-re-a   (CDLI P432280:219'-222')
    lú mu-sar-ra-na šu bí-ín-ùr-a mu-ni bí-íb-sar-a   (CDLI P216798:5-7)
    A person who shall erase this/his inscription and shall write his name on it

SYNTACTIC PECULIARITIES ASSOCIATED WITH THE PARTICIPLE OR INFINITIVE

1) Often one encounters a participial or infinitival construction which lacks a subject (patient) head noun or required agent. In many of these cases one may posit an
elliptical noun, typically <lú> or <níĝ>, to understand the underlying structure. A

    <lú> <níĝ> húl-húl-le-me-en <lú> <níĝ> du₁₀-du₁₀-ge-me-en
    <lú> giri₁₇-zal nam-nun-na u₄ zal-zal-le-me-en
    (A man) making all (things) joyous am I,
    (a man) making all (things) pleasant am I,

(a man) making all the days pass in splendor and pomp am I
(Šulgi B 175-176 Ur III)

With this compare a parallel passage without ellipsis of either patient or agent:

ᵈšul-gi lú níĝ lu-lu-me-en
Shulgi, a man who makes things numerous am I
(Šulgi A 55 Ur III)

Some other examples:

PN ugula íl-ne   {íl+(e)ne+Ø}
PN nu-bànda íl-ne
PN, the foreman/overseer of porters
(DP 140 3:2 & 142 3:3f. OS)
Elliptical for <lú/ùĝ> <níĝ> íl 'thing-carrying personnel'

mu nu-ĝál-la-ka   {nu+ĝál+a+ak+a}
mu hé-ĝál-la
In a year of (things) not being present (i.e. of want)
A year of (things) indeed being present (i.e. of plenty)
(Edzard, SRU No. 54 2:15/18 OAkk)

húl-húl-le-ĝá du₁₀-du₁₀-ge-ĝá   {dùg-dùg+e+ĝu₁₀+a}
About my causing (people) to rejoice and making (things) pleasant
(Šulgi E 33 Ur III)

ᵈnin-men-na-ke₄ tu-tu al-ĝá-ĝá   {tud-tud+Ø}
Ninmena was setting up birthing (people/animals)
(Hymn to the Hoe 27 OB)

uri₅ᵏⁱ-ma ur-bé úr bàd-da si-im-si-im nu-mu-un-ak-e
The dogs of Ur no longer sniff (things) at the base of the city wall
(Lament over Sumer and Ur 350 OB)

lá-a-ne-ne nu-ta-zi   {lá+a+(a)nene(+ta)}
From their surplus (items) it has not been deducted
(Nik I 271 4:1 OS)

2) When a marû participle serves as the regens of a genitive construction, the rectum represents the implicit subject or patient of the participle:

ùnu-dè du₉-du₉ ᵈᵘᵍšakir-ra-ka-na u₄ im-di-ni-ib-zal-e
The cowherd spends his day in his churning of the churn
(Enki and the World Order 30 OB)

zi-zi šú-šú tigi za-za-am-za-am-ma-ka ki bí-zu-zu-a
About how I always knew the places for the raising and lowering
of the *tigi* and *zamzam* instruments
(Šulgi E 34 Ur III)

3) A subject (patient), indirect object, or agent can be pronominalized, represented in the participial construction by a possessive pronoun:

é-gal-la-na níĝ-gu₇ la-ba-na-ĝál tuš-ù-bi nu-ub-du₇   {tuš+e+bi+Ø}
In his palace there was nothing for him to eat,
dwelling in it was not fitting for it
(Lament over Sumer and Ur 307 OB)

60 še gur ki dumu In-si-naᵏⁱ-ke₄-ne-ta ù še tuku-ni   {tuk+e+(a)ni+Ø}

60 gur barley from the citizens of Isin and the barley which is
<u>being held by him</u>
(TCS 1, 198:3-5 Ur III)

* * * * * *

EXAMPLES FOR STUDY ORGANIZED BY GRAMMATICAL CONTEXT

HAMṬU PARTICIPLE WITHOUT NOMINALIZING -a

The bare hamṭu stem is a component of numerous common and proper nouns, including many different occupation terms, for example:

apin-ús	plow follower	> plowman
gir₄-bil	oven heater	> oven tender
ĝír-lá	knife wearer	> butcher
gu₄-gaz	ox smiter	> cattle slaughterer
igi-nu-du₈	not-seeing (person)	> blind(ed) worker
kù-dím	silver fashioner	> silversmith
lú-éš-gíd(-k)	person of cord pulling	> field surveyor
lú-kaš₄	running person	> courier
lú-zàh	fleeing person	> fugitive
(lú-)má-gíd	boat pulling (person)	> boat tower
munu₄-mú	malt grower	> maltster
àga-ús(-ne)	crown follower(s)	> soldier(s), guard(s)
íl(-ne)	<load> carrier(s)	> porter(s)
ki-nú	lying place	> sleeping quarters
ki-tuš	sitting place	> residence
níĝ-gu₇	eating thing	> food item
níĝ-ba	alloting, distributing thing	> gift

It is also the stem seen in periphrastic compound verbs of the type ir si-im - a₅ 'to perform scent-sniffing' > 'to smell' ki su-ub - a₅ 'to perform ground-rubbing' > 'to prostrate oneself' or šu-tag - du₁₁ 'to do hand-touching' > 'to decorate'.

This kind of bare hamṭu participle is common both in ordinary contexts and particularly in earlier literary texts, where it conveys an aspectual nuance that is difficult for us to distinguish from that of a marû participle. Examples:

é-igi-<u>íl</u>-eden-na
Temple lifting (its) eye over the steppe
(Ent 16, 3:7 OS = temple name)

šu-níĝin 50 lú igi-níĝin ᵈba-ú ga kù munu₄ kù <u>ba-me</u>   {ba+me+(e)š}
They are a total of 50 supervisory personnel of Bau
distributing sacred milk and malt
(Genouillac TSA 5 13:1-4 OS)

še <u>hal-bi</u> íb-ta-zi zíz <u>ús-bi</u> šà-ba ì-ĝál
The (cost of the) distributing of the barley was deducted from it,
and the (cost of the) treading(?) of the emmer is included in it
(Gelb, MAD 4 No. 39:16-17 OAkk)

ama <u>nu-tuku</u>-me ama-ĝu₁₀ zé-me   {nu+tuku+me+(e)n} {zé+me+(e)n}
a <u>nu-tuku</u>-me a-ĝu₁₀ zé-me
I am one having no mother - you are my mother!
I am one having no father - you are my father!
(Gudea Cyl A 3:6-7 Ur III)

du₁₁-ga zi-da inim ki-bi-šè ĝar
(Nudimmud) he of the righteous command, putting the word into its place
(Šulgi D 316 Ur III)

diĝir-re-ne-er gub-bu gal zu-ĝá
In my knowing well (how) to stand (serving) before the gods
(Šulgi E 17 Ur III)

ᵈen-líl temen an-ki-bi-da
šibir ùĝ ge-en-ge-né šu du₈   {ge(n)-ge(n)+e}
su₄-un su₄-un-na-ni kur-ra dib-dib-bé
me ní-te-na-ke₄ kìri šu ĝál
Enlil, foundation of heaven and earth, holding onto (-e) the staff
which makes the people secure, whose beards pass over the mountains,
making obeisance to his own divine powers
(Šulgi E 1-4 Ur III)

ᵈnin-a-zu gu₄-sún naĝ-a ad-ba gù di-dam
Ninazu, like a wild cow that makes noise with its voice in drinking
(Šulgi X 94 Ur III)

mu en-nun-e ᵈama-ᵈsuen-ra ki-áĝ en eriduᵏⁱ ba-huĝ
Year: Noble-High-Priest-Loving-Amar-Suen was installed as high priest of Eridu
(Amar-Suen year 8 Ur III)

ᵈi₇-lú-ru-gú šà diĝir-re-e-ne
en ka-aš bar níĝ-érim-e hul gig
ᵈsuen-gin₇ níĝ-si-sá ki áĝ
Ordeal River, heart of the gods,
lord rendering decisions, hating evil,
loving justice like Suen
(Ibbi-Suen B Segment A 41'-43' Ur III)

su-ĝá á-sàg níĝ-hul ĝál-e a im-ma-ni-ib-tu₅   {-b- resumes -e}
In my body the evil-producing Asag demon took a bath
(Man and His God 74 OB)

ur-saĝ usu ir₉-ra me galam-ma šu du₇
diĝir me-dím gu₄-huš igi bar-bar-re-dè du₇
a-a-zu ᵈsuen-gin₇ zi ti-le ki ba-e-a-áĝ   {til+e, ba- resumes -e}
Hero, having mighty strength, making perfect the artful *me*'s,
god having the limbs of a fierce bull, fitting to be gazed at,
god, like your father Suen you loved to enliven life.
(Hymn to Numushda for Sîn-iqišam 37 OB)

gùd-bi-šè á dúb ì-ak-e   {dúb+Ø V+ak+e+Ø}
Toward its nest it (Bird) does wing-flapping
(Bird and Fish 111)

How this simple hamṭu-stem participle without suffixed -a differs in meaning from that
of the marû participle is not alwys clear, apart from what meaning may be deduced from
the difference in perfective vs. imperfective aspect. The compilers of the OB Lú lexical
series were certainly aware of some sort of difference. Compare the use of different
Akkadian expressions to render hamṭu vs. marû participles in the following pairs of
bilingual lexical entries (OB Lu B ii 7/9/23/25); the translations follow the Akkadian.

    lú níĝ tuku   = *ša-a-ru-ú-um*   rich, prosperous
    lú níĝ tuku-tuku   = *ra-a-šu-ú*   acquisitive, one who acquires

134

lú téš tuku	= *ša bu-uš-tam i-šu-ú*	one who has dignity
lú téš tuku-tuku	= *ba-a-a-šu-ú*	very decent(?)

HAMṬU PARTICIPLE WITH NOMINALIZING -a

iri-ka-gi-na lugal lagas^(ki) lú é-ninnu <u>dù-a</u>
Irikagina, king of Lagaš, who built the Eninnu temple
(Ukg 10-11 4:5-9 OS)

en-mete-na énsi lagas^(ki) ĝidri <u>šúm-ma</u> ^(d)en-líl-lá ĝéštu <u>šúm-ma</u> ^(d)en-ki-ka
šà <u>pà-da</u> ^(d)nanše
Enmetena, governor of Lagash, given the scepter by Enlil, given understanding
by Enki, chosen by the heart of Nanshe
(Ent 28-29 5:19-27 OS)

udu <u>gu₇-a</u> ur-du₆ šùš-kam
It is a sheep eaten (i.e. used) by Urdu the š.-official
(Nik I 150 2:4ff. OS)

5.0.0 še gur-saĝ+ĝál [...] é-gal-ta <u>er₁₄(DU.DU)-ra-ne</u> ì-gu₇   {er_x+a+(e)ne+e}
5 *g.*-measures of barley were eaten by the [...] who came
from the palace
(Nik I 133 3:1-5 OS)

mu nu-bànda ù gàr-du ^(d)amar-^(d)suen kaskal-ta <u>er-ra-ne-šè</u>   {er+a+(e)ne+šè}
(Small cattle) for the overseers and soldiers of Amar-Suen
who had come in from the road
(Legrain, TRU 334:2-3 Ur III)

gù-dé-a lú é <u>dù-a-ka</u> nam-ti-la-ni mu-sù
She shall prolong the life of Gudea, the man of the temple building
(Gudea Statue A 3:7-4:2 Ur III)

an numun <u>è</u> a-a níĝ-nam <u>šár-ra</u>
An, who made the seed come forth, father who made everything numerous
(Ur-Ninurta A 30 OB)
Unless the first participle is simply not nominalized note here that a single
-a suffix appears only on the last of two participles, a common occurrence.

Note also the somewhat rare nominalized roots used as nouns such as ti-la 'life'.

MARÛ PARTICIPLES WITHOUT NOMINALIZING SUFFIX -a

The bare marû stem is a component of numerous nouns, including many occupation names and proper nouns, for example:

balaĝ-di(d)	harp doer	> harpist
ga/ì-gùr-ru	milk/oil carrier	> milk/oil carrier
lú-búr-ru	person who reveals it	> dream interpreter
lú-kaš₄-e	person doing running	> runner
sig₄-dím-me	brick fashioner	> brickmaker
umbin-ku₅-ku₅	nail cutter	> manicurist
zi-du	righteous goer	> righteous person

é-me-ur₄-ur₄	Temple That Gathers (All) The *me*'s (or plural reduplication?)
i₇-lú-dadag	River That Purifies (<*dag-dag) a Person (the ordeal river)
i₇-NINA^(ki)-šè-du	Canal Going to NINA

nin-lú-ti-ti   Lady Who Makes A Person Live (PN)
lugal-níĝ-lu-lu   King Who Makes Things Numerous (PN)
me-al-nu-di   He Who Does Not Desire Divine Powers (PN)

Over and above its use in such nominal formation, the marû participle is a ubiquitous and productive feature of the Sumerian language, especially common in literary contexts. Marû participles have both verbal and nominal characteristics. In the collection of examples that follow it will be seen that they can be negated with the verbal preformative nu- and, as nominal chain attributives, they can appear with pronominal suffixes or the personal plural marker -(e)ne in addition to case markers.

MARÛ PARTICIPLES FOLLOWED BY POSSESSIVE OR DEMONSTRATIVE PRONOUNS

naĝa₄ mah ᵈnanše ki-gub-ba-bé <u>tag₄-e-ba</u>   {tag₄+e+bi+a}
Upon that one leaving the great mortar of Nanše on its pedestal
(Ean 62 side IV 3:7'-8' OS)

šà-ge du₁₁-ga eme-a ĝá-ra-a   {ĝar+a+ak}
a-ba-a ĝá-gin₇ <u>búr-búr-bi</u> mu-zu   {aba+e}
Of what is said by the heart or put upon the tongue,
who, like me, has known the interpreting of it?
(Šulgi C 110-111 Ur III)

balaĝ ki-áĝ-ni ušumgal kalam-ma ᵍⁱˢgù-di mu tuku níĝ ad <u>gi₄-gi₄-ni</u>   {gi₄-gi₄-(a)ni+Ø}
His beloved harp, Dragon of the Land, his instrument
which has a (famous) name, which makes the sound echo
(Gudea Cyl A 6:24-25 Ur III)

kur sig itima kù ki ní <u>te-en-te-en-zu</u>   {ten-ten+zu+e}
é-kur é za-gìn ki-tuš mah ní <u>gùr-ru-zu</u>
    {gùr+e+zu+e}
As for your deep mountain, the holy chamber, the place where you
refresh yourself, your Ekur, the lapis lazuli house, the exalted
residence bearing fearsomeness (Enlil A 76-77 OB)

u₄-da u₄ <u>ug₅-ge-ĝu₁₀</u> nu-un-zu   {ug₅+e+ĝu₁₀+Ø}
If she does not know my dying day
(Dumuzi's Death 12 OB)

gu₄-si-dili-gin₇ bàd <u>e₁₁-dè-zu-ù</u>   {e₁₁(d)+e+zu+e}
At your knocking down a wall like a battering ram
(CBS 11553:5' Šulgi hymn, cited PSD B 41 Ur III)

kíĝ-gi₄-a <u>du-né</u> šeg₉-bar-ra-àm ím-mi-da-né súr-dù^ᵐᵘˢᵉⁿ-àm   {du+(a)ni+e}
The messenger: at his going he is a wild ram,   {ím+e+d+(a)ni+e}
at his having to hurry he is a falcon
(Enmerkar and Ensuhgirana 40 OB)

MARÛ PARTICIPLES FOLLOWED BY ADVERBAL CASE MARKERS

Absolutive Subject -Ø

ki-sur-ra ᵈnin-ĝír-su-ka-ta a-aba-šè maškim <u>di</u> e-ĝál-àm   {di+Ø}
From the Kisurra of Ninĝirsu to the Sea there existed
one(s) who performed the function of maškim
(Ukg 4, 7:12-16 OS)

```
é-ki-šuku-bi uz-ga èš ĝá-ĝá                                    {ĝá-ĝá+Ø}
ne-saĝ-bi kur ĝeštin biz-biz-zé                                {biz-biz+e+Ø}
é-lùnga-bi ⁱ⁷idigna a-ù-ba ĝál-la-àm                           {ĝál+a+m+Ø}
```
Its ration-place house a treasure establishing shrines –
its first-fruits offerings a mountain always dripping wine –
(Gudea Cyl A 28:9-13 Ur III)

```
u₄-bi-ta inim im-ma gub-bu nu-ub-ta-ĝál-la                     {gub+e+Ø}
```
Though in those days words standing on clay did not exist
(Enmerkar and the Lord of Aratta 504 OB)

```
u₄-bi-ta <inim> im-ma gub-bu hé-ĝál im si-si-ge ba-ra-ĝál-la-am₃   {si(g)+si(g)+e+Ø}
```
Though in those days <words> standing on clay existed, putting
clay (tablets) into clay (envelopes) certainly did not exist
(Sargon Legend 53 OB)

```
piriĝ nam-šul-bi-ta nu-kúš-ù ne-ba gub-ba-me-en                {nu+kúš+e+Ø}
```
I am a lion never relaxing in its vigor, who stands (firm) in its strength
(Šulgi A 42 Ur III)

```
nin₉ mul-mul làl ama ugu-za-me-en                             {mul-mul+Ø}
```
Sparkling sister, you are the honey of the mother who bore you
(Inana-Dumuzi C 22)

```
kur gul-gul ga-ša-an é-an-na-ĝen                              {gul-gul+Ø}
```
I am the mountain destroyer, queen of the Eanna temple
(Eršemma No. 106:3 OB Emesal: ga-ša-an = nin, -ĝen = -me-en))

```
níĝ-GA buru₅ᵐᵘšᵉⁿ dal-dal ki-tuš nu-pà-dè-dam                  {dal-dal+Ø}
```
Possessions are flying birds which cannot find a place to alight
(Sumerian Proverbs 1.18 OB)

```
ní-zuh é bùru-bùru ᵍⁱšig gub-bu za-ra suh-ù        {bùru-bùru+Ø, gub+e+Ø, suh+e+Ø}
```
A thief, burrowing into houses, making doors
stand (open), pulling out door-pivots
JCS 24, 107 No. 1:12)

Absolutive Patient -Ø

```
i₇ kù-ga-am₆ šà-bi dadag-ga-am₆ ᵈnanše a zal-le hé-na-tùm
```
A canal which is holy, whose flood is pure, let it bring
constanting flowing water for Nanše
(Ukg 4-5, 12:41-44 OS)

```
lugal-ĝu₁₀ útug mah kur érim-ĝál-la saĝ sahar-re-eš dub-bu ki-bal-a ša₅-ša₅
e-ne-er mu-na-an-šúm en ᵈnu-nam-nir-re
```
To my king: a lofty mace which in the evil-doing land heaps up heads
like dirt and smashes the rebel land Lord Nunamnir did give to him
(Ur-Namma B 52-54 Ur III)

```
šeš-kal-la ù en-ú-bi-šu-e še ĝiš ra-ra ì-til                   {ra-ra+Ø}
```
Šeškala and Enubišu have finished threshing the barley
(SET No. 265:1-4 Ur III)

```
a zi-[šà]-ĝál numun zi ù-tu šu-šè im-ma-ab-lá                  {ù-tu(d)+Ø}
```
Lifegiving water, causing good seed to be born, he bound to the hand
(Bird and Fish 6 OB)
The late lexical list Nabītu I 17 describes ù-tu(d) as the marû stem of tu(d).

    é làl ì-nun ù ĝeštin ki sískur-ra-ka-na <u>nu-šilig-ge</u> mu-na-an-dù   {nu+šilig+e+Ø}
    The house (where) syrup, ghee, and grapes never cease at his
    place of offerings he built
    (Amar-Suen 11, 13-17 Ur III)

    šà-ge du₁₁-ga eme-a ĝá-ra-a a-ba-a ĝá-gin₇ <u>búr-búr-bi</u> mu-zu   {búr-búr+bi+Ø}
    Who knew, like me, the revealing of what has been spoken by the heart
    or put into upon the tongue
    (Šulgi C 110-111 OB)

Ergative -e

    šeš-a-ne-ne ku-li-ne-ne, èn <u>tar-re</u> im-mi-in-kúš-ù-ne   {tar+(e+)e}
    His brothers and friends exhaust him (-n-)   {Vm+b+n+kúš+e+ne}
    with questioning (-bi-)   {-bi- resumes -e}
    (Lugalbanda and Enmerkar 225-226 OB)
    Whether the stem of the verb is marû or hamṭu is not clear;
    either way an instrumental ergative -e is required.

    ᵈištaran ki-en-gi-ra šà-ta níĝ-nam <u>zu-ù</u> di kalam-ma ki-bi-šè ì-kud-re₆   {zu+e+e}
    He, the Ishtaran of Sumer who knows everything from birth,
    renders the verdicts of the country for that place
    (Šulgi X 142-143 Ur III) (or perhaps just hamṭu {zu+e}?)

    sig-ta <u>du</u> igi-nim-ta <u>du-e</u> á šed-bi-šè ní hé-eb-ši-te-en-te-en   {du...du+e}
    The one coming from above or from below refreshes himself
    under its cool branches
    (Šulgi A 32-33 Ur III)
    Note that the ergative marker appears only on the second participle, at
    the end of the ergative nominal chain, likewise in the following example.

    íl énsi umma^ki(-a) a-šà.GÁNA <u>kar-kar</u> níĝ-érim <u>du₁₁-du₁₁-ge</u>   {kar-kar..du₁₁-du₁₁(g)+e}
    e ki-sur-ra ᵈnin-ĝír-su-ka e ki-sur-ra ᵈnanše ĝá-kam ì-mi-du₁₁   {Vm+bi+n+du₁₁}
    Il, the ruler of Umma, taker of fields, doer of evil things,
    declared: "The boundary levees of Ningirsu and Nanše are mine!"
    (Ent 28 4:19-29 OS)
    Note ergative -e falls only on the 2nd participle, at the end of the chain.

    nin en <u>ù-tu-dè</u> lugal <u>ù-tu-dè</u> ᵈnin-men-na-ke₄ tu-tu al-ĝá-ĝá   {utud+e)}
    Queen who gives birth to en's, who gives birth to kings,   {tu(d)-tu(d)+Ø}
    Ninmenna(k) establishes birthing
    (Hymn to the Hoe 26-27 OB)
    Conversely, here ergative -e appears three times at the ends of parallel
    chains, unless the -e on utud+e is the marû formative. The participle
    tu-tu lacks an overt patient, for which one may posit an elliptical <lú>.
    This sort of ellipsis is especiall common in literary contexts.

    ᵈnu-nam-nir en nam <u>tar-tar-re</u> kur níĝ daĝal-la-ba mu-zu im-mi-in-mah   {tar-tar+e}
    Nunamnir, the lord who decides the fates, made your name great in
    the wide lands
    (Hymn to Numushda for Sin-iqišam 42-43 OB)

    gu₄ <u>gaz-gaz-e</u> dam-ni hé-en-gaz-e, udu <u>šum-šum-e</u> dumu-ni hé-en-šum-e   {gaz-gaz+e}
    May the man (elliptical <lú>) who slaughters cattle slaughter his wife,
    may the man (<lú>) who butchers sheep butcher his child!
    (Curse of Agade 237-238 OB)

Locative-terminative -e

    lú ninda tur ka-a gub-ba-gin₇ du-du-e nu-ši-kúš-ù

Like a man who has put little food in his mouth,
he does not tire at constantly going about
(Gudea Cyl A 19:26-27 Ur III)

buru₁₄ mah-ĝu₁₀ ní-bi íl-íl-i níĝ-ku₅ nu-ak-e   {íl-íl+e}
Upon my huge harvest, raising itself up, no tax is imposed
(Ur-Namma C 80 Ur III)

me-li-e-a u₄-dè   šu-ni-a im-ma-ši-in-gi₄
u₄ úru gul-gul-e   šu-ni-a im-ma-ši-in-gi₄
u₄ é gul-gul-e   šu-ni-a im-ma-ši-in-gi₄   {gul-gul+e}
Woe, he has handed it (the city) over to the storm,
he has handed it over to the city-destroying storm,
he has handed it over to the house-destroying storm
(Lament over Destruction of Sumer and Ur 175-177 OB)

u₄-bé á áĝ-ĝá kur-ra-ke₄ si sá-sá-e an hé-da-húl ki hé-da-húl   {sá-sá+e}
On that day, over the correct performing of the orders of the
netherworld may Heaven rejoice, may Earth rejoice!
(Incantation to Utu 260-261 OB)

ᵈen-líl temen an-ki-bi-da šibir uĝ ge-en-ge-né šu du₈   {ge(n)-ge(n)+e}
Enlil, foundation of heaven and earth, holding onto
the staff which makes the people secure
(Šulgi E 1-2 Ur III)

ì-ne-éš ᵈutu u₄-ne-a ᵈutu an-na gub-bé-e   {gub+e+e}
Now Utu, on this day, as Utu was standing in the sky,
(Enki and Ninhursaĝa 50-51 OB)
The plene writing suggests the stem is marû. The locative-
terminative here has adverbial force.

ur-bar-ra sila₄ šu ti-a-gin₇ ul₄-ul₄-le im-ĝen
Like a wolf capturing a lamb he came quickly.
(Enmerkar and Ensuhgirana 49 OB)
The locative-terminative here has adverbial force.

Locative -a

1 sila₄ ù-tu-da ba-úš   {utud+a}
1 kid, died while being born
(JCS 28, 222 No. 48:1 Ur III)

ki-bala kur bad-rá è-a-né sùh-sah₄-a u₄ mi-ni-ib-zal-zal-e
At his having gone forth into the rebel lands, the distant lands,
he spends his days in the crunching (of battle)
(Inana E 25)

ᵈnin-tu ki-tuš [giri₁₇]-zal-la ki-tuš níĝ lu-lu-a   {lu-lu+a}
ama ᵈnin-tu bára tuš-a-né
Nintu, mother Nintu, at her having sat down upon the dais,
the seat of splendor, the seat that makes things abundant
(Hymn to Nintu-Aruru 40 OB)

MARÛ PARTICIPLES FOLLOWED BY ADNOMINAL CASE MARKERS OR THE COPULA

dùrᵘʳ dili du-gin₇   {du+gin₇}
Like a donkey stallion going alone
(Šulgi A 74 Ur III)

mušen téš-bé nunuz zuh-zuh-gin₇ {zuh-zuh+gin₇}
Like birds stealing eggs together
(Civil, Or 54 (1985), 28 Ur III, possibly plural reduplication)

lú a-šà ur₁₁-ru-ke₄ a-šà hé-ur₁₁-ru {ur₁₁+e+ak+e}
Let the man of field plowing plow the field
(Proverbs 4.47 OB. Read the verb alternately as uru₄^ru)

an ki téš-ba sig₄ gi₄-gi₄-àm {gi₄-gi₄+(a)m+∅}
Heaven and earth were crying out together
(NFT 180 2:2 OS)

ĝiš-hum-bi é-gal i₇-mah-ha me-lám gùr-ru-àm {gùr+e+(a)m+∅}
Its (the boat's) cabin was like a palace in a great river,
bearing divine radiance
(Šulgi D 359 Ur III)

lú ĝá ì-šub-ba ᵈnanše-ka sig₄ dím-me-me {dím+e+meš}
They are men fashioning bricks in the brickmold shed of Nanše
(DP 122 2:4-5 OS)

ᵈŠul-gi lú níĝ lu-lu-me-en ninda ĝiš ha-ba-ni-tag {lu-lu+me+(e)n}
I, Shulgi, being a man who makes things abundant, offered bread there
(Šulgi A 55 Ur III)

an lugal-da bára an-na-ka di si-sá-e-me-en {sá+e+me+(e)n}
With An the king on the dais of An I administer justice correctly
(Enki and the World Order 74 OB)

MARÛ PARTICIPLES WITH PERSONAL PLURAL -(e)ne

    ninda-bi saĝ-apin apin-dur sur_x(ERIM) è-è-dè-ne šu ba-ti {è(d)-è(d)+(e)ne+e}
Those breads were received by the plow-leaders bringing in
the teams' cable-plows
(VS 14, 75 4:1-4 OS)

ì-bi lú ì nu-zu-(ù-)ne ì-im-du₉-du₉-ne {nu+zu+e+(e)ne+e}
Its butter was being churned by men who did not know butter,
(Lament over Destruction of Sumer and Ur 335-336 OB) (-ù- = variant)

nu-zu-ù-ne um-ši-húl-húl-e-eš {nu+zu+e+(e)ne+∅}
The ones who do not know <anything> shall greatly rejoice
(Uruk Lament E 28 OB)

ki-bi-šè ku₄-ku₄-da bí-in-eš en nam tar-re-ne {tar+e+(e)ne+e}
The lords decreeing destinies comanded that they (the
looted treasures) should be brought back into their places
(Nippur Lament 274 OB)

MARÛ PARTICIPLES FOLLOWED BY THE NOMINALIZING SUFFIX -a

i₇-NINA^ki-du-a
The Canal Going to NINA
(Ukg 1 3:6' OS)

lugal ninda sa₆-ga gu₇-gu₇-a šuku-re <šu> im-ma-an-dab₅ {gu₇-gu₇+a+e} {ba- = -e}
The king who used to eat fine food (now) took rations {Vm+ba+n+dab₅+∅}
(Lament over Destruction of Sumer and Ur 304 OB)

[u₄ x] x nam-lugal-la an-ta è-dè-a-ba {è(d)+e+a+bi+a}
men mah ᵍⁱˢgu-za nam-lugal-la an-ta è-a-ba {è(d)+a+bi+a}
On that [day] when the ... of kingship was about to descend from above,
when the exalted crown and throne of kingship had descended from above
(Flood Story Segment B 6-7 OB)

lú inim-inim-ma lú èn-du búr-búr-ra {búr-búr+a}
A man of incantations, a man who interprets songs
(Letter of Igmil-Sîn to Nudimmud-saga 8 OB)

ki-en-gi ki-uri bir-bir-re-a ki-bi-šè bí-in-gi₄-a {bir-bir+e+a+∅}
He who restored Sumer and Akkad which had been repeatedly scattered
(Formula for Hammurapi Year 33 OB)

MARÛ PARTICIPLES WITH MODAL ELEMENT /d/

ᵈsuen mu-ni lú nu-du₈-dè {ergative -e}
Suen, whose name no one can explain
(Gudea Statue B 8:48 Ur III)

nin an-ki-a nam tar-re-dè ᵈnin-tu ama diĝir-re-ne-ke₄ {ergative -e}
The lady, when she was to decide fate in heaven and earth,
Nintu, mother of the gods,
(Gudea Statue A 3:4-6 Ur III)

lú a-šà ur₁₁-ru-ke₄ a-šà hé-ur₁₁-ru {ur₁₁+e+ak+e}
lú še šu su-ub-bu-da-ke₄ še šu hé-eb-su-ub-bé {su-ub+e+d+ak+e}
Let the man of field plowing plow the field
Let the man who is to collect (esēpu) barley collect the barley
(Proverbs 4.47 OB)

níĝ-GA buru₅ᵐᵘˢᵉⁿ dal-dal ki-tuš nu-pà-dè-dam {nu+pàd+e+d+(a)m}
Possessions are flying birds which cannot find a place to alight
(Proverbs 1.18 OB)

di-ku₅ ka-aš bar-re-dè igi mi-ni-in-ĝál lul zi-bi mu-zu {bar+e+d+e}
She (Ninegala) has set her eye upon (-e) the judge about to render
the decision and will make known the false and the true
(Nungal A 37 OB)

mu kìšib lugal-é-mah-e tùm-da-šè kìšib lú-igi-sa₆-sa₆ {tùm+(e)+d+a+šè}
Instead of the seal that Lugalemahe is to bring is the seal of Lu'igisasa
(Sigrist, Princeton 1, 522:3-5 Ur III)

INFINITIVE {√(marû)+d+e} WITHOUT NOMINALIZING -a

1) Dependent upon a finite verb of speaking or commanding

me kù sikil-zu pa-è kè-dè á-bi mu-un-da-áĝ {AK+e+d+e}
He instructed him to make your holy, pure me's resplendent
(Enlil's Chariot = Išme-Dagan I 5 OB)

úr kù nam-ti-la si-a-ĝu₁₀ u₄-zu sù-sù-dè {si+a+ĝu₁₀+e}
šul ᵈen-líl-le é-kur-ta á-bi mu-un-da-an-áĝ
Enlil instructed him from the Ekur temple, O youth, to prolong
your days upon my holy lap filled with life
(Ur-Ninurta A 83f. OB)

    ᵈur-ᵈninurta lugal-e di-bi pu-úh-ru-um nibruᵏⁱ-ka dab₅-bé-dè bí-in-du₁₁
    Ur-Ninurta the king ordered that this case was to be
    tried in the assembly of Nippur
    (OB Homocide Trial 17-19)

    ki-nu-nir-ša^{ki} iri nam-dumu-gi₇-ra-ka-ni kar-kar-re-dè ba-ab-du₁₁   {-b- = -e}
    Kinunirša, her city of noble citizens, was ordered to be plundered
    (Lament Over the Destruction of Sumer and Ur 179)

2)   More loosely dependent upon another finite verb

    tukumbi lú lú-ù kiri₆ ĝiš gub-bu-dè ki-ĝál in-na-an-šúm
    If a man gave uncultivated land to another in order to plant
    an orchard with trees
    (Code of Lipit-Ištar 12:50-53 OB)

    gaz-dè ba-šúm   {ba- = -e}
    He was given over to be executed
    (Durand, RA 71, 125:6 OB)

    gaz-dè ba-an-šúm-mu-uš   {ba- = -e}
    They gave him over to be executed
    (AnBib 12, 130ff.:59 OB)

    PN PN₂-ra su-su-dè ba-na-gi-in
    PN was certified as having to replace it for PN₂
    (NSGU 188:12'-14' Ur III)

    šu-tur-bé mu-bé šu uru₁₂-dè ĝèštu hé-em-ši-gub   (-ši- = -e}
    If he shall set his mind to erasing the name on this inscription
    (Gudea Statue B 9:12f. Ur III)

    1 ma-na kù-luh-ha igi-nu-du₈-a sa₁₀-sa₁₀-dè PN, dam PN₂-ke₄ ba-de₆
    PN, wife of PN₂, took 1 mana refined silver to buy an *iginudu*-slave
    (Edzard, SRU 42 1:1-5 OS)

    1 udu-nita PN níĝ gu₇-dè ba-de₆
    PN took 1 ram for eating (lit. for a thing to be eaten)
    (Selz FAOS 15/1 157 1:1ff. OS)

    bar-udu siki PN-e garig kè-dè e-ne-lá
    PN weighed out to them wool sheep fleeces to be combed
    (Selz, FAOS 15/2 No. 95 4:1-2 OS)

    gù-dé-a é ᵈnin-ĝír-su-ka hur-saĝ nu₁₁-bar₆-bar₆-ra-gin₇ ù di-dè ba-gub
    Gudea made the temple of Ningirsu stand to be marveled at
    like a mountain of white alabaster
    (Gudea Cyl A 24:17ff.)

    PN ù PN₂ su-su-dè PN₃-ra ba-an-ši-ku₄-re-eš
    PN and PN₂ were made liable to PN₃ for replacing it (this money)
    (Steinkeller, Sales Documents 330:12-14 Ur III)

    ár kè-dè la-ba-ab-du₇-un
    You are not fit for doing praising (of yourself)
    (Dialogue 2:59, JCS 20, 124 OB)

    lú-zàh dab₅!-dè ĝen-na
    (Rations for PN) who had gone to seize a runaway
    (Lafont, DAS No. 197:6 Ur III}

Compare the following exactly parallel passage:

lú-zàh dab₅-dab₅-dè ĝen-na
(Rations for PN) who had gone to seize runaway persons
(Lafont, DAS No. 199:18 Ur III) {pl. reduplication}

3) Adverbial clauses (usually marked with -e) independent of a main verb

ù níĝ en-na ĝál-la-aš é-a-na lú nu-ku₄-ku₄-dè ama-ar-gi₄ mu-ĝar¹⁷
Moreover, regarding whatever property of the lord that may exist, so that
no one might enter his house (to take it) he established (his) freedom
(Gudea Statue R 2:6-7 Ur III)

20 ĝuruš u₄-4-šè e kuru₅ gi-né-dè   {kudr+e(+d)?} {gin+e+d+e}
20 workers for 4 days to cut and make secure ditches
(Oberhuber Florence 29 Ur III)
(kudr here may feature a concealed /d/; the case marker
that could reveal it is placed only on the last infinitive.)

mu-ĝu₁₀ u₄ ul-li-a-aš ĝá-ĝá-dè ka-ta nu-šub-bu-dè   {nu+šub+e+d+e}
ár-ĝu₁₀ kalam-ma a₅-a₅-dè
ka-tar-ĝu₁₀ kur-kur-ra si-il-le-dè
In order that my name be established for distant days
and that it not fall from mouths,
that my praises be performed in the nation,
that my glory be proclaimed in all the lands,
(Šulgi A 36-38 Ur III)

nam kur-kur-ra tar-re-da-né   {tar+e+d+ani+e}
u₄ saĝ zi-dè igi kár-kár-dè u₄-nú-a me šu du₇-du₇-dè
zà-mu u₄ biluda-ka nin-ĝu₁₀-ra ki-nú ba-da-an-ĝar
As he was about to (or that he might?) decree the fate of all the lands,
to inspect the good first day, to perfect the *me* on the day of the new moon,
he put down a resting place for my lady at the new year, on the day of rites
(Iddin-Dagan A 169-175 OB)

gù-dé-a é-ĝu₁₀ dù-da ĝiskim-bi ga-ra-ab-šúm   {dù+e+d+ak}
Gudea, I will give you the sign of the building of my house
(Gudea Cylinder A 9:9-10 Ur III)

inim ᵈen-líl-lá zi-da gel-èĝ-dè gùb-bu zu-zu-dè   {Emesal for ha-lam+e+d+e}
ᵈen-líl lú nam tar-tar-re-dè a-na bí-in-ak-a-ba
To make the word of Enlil destroy on the right and make it known to the left,
Enlil, he about to determine all the fates, what did he do?
(Lament of the Destruction of Sumer and Ur 164f. OB)

INFINITIVE FOLLOWED BY NOMINALIZING -a OR LOCATIVE -a

Some infinitives ending in /a/ can easily be understood from their syntax as relative
clauses featuring the nominalizing suffix -a:

lú umma^ki-a e ki-sur-ra ᵈnin-ĝír-su-ka-ka e ki-sur-ra ᵈnanše-ka
ᵃ⁻šᵃaša₅ tùm-dè an-ta bal-e-da ... ᵈen-líl-le hé-ha-lam-me   {bal+e+d+a}
May Enlil destroy the man of Umma who may come from above
across the boundary ditch of Ningirsu, or the boundary ditch of Nanše,
in order to take away fields
(Entemena 28-28 6:9-16 OS, others read as a finite verb am₆-ta-bal-e-da)

    2/30 4 sìla ì-ĝiš mu ì túg-gé kè(AK)-da-šè   {AK+e+d+a+ak+šè}
    2/30 (gur) 4 silas of sesame oil for oil that is to be put on cloth
    (CT 5, 38 2:2f. Ur III)

    mu kišib lugal-é-mah-e tùm-da-šè kišib lú-igi-sa₆-sa₆   {tùm(u)+d+a+ak+šè}
    Seal of Lu-igisasa instead of the seal of Lugal-emahe which is to be brought
    (Sigrist, Princeton 522:3-5 Ur III) With this compare the following:

    mu kišib lugal-níĝ-lagar-e tùmⁱ-a-šè kišib a-gu ì-ĝál   {tùm(u)+a+ak+šè}
    Instead of the seal of Lugal-niĝlagare, which will be brought,
    the seal of Agu was produced
    (Sigrist, Princeton 1, 229:5-7 Ur III)

    nam é dù-da lugal-na-šè ù ĝi₆-an-na nu-um-ku₄-ku₄   {dù+e+d+a}
    For the sake of the house that is to be built of his king
    he does not sleep (even) at midnight
    (Gudea Cylinder A 17:7-8 Ur III)

Other infinitives show a locative suffix -a, which should be distinguished from the
nominalizing element -a in more careful analysis of texts. We must assume that since all
the following feature relative clauses, they are marked with a nominalizing -a in
addition to a final (elided) locative -a:

    mu šar-kà-li-šarri púzur-eš₄-tár šagina é ᵈen-líl dù-da bí-gub-ba   (bí- = -a}
    The year that Šar-kali-šarri stationed Puzur-Eštar the general
    at the temple of Enlil which was to be built
    (Goetze, JAOS 88 (1968) 56 OAkk)

    u₄ zà-mu ezem ᵈba-ú níĝ-MÍ.ÚS.SÁ kè(AK)-da
    On new year's day at the festival of Bau when the betrothal gifts are to be made
    (Gudea Statue E 5:12-13 Ur III)

    u₄ a[n-k]i-a nam tar-[(tar-)re-d]a   {tar(-tar)+e+d+a)
    On the day when (all) the fates were to be decided in heaven and on earth
    (Gudea Cylinder A 1:1 Ur III)

    u₄ diĝir-zi-da du-da   {du+d+a+a}
    On the day when the righteous god was to come
    (Gudea Cylinder B 3:25)

    kù-bi ki-su₇-ta šúm-mu-da <inim> bí-in-du₁₁   (bí- = -a}
    "That silver is to be given from the threshing field," he said
    (Çiğ et al., ZA 53, 86-87 No. 24:8-9 Ur III)
    Though the patient inim is often omitted with this compound verb, the original
    locative rection is normally preserved in the nominal and verbal chains.

    dub-šen kù lú igi nu-bar-re-da lú SUᵏⁱ elamᵏⁱ lú ha-kam-ma-ke₄ [igi i-ni]-in-bar
    The holy treasure box, upon which no person should look,
    the people of Simaški and Elam, the destroyers, looked upon
    (Eridu Lament A 86-87 OB)

INFINITIVE ENDING IN A COPULA

"Infinitives" featuring copulas are very common among the laconic remarks found in
economic and administrative texts, e.g.

        dah-dam   (interest) is to be added
        gi-né-dam   (testimony) is to be confirmed   {gi(n)+e+d+am}
        kud-ru-dam   (reed) is to be cut   {kudr+e+d+am}

```
su-su-dam              (grain) is to be replaced
tùmu-dam               (item) is to be taken
tur-re-dam             (money) is to be subtracted
ze-re-dam              (tablet) is to be broken
maš ĝá-ĝá-dam          (loan) is to bear interest
kišib ra-ra-dam         seal is to be impressed
```

Frequently in economic texts one sees copular infinitives varying with an ordinary infinitive ending in locative-terminative -e, even though the syntax properly favors one or the other form. That the difference between the two constructions was felt to be slight is suggested from the following Ur III passage where the text has two infinitives ending in -e, dependent on a verb of speaking, while the repeated passage on the clay envelope covering the tablet shows the same infinitives ending in copulas:

```
itu šu-numun-a saĝ-šè lá-e-dè    (envelope: lá-e-dam)
tukumbi nu-lá 2-àm tab-bé-dè     (envelope: tab-bé-dam)
mu lugal ì-pà
To pay it (the silver) in the month Šu-numun-a, at the beginning(?),
and that if he has not paid it, to double it two-fold,
(so) he swore by the name of the king
(Oppenheim, Eames Collection P1 7-11 Ur III)
```

A few further examples:

```
en-en-né-ne-šè hal-ha-dam                                          {hal-ha(l)+d+am}
(The offerings) are to be distributed to all the (ancestral) lords
(DP 222 12:1'-2' OS)

ig ĝišeren-na é-a šu₄-ga-bi diškur an-ta gù-nun di-da-àm
Its doors of cedar that stood in the temple were (like) Iškur (the rain god)
making a loud noise from the sky
(Gudea, Cylinder A 26:20-21 Ur III)

šimna4 é-a šu₄-ga-bi é gudu₄ kù a nu-šilig₅-ge-dam
Its stone basins which stood in the temple were (like) the holy house
of the lustration priest where water must never cease
(Gudea, Cylinder A 29:5-6 Ur III)

lugal-hé-ĝál-e ezem-mah-šè tùm-mu-dam tukum-bi nu-mu-de₆ sú-sú-dam
It is to be brought in to the Great Festival by Lugal-heĝal;
if he has not brought it in (by then), it is to be replaced
(Fish, Catalogue 534:4-9  Ur III)

(i₇-zu) i₇ mah ki-utu-è igi nu-bar-re-dam
(Your river) is the great river at the place of sunrise, which is not
to be looked upon
(Ibbi-Suen B Segment A 24' Ur III)

lú é lugal-na dù-dam énsi-ra
To the person who was about to build his king's house, the governor,
(Gudea Cyliner A 16:18f. Ur III)
```

POSSIBLE INSTANCES OF INFINITIVES/PARTICIPLES FEATURING A CONCEALED /d/

```
še-numun še gu₄ gu₇-šè PN-e GN-šè ba-de₆                            {gu₇+e+d+šè}
PN took away to GN seed barley and barley for feeding the oxen
(Bauer, AWL 24 OS)
Compare the following parallel where the unusual terminative is replaced
```

by the normal locative-terminative:

še-numun še anše gu₇-dè PN-ra PN₂-e ĝanun-gibil-ta e-na-ta-ĝar {gu₇+e+d+e}
PN₂ set out for PN from the New Storehous seed barley
and barley to feed the donkeys
(Bauer, AWL 21 OS)

é-a-ni dù-ba mu-na-du₁₁ {dù+e+d+bi+a)
He spoke to him about that building of his house
(Gudea Cylinder A 1:19
Compare the following parallel with explicit /d/:

é-a-ni dù-da mu-na-du₁₁ {dù+e+d+a)
He spoke to him about the building of his house
(Gudea Cylinder A 4:20)
In this and the preceding line the verbal chain abbreviates an
underlying verb <inim> mu-na-ni-in-du₁₁, with -ni- resuming -a.

igi utu-è ki nam tar-re-ba {tar+e+d+bi+a}
Facing sunrise, the place where the fates are to be decided
(Gudea Cylinder A 26:3)

inim nu-kúr-ru-da-na ù-tu-ba bí-in-du₁₁ {nu+kúr+e+d+ani+a}
He commanded its having to be created {utud+d+bi+a}
with his unalterable word
(Numušda Hymn for Sîn-iqišam A 47 OB)

é-kur èš mah-a-na dím-me-za bí-in-du₁₁ {dím+e+d+zu+a}
(Enlil) spoke about your having to be fashioned in his Ekur, the exalted shrine
(Enlil's Chariot 2 OB)

é-e kur ĝišeren kuru₅ nu-me-a {kudr+e+d+Ø}
uruduha-zi-in gal-gal ba-ši-in-dé-dé
As for the temple, though it was not a mountain where cedar was to be cut,
he poured out (molten bronze in the form of) great axes against it
(Curse of Agade 112-113 OB)

é dù máš-a nu-mu-un-dè-ĝál {dù+e+d+Ø}
He could not produce a "must-build-a-temple" in the extispicy
(Curse of Agade 95 OB)

(èn-du-ĝu₁₀) ĝeštu-ge nu-dib-bé ka-ta nu-šub-bu-dè {nu+dib+e+d, nu+šub+e+d+e}
So that (my songs) not pass by ears, not fall from mouths
(Šulgi X 57 Ur III)
In this and the next two references the case marker -e (and also -d- as well?)
is suffixed only to the last of the two infinitives at the end of the chain.

kalam gi-né sig-nim gúr-e-dè {gin+e+d} {gam+e+d+e}
In order to make the land just and subdue the lower lands
(Ibbi-Suen 1-2 1:12-13)

eger-bé níĝ-na-me nu-ša₆-ge-dè
é tuk₄-e èrim ság di-dè {tuk₄+e+d} {di+d+e}
ᵈna-ra-am-ᵈsîn máš-ĝi₆-ka igi ba-ni-in-du₈-a {ba- resumes -e}
When Naram-Sîn had seen in a dream that after this nothing would be pleasant,
that the houses would shake and the storehouses would be scattered
(Curse of Agade 84-86)

* * * * *

THE PRONOMINAL CONJUGATION

The pronominal conjugation refers to hamṭu or marû participles conjugated by means of possessive pronouns. These constructions form simplified kinds of temporal relative clauses. They are mostly encountered in OB literary contexts, especially marû forms. There are two paradigms, one built on the hamṭu stem with nominalizing -a suffix, the other built on the marû stem with the modal /d/ extension and nominalizing -a suffix, both then followed by pronominal suffixes. See Edzard 2003, p. 137-142 and Thomsen §519-521 for their descriptions of these forms with examples and discussion of some unresolved questions. The paradigms are as follows:

hamṭu	1 sg.		ku_4-ra-ĝu_{10}(-ne)	{kur_9+a+ĝu_{10}+ne}
	2 sg.		ku_4-ra-zu(-ne)	{kur_9+a+zu+ne}
	3 sg.	p.	ku_4-ra-ni	{kur_9+a+(a)ni}
		i.	ku_4-ra-bi	{kur_9+a+bi}
	1 pl.		ku_4-ra-me*	{kur_9+a+me}
	2 pl.		—	
	3 pl.		ku_4-ra-ne-ne	{kur_9+a+(a)nene}
marû	1 sg.		ku_4-ku_4-da-ĝu_{10}-ne	{kur_9+kur_9+d+a+ĝu_{10}+ne}
	2 sg.		ku_4-ku_4-da-zu-ne	{kur_9+kur_9+d+a+zu+ne}
	3 sg.	p.	ku_4-ku_4-da-ni	{kur_9+kur_9+d+a+(a)ni}
		i.	ku_4-ku_4-da-bi	{kur_9+kur_9+d+a+bi}
	1 pl.		—	
	2 pl.		ku_4-ku_4-da-en-zé-en**	{kur_9+kur_9+d+a+enzen}
	3 pl.		—	

*For this form, described as not attested by Edzard, cf. possibly šu nu-du_{11}-ga-me, sa-bíl-lá nu-ak(a)-me 'despite our not having touched it', 'despite our not having plastered it', in LSUr 241-242 OB.

**For this form, described as not attested by Edzard, see Michalowski, JCS 30 (1978) 115:4 (OB literary letter). This is probably an OB artifical creation.

The final suffix on 1st and 2nd sg. forms was previously read as -dè and connected with comitative -da (so Thomsen). Edzard 2003, following J. Krecher, reads it instead as -ne, with a locative meaning, based on a variant writing -né in a few eme-sal contexts. C. Wilcke now identifies this -ne as the demonstrative suffix -ne in RAI 53 (2010) 29-32. Jagersma 2010 §20.2 calls it an "old locational case marker ... without doubt cognate with the local prefix [ni] 'in', a "fossilized case marker" (§28.8). Compare the adverbial expression dili-zu-ne 'you alone, by yourself' usually read dili-zu-dè?

In 3rd person occurences the possessive suffixes generally hide a locative-terminative postposition used with adverbial force. The -ne suffix on 1st and 2nd person forms may have served the same function. Hamṭu forms may usually be translated "when, or while, someone did something," while the marû forms are normally given present-future translations occasionally with modal ideas like obligation or necessity, "when, or while, someone does, or has to do, or is about to do something." Examples:

    PN ti-la-né šu ba-ti   {tìl+a+(a)ni+e}
    PN, when he was still alive, received it (the purchase price)
    (BIN 8, 352 2:1-3 OS)

    kaš-a gub-ba-né níĝ $giri_{17}$-zal kaš-ta tuš-a-né mud_5-me-ĝar   {gub+a+(a)ni+e}
    When she (the beer goddess) stood in the beer there was delight,
    when she sat in the beer there was joy
    (Lugalbanda and Enmerkar 19-20 OB)

    umma^{ki} e-bé bal-e-da-bé   {bal+e+d+a+bi+e}
    Whenever Umma might cross over this ditch
    (Ean 1 rev. 5:37-38 OS)

    lú muš-mir-te-gin₇ bal-bal-e-da-né　　　　　　　　　　　　　　{bal+bal+e+d+a+ni+e}
    As for the man who was turning over and over like an *m.*-snake
    (Šulgi D 173 Ur III)

    im tur-tur-e iri-a du-da-bé im gal-gal-e ság di-da-bé　　　　　{du+d+a+bi+e}
    za-e é-ubur-ra ma-ra-an-dù-ù-ne
    When light winds go through the city, when great winds produce scattering,
    for you indeed they build a milking house
    (Sheep and Grain 134-136 OB)

    še gur₁₀-gur₁₀-ru-da-zu-dè　　　　　　　　　　　　　　　　　　{gur₁₀-gur₁₀+e+d+a+zu+dè}
    When you have to reap the barley
    (Farmer's Instructions 74 OB)

With the Sumerian locative-terminative postposition in this construction compare the use of the preposition *ina* 'in' in the following Akkadian glosses to an OB Nisaba hymn:

    é-engur-ra ki tuš-a-né : *a-gu-ur i-na wa-[ša]-bi-šu*
    abzu eridu^ki-ga dù-dù-a-né : *ap-sa-am e-ri-du i-na e-pe-ši-i-šu*
    hal-an-kù šà kúš-ù-da-né : *i-na ha-al-la-an-ku i-na mi-it-lu-ki-šu*
    When he (Enki) took his place in the Engur Temple,
    when he had built all of the Abzu of Eridu
    as he was about to deliberate in the Halanku (Nisaba A 40-42)

Finally, OB literary texts are replete with neologisms, providing anomalous forms which confound attempts to create universal paradigms. Here the pronominal conjugation co-occurs with a finite verbal form to give an uncertain temporal nuance to the clause:

    eger-bi-šè ug-àm saĝ-bi-šè piriĝ-àm
    ug-e piriĝ im-sar-re
    piriĝ-e ug [im]-sar-re
    ug-e piriĝ im-[sar]-re-da-bé
    piriĝ-e ug im-[sar]-re-da-bé
    u₄ nu-um-zal ĝi₆-[u₃-na] nu-ru-gu₂
    By its back it was an *ug*-lion, by its front it was a *piriĝ*-lion
    That *piriĝ*-lion chases after the *ug*-lion,
    that *ug*-lion chases after the *piriĝ*-lion.
    While that *piriĝ*-lion was chasing after the *ug*-lion,
    while that *ug*-lion was chasing after the *piriĝ*-lion
    day did not pass, midnight was not opposed(?)
    (Enmerkar and Ensuhgirana 82-87 OB)

Here, combined *marû* and *hamṭu* features produce an odd hybrid form:

    tu-tu-a-zu ha-ra-gub-bu-ne　　　　　　　　　　　　　　　　{tu(d)-tu(d)+a+zu+e}
    Let them stand by you while you are giving birth
    (Enki and Ninmah 36 OB)

PRONOMINAL SUFFIXES ON FINITE VERBS

Perhaps comparable with pronominal conjugation constructions are a certain class of finite verbal forms featuring possessive pronoun suffixes. Confident translation of the stylistic nuance involved is often difficult. For example:

    u₄ ba-zàh-dè-na-ĝá NIR-da hé-a bí-in-du₁₁　　　　　　　　　{ba+zàh+e+d+en+a+ĝu₁₀+a}
    "On my day when I should flee may it be a felony" he declared
    (BE 3/1, 1:4-6 Ur III}

PN še hé-ĝál bí-du₁₁-ga-ĝu₁₀ hé-na-ab-šúm-mu   {b+Ø+dug₄+a+ĝu₁₀+e?}
Let him give (the barley) to PN, at(?) my having
commanded "Let there be barley!"
(Sollberger, TCS 1, No. 115:2-6 Ur III)

ᵈen-líl sipa saĝ-gi₆-ga-ke₄ a-na bí-in-ak-a-bi
Enlil, the shepherd of the Black-Headed, this (is) what he did to them
(Lamentation over Sumer and Ur 72 OB)

VOCABULARY NOTE 3

<u>Multiple Rection Verbs</u>

Many verbs show variation in rection (indirect object case preference) in some cases
possibly owing to the influence of Akkadian syntax. Common examples are si 'to fill into
(-a)', ra 'to beat upon (-e)', and sìg 'to hit upon (-e/a), strike, smite'. In the
following three example sets, the (a) passages demonstrate the normal rection, the (b)
passages demonstrate rection altered in the direction of instrumental ideas, and the (c)
passages show ungrammatical conflations of rection marked by double case postpositions.
One must always remain patient and flexible when reading Sumerian!

(a)   li ᵍⁱˢú-sikil kur-ra-kam izi-a bí-si-si
      Juniper, the pure plant of the mountains, he filled repeatedly into the fire
      (Gudea Cyl A 8:10 Ur III)

(b)   ᵍⁱˢig-bi mah-àm ul-la mi-ni-in-si
      Its doors (which) were lofty: he filled them with (-a) flowers
      (Ur-Namma B 26 Ur III)

(b)   GÁNA šuku surₓ(ÉREN)-ra, GÁNA gig-ga, a-e íb-si
      The subsistence field of the workers, a field of wheat, has filled with (-e) water
      (ITT 2 3116 = FAOS 19 Gir16 OAkk letter)

(a)   saĝ-du-bé tíbir im-mi-ra
      He caused (his) palm (-Ø) to strike upon (-e) their heads
      (JCS 21, 30 4:24f. Šū-Sîn inscription Ur III)

(b)   ká silim-ma-bi ᵍⁱˢal-e bí-in-ra
      He struck the Gate of Well-Being with (-e) a pickax
      (Curse of Agade 125 OB)

(c)   é-kur za-gìn-na dù-a-ba ᵍⁱˢal-e hé-em-mi-in-ra
      He struck with (-e) a pickax upon (-a) that lapis lazuli Ekur, all of it
      (Eridu Lament C 26 OB)

(a)   u₄ ᵍⁱˢtukul elam-a ba-sìg-ga
      The day when weapons struck in(to) Elam
      (BIN 9, 4-7, JCS 30, 196 n. 17))

(b)   umuš-bi in-sùh-àm líl-e bí-in-sìg-ga-àm
      He confused its judgment, he smote it with (-e) a wind-phantom (or: to the wind)
      (Nippur Lament 104 OB)

(c)   ᵈen-líl-le dur-an-ki-ka ᵍⁱˢmitum-a ba-an-sìg
      Enlil struck upon Duranki (-a) with (-a) a divine weapon
      (Lament over Sumer and Ur 139 OB)

THE SUMERIAN VERBAL PREFIX CHAIN

MODAL PREFIXES	VENTIVE	DATIVE		DIMENSIONAL PREFIXES DA TA ŠI RA	CORE PREFIXES L-T	Erg
		M	BA	SINGULAR	Comitative, Terminative, and Ablative-Instrumental may be preceded by a pronominal element (mu, e, n, b, ne)		
hé							
		->		1 ma			
ga	C						
	o			2 ra			
na	n				Terminative		
	j			3p na	Comitative	ši (šè)		
na	u				da			
	n		->	3i ba	(dè, di)	Ablative	Ablative-		
ba-ra	c					ra	Instrumental	ri	e/Ø
	t					(re, ri)	ta (te, ti)		
nu	i			PLURAL			
	v				Ablative ra appears only after a sg. Dative prefix except in emphatic Ablative sequences such as ma-da-ra-ta-è		
ù	e	->		1 me		ni	n
ši	nga			2 e-ne?			
nu-uš				3p ne	<-------------------------->	ne	n--š
		->		mu- with Loc.-Term. function may only be preceded by a preformative	mu	Ø
Imperative Transform.				Loc.-Term. bi- may only be preceded by the ventive or a preformative	bi	b

Stative al   (exceptionally preceded by ù- or nu-)

THE EMESAL DIALECT

Eme-sal 'fine tongue' is usually described as an example of a linguistic women's language or dialect (sociolect), since it is mainly seen used in the speech of female deities in Sumerian literary contexts and in the language of 2nd and 1st millennium temple liturgies performed by the gala 'lamentation priest', an occupation almost exclusively of males of uncertain sexual orientation. Women's dialects are well known among the world's languages, some having linguistic features in common with the Sumerian example. There is, however, almost no evidence to show that eme-sal was actually spoken by Sumerian women in historical times. Furthermore, it has even been suggested that it may instead have served, or at least originated, as a geographical dialect (see most recently Josef Bauer in OBO 160/1 [1998] 435f. regarding OS Lagaš-Ĝirsu). Earlier scholars attempting to explain eme-sal were to some extent misled by the fact that the term sal is written with the MUNUS 'woman' sign, and until fairly recently it was thought that the Sumerian term for 'woman' was in fact sal, not munus. Now it is understood that eme-sal has something of the sense of 'fine, delicate, genteel, sweet speech', referring certainly to what might be described as a kind of softening of the spoken language brought about by the kind of phonological modifications that characterize the dialect. See the exhaustive study of Manfred K. Schretter, *Emesal-Studien* (IBK Sonderheft 69, Innsbruck, 1990. also the 3-tablet Emesal Vocabulary, Materials for the Sumerian Lexicon IV (Rome, 1956) 1-44, for an overview of the sound correspondences in context.

Eme-sal differs from the main dialect eme-gir$_{15}$ 'native tongue' in two ways. In a few cases completely different words are employed. More often one sees certain types of phonological modification of both consonants and vowels. Since eme-sal modifies the pronunciation of common words, eme-sal words cannot be written logographically but must be spelled out syllabically, and syllabic spellings are a good sign that one is in an eme-sal context even if not all words in a particular text are consistently given proper eme-sal spellings. The following illustrate a few of the known eme-sal spellings.

Some word substitutions include:

ga-ša-an =	nin 'mistress'		mu-lu =	lú 'person'
ir	túm 'to bring'		ta	a-na 'who'

Some phonological modifications include:

/m/ < /ĝ/

da-ma-al =	daĝal 'wide'
dìm-me-er	diĝir 'god(dess)'
èm(ÁĜ)	níĝ 'thing'
ma-al	ĝál 'to be'
-mà(ĜÁ)	-ĝá 'in/of my'
mar	ĝar 'to place'
me-ri	ĝìri 'foot'
mu	ĝiš 'wood'
-mu	-ĝu$_{10}$ 'my'
na-ma	naĝa 'alkali'

/ĝ/ < /m/

e-ne-èĝ =	inim 'word'
na-áĝ-	nam- (abstract formative)
zé-èĝ	šúm 'to give'

/b/ < /g/

a-ba =	a-ga (àga) 'rear'
zé-eb	dug$_3$ 'good'
i-bí	igi 'eye'
šà-ab	šag$_4$ 'heart'

/u/ < /i/

su$_8$-ba(d) =	sipa(d) 'shepherd'
u$_5$	ì 'oil'
ù-mu-un	en 'lord'
uru	iri 'city'

(other)

e-zé =	udu 'sheep'
ka-na-áĝ	kalam 'nation'
li-bi-ir	niĝir 'herald'
ši-pa-áĝ	zi-pa-áĝ 'breath'
šu-um-du-um	nundum 'lip'
du$_5$(?)-mu	dumu 'son'

INDEX

a- (= ù- before ba-) 106f.
-a (nominalizing) 95ff., 135f.
-a-ka-nam 101
a-ba 36
a-da-al/lam 52
a-na 36
a-rá (multiplication) 53
abilitative -da- 79
ablative -ra- 80f.
ablative -ra/re/ri- 81
ablative-instrumental prefix 80
ablative-instrumental postposition 58
adverbial expressions
   causal 52, 101
   local 52
   temporal 52, 100f.
adverbs 51f.
al- (stative prefix) 67f.
anticipatory genitive 42
auxiliary verbs 72
ba- 74-77
ba-a-, ba-e- = /bay/ < ba-an 83
ba-ra- (preformative) 105
bahuvrihi modifiers 30
-bi (demonstrative, adverbial) 35, 51
-bi-da (conjunctive) 57
comitative postposition 57f.
comitative prefix 78f.
compound verbs, rection 60
copula 30, 46ff.
dative postposition 55f.
demonstrative adjectives 35f.
didli 53
-e (adverb formative) 51, 54
-e (casus pendens, vocative) 55
/(e)d/ in non-finite forms 127-130
/(e)d/ in finite forms 124-6
emesal dialect 22, 151
equative 44f.
ergative 61f.
ergativity 83ff.
-eš(e) (adverbiative) 59
finite copula 49f.
ga- 105f.
gender 24
genitive as implicit agent 43
genitive construction 39ff.
genitive without regens 42f.
hé- 104f.
i-gi₄-in-zu, igi-zu 52
ì- (conjugation prefix) 66f.
ì- (= ù- before bí-) 106f.
ì-ne-éš 52
im-√ = Vm+b 91f.
imperative 109ff.
in-nu 50
infinitives 141ff.

interrogative pronouns 36
-kam, -kam-ma-ka 53
locative -a 56f.
locative -ni- 86f., 114-116
locative -n- and -b- 87f., 114-116
instrumental agent 88
loss of final /n/ 126
ma-na-, ma-ra- 92
marû finite verbs 117
marû stem formation 117-119, 130f.
me-a 36
Mesanepada construction 97
mi-ni-, mi-ri- 92
-n-ga- (conjunctive) 108
na- (negative) 105
na- (positive) 106
-na-an-na 101
na-me 37
-ne (demonstrative adjective) 35, 147
ní 'self' 36
nu- 102
nu as verbal root (in-nu) 50
nu-uš- 107
number 24
numerals 53
participles 127ff.
periphrastic verbs 72
plural verbs 82, 118f.
predicative genitive 43
pronominal conjugation 146-148
pronouns
   dimensional prefixes 69, 78
   dative paradigm 73
   demonstrative 35
   hamṭu agent 64-6
   hamṭu subject/patient 63
   independent 31
   marû agent and object 120f.
   possessive 32f., with verbs 148
   relative 37
   summary chart 38
reduplication 26f., 63f.
relative clauses 95ff.
-ri (demonstrative adjective) 35
second agent 88
sentence adverbs 52
subordinate clauses 99f.
syllabic sign values chart 16f.
-šè (adverb formative) 51, 59
ši- 107
terminative postposition 58f.
terminative prefix 79f.
ù- 106f.
ur₅ (demonstrative pronoun) 36
ventive 90ff., imperatives 111-113
verbal prefix chain chart 150
vowel harmony, OS Lagaš 19, 67, 79

EXERCISE 1

NOUNS, NOUN PLURALS, ADJECTIVES

Analyze morphologically using plus (+) symbol and translate, noting any possible alternate translations. All forms are absolutive nominal chains whose analyses must end with the marker -Ø. Some forms are nominal compounds, so check the glossary carefully.

1   lú-ne

2   é-é

3   dumu-dumu-ne

4   diĝir gal

5   diĝir-re-ne

6   diĝir gal-gal-le-ne

7   dumu zi

8   hur-saĝ galam-ma

9   níta kal-ga

10 munus sa$_6$-ga

11 nam-lugal

12 ki-sikil tur

13 ki Lagaš^{ki}

14 gu$_4$-áb-hi-a

15 šu sikil

16 bàd sukud-rá

17 níĝ-ba

18 šeš bànda

19 nu-^{giš}kiri

20 níĝ-gi-na níĝ-si-sá

21 dumu-níta

22 a-ab-ba sig

23 dumu-munus

24 dub-sar mah

25 é-bappir

26 ^{uzu}ti, ^{uzu}ti-ti

153

EXERCISE 2

NOUN PLURALS, POSSESSIVE AND DEMONSTRATIVE PRONOUNS

Analyze carefully and translate. Use the Glossary to identify any nominal compounds. Don't forget to put an absolutive -Ø at the end of each analyzed chain.

1. diĝir-zu

2. á dugud-da-ni

3. dumu-bi

4. ama kal-la-ĝu$_{10}$

5. lugal-zu-ne-ne

6. ama-ne-ne

7. diĝir-bé-ne

8. diĝir-ra-né-ne

9. lú mah-bi

10. gú-ri

11. iri gal-me

12. nam-ti-ĝu$_{10}$

13. nam-ti-la-ni

14. ur-saĝ-zu-ne

15. níĝ-na-me

16. igi zi-da-ni

17. dub-sar tur-ĝu$_{10}$-ne

18. ki-tuš kù-ga-ni

19. a-a kal-la-ni

20. nin igi sa$_6$-sa$_6$-ĝu$_{10}$
    (Enlil and Sud 25 OB)

EXERCISE 3

ADNOMINAL CASES
POSSESSIVE AND DEMONSTRATIVE PRONOUNS

Analyze and translate; note all possible alternative analyses. Remember to use the absolutive postposition -Ø in the absence of any other case. This exercise employs the following case postpositions:

        locative   -a   'in'
        terminative -šè 'to, towards, for'

1   é lugal-la
2   é lugal-la-na
3   é lú
4   é dumu-ne
5   é lú-ka
6   é lú-ne-ka
7   é-gal lugal-la
8   é-gal lugal-ba-ka
9   é-gal lugal-ĝá-šè
10   é diĝir mah-e-ne
11   é diĝir-ra-bi
12   é diĝir-ba-gin₇
13   é mah diĝir gal-gal-le-ne-ka
14   nam-lugal iri
15   é-gal nam-lugal-la-ĝu₁₀-šè
16   ama dumu-dumu-ne
17   ama dumu-dumu-ke₄-ne-gin₇
18   ir₁₁-zi dam lugal-la-ka
19   lugal kal-ga diĝir-ra-ni
20   lugal-ĝá nam-kal-ga-ni
21   é-ba diĝir mah-bi
22   dumu-ne ama kal-la-ne-ne
23   é-ĝá ᵍⁱšig-bi
24   lú iri-ke₄-ne é-é-a-ne-ne

25   i₇ a-šà-ba-ka gú gibil-bi
26   ká iri-šè
27   ᵍⁱšig ká iri-ka
28   lú é-gal iri-ba-ka-ke₄-ne-gin₇
29   é ᵈnin-ĝír-su-ka
30   dumu ᵈnin-hur-saĝ-ĝá-ka-ke₄-ne
31   nam-ti énsi-ka-šè
32   ᵈInana nin kur-kur-ra nin
      É-an-na-ka
33   é me huš gal an-ki-ka-ni
34   nu-bànda kù-dím-ne
      (OSP 2, 50 1:6/3:9 OAkk)
35   ki-a-naĝ lugal-lugal-ne
      (RTC 316 Ur III)

EXERCISE 4

COPULA, INDEPENDENT PRONOUNS

Deities
- ᵈEn-líl — highest earthly god, patron of the city Nippur
- ᵈInana — goddess of passion and conflict, patron of Uruk
- ᵈIškur — god of rain, patron of Karkar
- ᵈNin-urta(-k) — son of Enlil, farmer god and war god, patron of Ĝirsu
- ᵈŠákkan — god of wild animals

Places
- Ènnigi^ki — Ennigi, cult center of the chthonic healing god Ninazu
- Ki-en-gi(r) — Sumer
- Úri(m)^ki — Ur, cult center of the moon god Nanna(r)

1 bàd sud-rá-bi bàd é-gal-ĝá-kam

2 lugal nin Ki-en-gi-ra ì-me-en-dè-en

3 é-bi é-ĝu$_{10}$ nu-um, ki-tuš kù en Úri^ki-ma-ka-kam

4 nin-ĝu$_{10}$ ᵈInana á-dah-ĝu$_{10}$-um
   (Annal of Utuheĝal 29 Ur III)

5 za-e: ᵈIškur lugal-zu-um ᵈŠákkan šùš-zu-um bar-rim$_4$ ki-nú-zu-um
   (Sheep and Grain 171 OB)

6 nar za-pa-áĝ-ĝá-ni du$_{10}$-ga-àm e-ne-àm nar-àm
   (Proverbs 2+6 A 73 OB)

7 ᵈIškur-ra á-dah-ha-ni-me-eš
   (Lugalbanda and Hurrum 401 OB)

8 a-ne-ne dumu Ènnigi^ki dumu Úri^ki-ma-me-éš
   (Šulgi D 373 Ur III)

9 ᵈEn-líl en za-e-me-en lugal za-e-me-en
   (Enlil and Ninlil 144 OB)

10 ur-saĝ an-eden-na men-bi-im eden-na lugal-bi-im
   (Enki and the World Order 354 OB)

11 ĝá-e ù za-e šeš-me-en-dè-en
   (Proverbs 8 D 2 OB)

12 an-na dili nun-bi-im ki-a ušumgal-bi-im
   (Enlil A 100 OB)

13 ᵈNin-urta ur-saĝ ᵈEn-líl-lá za-e-me-en
   (Ninurta B 29 OB)

14 sá-du$_{11}$ kas gíg du$_{10}$-ga-kam
   (Nik I 59 3:9 = TSA 34 3:10 OS)

15 me-bi kù-kù-ga-àm
   (Ibbi-Suen B Segment B 11 Ur III)

EXERCISE 5

ADVERBAL CASES, ADVERBIAL EXPRESSIONS, DEMONSTRATIVES

Analyze and translate these nominal chains

1. u₄-bi-ta
2. u₄-ba
3. u₄-ul-la-ta
4. u₄-ri-a
5. gù nun-ta
6. á kal-ga-ni-ta
7. šà-húl-la-zu-ta
8. šà iri-ka
9. šà iri-ba-ta
10. šà-bi-ta
11. bar iri-ka
12. eger é-ĝá-ta
13. igi é-babbar-ra-ka
14. igi-zu-šè
15. igi-ba
16. ugu-ba
17. gú i₇-da-ke₄
18. gaba hur-saĝ-ĝá-šè
19. da é-za-ke₄
20. da-bi-šè
21. saĝ-bi-šè
22. ul-šè
23. mah-bi-šè
24. galam-šè
25. gal-le-eš
26. ul₄-la-bé
27. nam-bi-šè
28. téš-bi-šè
29. u₄-dè-eš
30. ní-bi-šè
31. dili-zu-šè
32. an-ta ki-šè
33. ugu saĝ-ĝá-na-ke₄
34. gú-e-ta gú-ri-šè
35. ì-ne-éš
36. hur-saĝ an-ki-bi-da-ke₄
    (Grain and Sheep 1 OB)
37. 1/6 (gur) zíz ninda
    Géme-ᵈNanše
    Munus-sa₆-ga-bi
    (DP 149 8:4-6 OS)

157

EXERCISE 6

SIMPLE PERFECTIVE VERBS, COPULA, ADVERBIAL EXPRESSIONS

1. za-e iri Lagaš^{ki}-a ba-tu-dè-en?

2. dumu iri-ba nu-me-en, ama-ĝu$_{10}$ Úri^{ki}-ma in-tu-dè-en

3. tukumbi lú énsi Lagaš^{ki}-a-ka ì-me-en, énsi-ra a-na e-a$_5$?

4. ĝa-e, šitim saĝ iri-me-en, é-gal énsi kalam-ma-ka ì-dù

5. ù ku-li sumun-zu iri-me-a a-na in-a$_5$?

6. ku-li-ĝu$_{10}$, naĝar-ra-àm, ^{giš}gu-za ^{giš}banšur é-gal énsi-ka-ka in-dìm-dìm

7. a-na-gin$_7$ é-gal Lagaš^{ki}-a e-dù?

8. dili-ĝu$_{10}$-šè nu-dù, ĝiš-hur-bi ì-a$_5$, uĝ iri-ke$_4$ kíĝ íb-a$_5$

9. ir$_{11}$ énsi-ke$_4$ im ^{giš}ù-šub-ba íb-ĝar, sig$_4$ ki-sikil-la íb-du$_8$

10. lú iri-ke$_4$-ne téš-bi-šè é-gal sig$_4$-ta in-dù-uš

11. énsi é ^{d}Nin-ĝír-su diĝir Lagaš^{ki}-a-ka-ka ì-ku$_4$, dam dumu-ni e-ne-da ì-ku$_4$-re-eš

12. igi bára kù-ga-ka ì-gub, šu-ni alaĝ diĝir-ra-šè in-zi sizkur in-a$_5$

13. énsi šà-húl-la-ni-ta é-ta u$_4$-dè-eš ba-è, saĝ-ĝá-ni an-šè in-íl

14. zi-da gùbu-na piriĝ ì-nú-nú
    (Gudea Cyl A 5:16 Ur III)

15. Gù-dé-a ì-zi, ù-sa-ga-àm! ì-ha-luh, ma-mu-dam!
    (Gudea Cyl A 12:12-13)

16. é-bi Ambar^{ki}-a ì-dù-dù
    (Ukg 6 1:8'-9' OS))

17. ĝalga kalam-ma sug-ge ba-ab-gu$_7$
    (Lamentation over Ur 232 OB)

18. mu ^{d}Amar-^{d}Suen lugal-e ^{giš}gu-za ^{d}En-líl-lá in-dím
    (Date formula for Amar-Suen year 3 Ur III)

19. ^{d}Ba-ú-al-sa$_6$
    (OS personal name; ^{d}Ba-ú is the chief goddess of the city Ĝirsu)

20. Šu-ni-al-dugud
    (OS personal name)

21. inim-bi al-til
    (Edzard, SRU 54 3:27 Sargonic legal text)

22. Ka-tar nu-bànda-gu$_4$ ù Ur-^{d}Ma-mi šu-ku$_6$-e íb-gi-in
    (Falkenstein, NSGU 189, 4-6 Ur III legal text)
    (What is grammatically interesting in this line?)

EXERCISE 7

PERFECTIVE VERBS, DIMENSIONAL PREFIXES

1. šu-nígin 5 udu nita eger gúrum-ma-ta udu siki-šè ba-dab₅
   (Nik I 155 4:1-4 OS)

2. ùĝ e-da-lu ùĝ e-da-daĝal
   (Iddin-Dagan B 55 OB)

3. 3 lú anše sur$_x$(ÉREN)-ke₄ ba-su₈-ge-éš
   (HSS 3, 24 4:14-16 OS)

4. ᵈEn-líl lugal kur-kur-ra ab-ba diĝir-diĝir-ré-ne-ke₄
   inim-gi-na-ta ᵈNin-ĝír-su ᵈŠára-bi ki e-ne-sur
   (Ent 28-29 1:1-7 OS)

5. 1 sila₄ é-muhaldim-ma ba-sa₆
   (Nik I 197 1:6-2:2 OS)

6. en a-ba e-diri a-ba e-da-sá?
   (Sjöberg, Mondgott Nanna-Suen 45:25 OB)

7. aga-zi nam-en-na mu-da-an-kar
   (Exaltation of Inana 107 OB)

8. ad-da-ĝu₁₀ mu-da-sa₆
   (Schooldays 11 OB)

9. dub-a-ni mu-da-ĝál
   (TCS 1, 353:6 Ur III)

10. ᵈBa-ú-ma-ba
    (personal name)

11. lú Umma^{ki}-ke₄ E-ki-sur$_x$(ÉREN)-ra-ke₄ izi ba-szúm
    (Ukg 16 1:1-3 OS) (sur$_x$ is here a variant writing for sur)

12. mu a-rá 3-kam-aš Simurrum^{ki} ba-hul
    (Šulgi year 33 Ur III)

13. utu-è-ta utu-šú-uš èrim-bi ba-tur
    (Curse of Agade 195 OB)

14. èn ì-ne-tar
    (TCS 1, 135:9 Ur III - 1st sg. agent)

15. ad-da dumu-ni-ta ba-da-gur
    (Lamentation over Sumer and Ur 95 OB)

16. ki-sikil-bé ki-e-ne-di ba-an-šúm
    ĝuruš-bé á ^{giš}tukul-la ba-an-šúm
    di₄-di₄-lá-bé šà-húl-la ba-an-šúm
    (Curse of Agade 31-33 OB)

EXERCISE 8

DIMENSIONAL PREFIXES, COMPOUND VERBS

Proper nouns:

An	The sky god, source of kingship (written without a divine determinative)
ᵈIškur	The god of rain
ᵈEnlil	Highest earthly god, source of governing power
ᵈNanna(r)	The moon god, patron of the city-state of Ur
Nibruki	Nippur, the city of Enlil, Sumer's religious capital
Ur-ᵈNamma(-k)	First king of the 3rd Ur dynasty (2112-2095 BC)
Šulgi(r)	Second king of the 3rd Ur dynasty (2094-2047 BC)

When you have identified the nominal chain representing a patient, use the glossary to check whether the patient and verbal root are considered to be a *compound verb* with a special meaning.

1   u_4-ri-a ᵈnanna dumu ᵈen-líl-lá-ke_4 an-ta ki-šè igi zi-da-ni íb-ši-in-bar.

2   ᵈnanna diĝir uríki-ma-ke_4 šul-gi dumu ur-ᵈnamma-ka šà kù-ga-na in-pà.

3   lú 36,000-ta šu-ni íb-ta-an-dab_5, gù ì-na-an-dé:

4   "šul-gi-ĝu₁₀, šà kù-ĝá ì-pà-dè-en, ukkin diĝir-re-ne-ka nam-zu ba-tar!"

5   an-e nam-lugal an-ta ba-ta-an-e_{11}, šul-gi lugal uríki-ma-šè in-ši-in-ku_4

6   ᵈnanna-re suhuš ᵍⁱšgu-za-na ì-na-an-gi, bala-sù(d)-rá nam-šè ì-na-an-tar.

7   ᵈen-líl-le é nibruki-ka-ni-ta nam-ur-saĝ nam-kal-ga níĝ-ba-šè ì-na-an-ba.

8   ᵈiškur-re a hé-ĝál-la i_7-da in-ĝál, bala hé-ĝál-la ì-na-an-šúm.

9   diĝir-gal kalam-ma-ke_4-ne uĝ uríki-ma-ke_4 nam-du_{10} ba-an-tar-re-eš.

10 nam-bi-šè lugal-le diĝir-ra-né-ne-ra gal-le-eš ki ì-ne-en-áĝ.

11 šul-gi sipa kalam-ma-ke_4 níĝ-si-sá-e ki ba-an-áĝ, níĝ-gi-na uĝ-ĝá-né ba-an-ĝar.

12 á ᵈen-líl-lá-ta ur-saĝ kal-ga ki-bala ᵍⁱštukul-ta in-gaz, lugal-bi in-dab_5.

13 ki-bala-ta kù-sig_{17} kù-babbar-bi íb-ta-an-e_{11}, kisal ᵈnanna-ra-ka in-dub.

14 u_4-ba lugal-le sig_4 in-šár, bàd iri-na in-dù, saĝ iri an-šè íb-ši-in-íl.

15 é-mah ᵈnanna diĝir-ra-ni-ir ì-na-an-dù, alam diĝir-ra é-a in-ku_4.

16 u_4 zà-mu-ka-ka dili-ni-šè é diĝir-ra-na-šè ib-ši-ĝen, šùd ì-na-an-rá.

17 "diĝir-ĝu₁₀, igi nam-ti-la-zu mu-ši-bar, inim-zu-uš ĝeštú íb-ši-ĝar";

18 "nam-lugal kalam-ma ma-(a-)šúm. u_4-ul-lí-a-šè mu-zu kur-kur-ra mah-àm!"

19 inim-ma-ni diĝir-ra-ni-ir ì-na-sa_6. šul-gi lugal-àm é-gibil-ta íb-ta-è.

20 e-ne ì-húl. lú iri-ke_4-ne téš-bi-šè lugal-la-ne-ne-da in-da-húl-le-eš.

160

EXERCISE 9

CORE PREFIXES

1. 1 sila₄-ga ne-mur-ta ba-šeĝ₆, ki lugal-šè ba-an-ku₄
   (Legrain TRU 327 1-3 Ur III)

2. 2 gu₄ ú 26 u₈ 8 udu nita 2 sila₄ nita, 1 uzud, 1 máš gal 1 máš
   ug₇-ug₇-ga-àm géme uš-bar-e-ne ba-an-gu₇-éš
   (Hilgert, OIP 115 66:11-10 Ur III)

3. ⁱˢmes-e saĝ bí-sa₆
   (Gudea Cyl A 7:17 Ur III)

4. munus-e lú-igi-níĝin-ne ninda e-ne-gu₇
   (DP 166 iii 6-iv 1 OS)

5. niĝir-e sila-sila-a si gù ba-ni-in-ra
   (Sumerian Letters B 12:3 OB)

6. bàd Unuᵏⁱ-ga gu mušen-na-gin₇ eden-na ba-ni-lá-lá
   (Lugalbanda and Enmerkar 305 OB)

7. érin-e di bí-íb-du₁₁ ba-ab-de₆
   (NSGU 215:16 Ur III)

8. "udu-ĝu₁₀-um" bí-in-du₁₁
   (NSGU 120a:9 Ur III)

9. kišib Lú-ᵈEn-líl-lá di-ku₅ íb-ra
   (UET 3, 41 rev. 3 Ur III)

10. šu-níĝin 60 máš-gal 8 uzud ur-gi₇-re ba-ab-gu₇
    (PDT 346 rev. 13'-14' Ur III)

11. še-šuku engar-re šu ba-ab-ti
    (Gomi, ASJ 3, 157 No. 119:6 Ur III)

12. ⁱˢeren-bé tùn gal-e im-mi-ku₅
    (Gudea Cyl A 15:22 Ur III)

13. im-ba igi ì-ni-bar
    (TCS 1, 224:17 Ur III)

14. 1 é sar iri bar abul tur-ra-ka an-ĝál
    (Edzard, SRU No. 36:1-3 Sargonic)

15. 12 sìla ésir-é-a dug-ĝeštin(-e) ba-ab-su-ub
    (Contenau Umma 99:1-2 Ur III)

16. nam-lú-ùlu-bé ⁱˢtukul ki bí-íb-tag
    (Lamentation over Sumer and Ur 394 OB)

17. eden-eden-na ú-làl bí-mú-mú
    (Nisaba Hymn for Išbi-Erra, D.D. Reisman Diss. (1970) 111 OB)

EXERCISE 10

CORE PREFIXES, LOCATIVE, VENTIVE, PLURAL VERBS

Proper Nouns: Unu(g)^{ki} The city of Uruk
               An   The patron god of Uruk

Plural Verbs: Singular   Plural
  (hamṭu)   de$_6$ lah$_4$ 'to bring, take'
                du$_{11}$(g)   e   'to do'
                gub   su$_8$(g)   'to stand'
                tuš   dúr(-ru-un)   'to sit, reside'
                ĝen   re$_7$ 'to come, go'

1   lugal sumun unu^{ki}-ga ba-úš. An-né dumu lugal-ba ^{giš}gu-za ad-da-na-ka
    bí-in-tuš.

2   é-gal sumun-na ^{giš}ùr-bi ba-šub, sig$_4$-bi ki-šè ba-ši-šub.

3   lugal gibil-le lú ^{giš}tir-ra-ke$_4$-ne ^{giš}tir-šè íb-ši-in-re$_7$-eš.

4   lú-bé-ne ^{giš}tir-ra ĝiš bí-in-kud-re$_6$-eš, ĝiš-bi ad-šè íb-ši-in-a$_5$-ke$_4$-eš.

5   ad-bi iri-šè mu-un-de$_6$-eš, šà iri-ka im-mi-in-dub-bé-eš.

6   ĝuruš kalam-ma-ke$_4$ é-gal gibil šà unu^{ki}-ga-ka mu-na-ni-ib-dù.

7   za-dím kalam-ma-ke$_4$ šà é-gal-ba-ke$_4$ ^{na_4}za-gìn-na šu-tag ba-ni-ib-du$_{11}$.

8   u$_4$-ba lugal-e šà-húl-la-ni-ta uĝ-e ĝišbun im-ma-an-ĝar.

9   šeš-a-ni ku-li-ni téš-bi-šè kisal é-gal-la-ka ib-su$_8$-ge-eš,
    silim mu-na-né-eš. (= -an-e-eš)

10 da ^{giš}banšur-gal-la-ke$_4$ im-mi-in-dúr-ru-né-eš, e-ne zà-gu-la-a dili-né ib-tuš.

11 kaš mu-ne-en-bal, lú-ù-ne in-naĝ-ĝe$_{26}$-eš.

12 gúg ku$_7$-ku$_7$ ^{giš}banšur-ra mu-ne-ni-in-ĝar-ĝar, lú-ù-ne in-gu$_7$-uš.

13 gúg kaš-bi-ta šà-ga-ne-ne íb-ta-an-húl-le-eš;

14 ĝissu daĝal é-gal-la-na-šè ní íb-ši-in-te-en-eš.

15 u$_4$-bi-ta lú kalam-ma-ke$_4$-ne iri-iri-ne-ne-a silim-ma bí-in-dúr-ru-né-eš.

16 lugal-le mu-ni kur-kur-ra ì-ni-in-mah,

17 ù lú-né-ne mu lugal-la a-ab-ba igi-nim-ta a-ab-ba sig-šè mu-ni-in-zu-uš

18 nam-bi-šè ^{d}En-líl itima kù-ga ba-an-ku$_4$ šà-ka-tab-ba ba-an-nú
    (Curse of Agade 209 OB)

19 ká silim-ma-bi ^{giš}al-e bí-in-ra
    (Curse of Agade 127 OB)

20 en iri-bar-ra en iri-šà-ga líl-e ba-ab-lah$_4$-eš
    (Lamentation over Sumer and Ur 345)

EXERCISE 11

VENTIVE

1. a-a-ĝu₁₀ ᵈEn-líl-le mu-un-túm-en
   (Lugalbanda and Enmerkar 101 OB)

2. ù-šub mu-dúb sig₄ u₄-dè ba-šub
   (Gudea Cyl A 19:13 Ur III)

3. ki šà-húl-la ᵈNin-líl-lá-šè ᵈEn-líl ᵈNin-líl-da mu-dì-ni-in-u₅
   (Šu-Sin B 12:9-11, JCS 21, 34 Ur III)

4. e-bi I₇-nun-ta gú-eden-na-šè íb-ta-ni-è; e-ba na-rú-a e-me-sar-sar
   (Ent 28-29 2:1-5 OS)

5. ur₅ mu-du₈ šu-šu mu-luh
   (Gudea Statue B 7:29)

6. hur-saĝ Ur-in-gi-ri-az a-ab-ba igi-nim-ta ⁿᵃ⁴nu₁₁-gal-e
   mu-ba-al im-ta-è útug ur-saĝ-3-šè mu-na-dím
   (Gudea 44 2:2-3:4, a sculpted mace-head)

7. PN₁ PN₂ šu-[i] lú-inim-ma-bi-[šè] im-ta-è-è-[eš]
   min-a-bé é ᵈŠára-ka nam-érim-bi íb-ku₅
   (NSGU 40:3'-8' Ur III)

8. ᵈEn-ki-ke₄ An ki mah-a im-ma-an-tuš
   An-ra ᵈEn-líl im-ma-ni-in-ús
   ᵈNin-tu zà-gal-la im-mi-in-tuš
   ᵈA-nun-na ki-ús ki-ús-bé im-mi-in-dúr-ru-ne-eš
   (Enki's Journey 106-109 OB)

9. abul-la-ba izi mu-ni-in-ri-ri
   (Exaltation of Inana 44 OB)

10. u₄ é ᵈNin-ĝír-su mu-dù 70 gur₇ še é bi-gu₇
    (Ur-Nanše 34 3:7-10 OS)

11. u₄-bi-a ku₆-e ambar-ra nunuz ki ba-ni-in-tag
    mušen-e ka ĝiš-gi-ka gùd im-ma-ni-in-ús
    (Bird and Fish 22-22 OB)

12. šà-ba gi-gun₄ ki-áĝ-ni šim-ᵍⁱˢeren-na mu-na-ni-dù
    (Gudea Statue B 2:9-10 Ur III)

13. ú-du₁₁ sa₆-<ga->ni igi-šè mu-na-ĝen; ᵈLamma sa₆-ga-ni eger-né im-ús
    (Gudea Cyl B 2:9-10)

14. áb-zi-da amar-zi mu-ni-šár-šár ùnu-bi bí-ús
    u₈-zi-da sila₄-zi mu-ni-šár-šár sipa-bi im-mi-ús
    (Gudea Statue F 3:16-4:4 Ur III)

15. é-kur èš-mah-a mi-ni-in-ku₄-re-en
    (Römer SKIZ 7:10 OB)

16. igi-bi šim-bi-zi-da mi-ni-gùn
    (Lugalbanda I 58 OB)

EXERCISE 12

RELATIVE CLAUSES, NOMINALIZING SUFFIX -a

Proper Nouns: ᵈBa-ú   Consort of the godNinĝirsu, chief goddess of Ĝirsu,
               ᵈNin-líl   Consort of the god Enlil, patron of Nippur
               Šarrum-kīn Sargon, most famous of the Old Akkadian kings
               ᵈŠu-ᵈSuen (Divinized) 4th king of the 3rd Ur dynasty

1   uĝ saĝ-gíg-ga numun zi íb-i-i-a
    (Nippur Lament 17 OB)

2   En-an-né-pà-da
    (OS personal name)

3   4 ĝuruš engar šà-gu₄ itu Šu-numun-ta u₄ 26-àm ba-ra-zal-la-ta
    itu Ezem-ᵈŠul-gi u₄ 21-àm zal-la-aš
    (Sigrist, Princeton No. 513:1-5 Ur III)

4   PN lú-ni, PN₂-da mu-da-ĝen-na-a, mu-túm
    (RTC 19 3:3-7 Ur III)

5   šu-níĝin 20 lá-4 lú, lú ᵈba-ú kur-re lah₅-ha-me
    (DP 141 6:1-2 OS)

6   má-gur₈ ur₅-gin₇ dím-ma u₄-na-me lugal-na-me ᵈen-líl ᵈnin-líl-ra nu-[mu-ne]-dím
    (Civil, JCS 21, 34 13:6-11 Ur III)

7   kù-luh-ha saĝ-da sá-a
    (Nik I 294 i 4 OS)

8   5 ĝuruš gu₄-e ù anše ús-sa
    (Yildiz-Gomi UTAMI 2233:2 Ur III)

9   50 (silà) ninda-šu éren ᵍⁱˢkiri₆ ᵈŠu-ᵈSuen-ka gub-ba ib-gu₇
    (Oppenheim Eames C 13:1ff. Ur III)

10 mušen ᵍⁱˢtukul kal-ga-zu bí-dab₅-ba-šè ...
    (Ninurta and the Turtle B 17 ON)

11 ur-mah ᵍⁱˢtukul-la bí-til-a-ĝu₁₀
    (Šulgi B 76 Ur III)

12 kišib ra-a-bi
    (Oppenheim Eames 158f. Ur III)

13 ᵍⁱˢtukul-e gub-ba ᵍⁱˢtukul-e in-gaz
    (Lamentation over Ur 224 OB. Is there an error here?)

14 nin An-ra diri-ga
    (Exaltation of Inana 59 OB)

15 aša₅ zà Ambarᵏⁱ-ka ĝál-la-a
    (DP 387 5:2-4 OS)

16 mu Šar-rum-kīn Si-mur-umᵏⁱ-šè ì-ĝen-na-a
    (ECTJ 151:10-13 OAkk year name)

EXERCISE 13

PREFORMATIVES

1 énsi-bi ku-li-ĝu₁₀ hé!
  (En I 35 5:2-3 OS)

2 PNN ᵍⁱˢkiri₆ ĜÁ-dub-ba-ka aša₅-ga nu-gub-ba-me
  (MVN 7, 224 rev. 7 Ur III)

3 diĝir-re-e-ne-er šu-mu-un-ne-mah-en
  (Išme-Dagan X 17 OB)

4 kal-ga-me-en lugal-ĝu₁₀ ga-ab-ús
  (Letter Collection B 1:9 OB   Is there an error here?)

5 níĝ-na-me á-bé la-ba-ra-è
  (Curse of Agade 160 OB)

6 PN-šè ĝéštu-ga-ni ha-mu-šè-ĝál
  (VAT 4845 4:3-5 OS)

7 ĝìr-pad-rá-zu bàd-da hé-eb-lá
  (Šulgi N 43 OB)

8 lú-na-me níĝ-na-me ugu-na li-bí-in-tuku
  (Letter Collection B 12:4)

9 A-tu-e "Á-ta má nu-ra-šúm" in-na-an-du₁₁
  (NSGU 62:9-10 Ur III - two persons involved)

10 ga-e-gi₄ Éreš^ki iri ᵈNisaba-šè
   (Enlil and Sud 29 OB)

11 an-ta hé-ĝál ha-mu-ra-ta-du
   (Gudea Cyl A 11:8 Ur III)

12 "ìr nu-me-en" bí-in-du₁₁
   (NSGU 34:4 Ur III)

13 bàd Zimbir^ki sahar-ta hur-saĝ gal-gin₇ saĝ-bi hé-mi-íl,
   ambar-ra hu-mu-ni-in-níĝin. ⁱ⁷Buranun Zimbir^ki-šè hu-mu-ba-al,
   Kar-silim-ma-ke₄ hu-mu-ni-ús
   (Hammurapi Sippar Cylinder, KVM 32.1167 OB. The king is speaking)

14 gala hé lú-bàppir hé agrig hé ugula hé ...
   (Ukg 1 4:26-29 OS)

15 im-zu abzu-ba hé-eb-gi₄, im ᵈEn-ki-ke₄ nam kud-rá hé-a!
   še-zu ab-sín-ba hé-eb-gi₄, še ᵈEzinu-e nam kud-rá hé-a!
   (Curse of Agade 231-234 OB)

16 saĝ-ur-saĝ-ĝu₁₀-ne igi hu-mu-un-du₈-uš
   (Šulgi A 77 OB)

17 ĝá-ka-nam-hé-ti
   (VS 14, 86 2:3 OS personal name referring to a child's birth)

165

EXERCISE 14

THE IMPERATIVE

1. kù là-ma!
   (Ukg 4-5, 11:26-27 OS)

2. "é-dub-ba-a-šè ĝen-ù" mu-e-du$_{11}$
   (Scribe and His Perverse Son 22 OB)

3. "bára kù-zu, húl-la-bé diri-bé, tuš-a!" hu-mu-ra-ab-bé   {hé+mu+ra+b+e+Ø}
   (Eridu Lament C 48)

4. PN$_1$ nu-bànda-ar "túm-mu-un!" ba-na-ab-du$_{11}$
   PN$_1$ "ì-túmu" bí-in-du$_{11}$
   PN$_2$ nu-bànda-ar lú Naĝ-su^{ki} PN$_3$-da in-da-ĝen-na "túm-mu-un!" in-na-an-du$_{11}$
   (NSGU 121:10-17 Ur III)

5. a-šà gala-a *Awīlum-ša-lim*-ra érin-e "uru$_4$-a!" in-na-ab-du$_{11}$
   (NSGU 215:44 Ur III. The -a on gala must be a genitive.)

6. a naĝ-mu-ub-zé-en, ninda šúm-ma-ab-zé-en!
   (Schooldays 13-14 OB)

7. ù za-e ù-sà-ga nú-ni!
   (Šulgi N = Lullaby 92 Ur III)

8. ù-sá ĝe$_{26}$-nu ki du$_5$-mu-ĝá-šè!
   (Šulgi N = Lullaby 14 Ur III. Partly in Emesal dialect)

9. eden i-lu ĝar-ù! ambar inim ĝar-ù!
   (Dumuzi's Dream 6 OB)

10. èš Nibru^{ki} Dur-an-ki-ka saĝ íl-la ĝen-né!
    (Ur-Ninurta E 42 OB)

11. ninda gu$_7$-ni-ib!
    (VS X 204 6:7 OB)

12. ^{d}Nanna nam-lugal-zu du$_{10}$-ga-àm ki-za gi$_4$-ni-ib!
    (Lamentation over Sumer and Ur 514 OB)

13. lugal-ra igi-zi bar-mu-un-ši-ib!
    (Rīm-Sîn B 50 OB)

14. e-ne-ra du$_{11}$-mu-na-ab!
    (Enmerkar and the Lord of Aratta 135 OB)

15. "uzu níĝ sìg-ga ^{giš}gag-ta lá-a šúm-me-eb!" du$_{11}$-ga-na-ab-zé-en!
    (Inana's Descent 248 OB)

16. tukum-bi lú-na-me "dumu-ĝu$_{10}$ túm-ù-um!" ba-na-an-du$_{11}$
    (ZA 97, 4:9-10 OB legal)

EXERCISE 15

IMPERFECTIVE FINITE VERBS

1. ᵈEn-ki-da bára kù-ga za-e ša-mu-un-dè-dúr-en
   (Ninurta G 15f. OB)

2. ᵈDumu-zi-abzu nin Ki-nu-nir^(ki)-ke₄ diĝir-ĝu₁₀ ᵈNin-ĝiš-zi-da-ke₄
   nam-tar-ra-ni hé-dab₆-kúr(u)-ne
   (Gudea Statue B 9:2-5 Ur III)

3. kíĝ nu-mu-ra-ab-ak-en
   (Winter and Summer 180 OB)

4. ᵈGílgameš en Kul-aba^(ki)-ke₄ ur-saĝ-bé-ne-er gù mu-ne-dé-e
   (Gilgameš and Agga 51-52 OB)

5. šìr kù-ĝá-ke₄-eš ì-ug₅-ge-dè-en?
   (Exaltation of Inana 99 OB)

6. iši Za-bu^(ki)-a nir ba-ni-in-ĝál
   ama nu-mu-un-da-an-ti na nu-mu-un-de₅-de₅
   a-a nu-mu-un-da-an-ti inim nu-mu-un-di-ni-ib-bé
   zu-a kal-la-ni nu-mu-un-da-an-ti
   (Lugalbanda and Enmerkar Epic 2-5 OB)

7. níĝ di-ba en-na ĝál-la íb-su-su
   (Code of Urnamma IV 46 Ur III legal text)

8. ᵈNin-ki Umma^(ki) muš ki-ta ĝìr-ba zú hé-mi-dù-dù-e!
   (Ean 1 rev. r:34-36 OS)

9. ᵈHa-ìa lú šìr-ra-ke₄ zà-mí-zu ka-bi-a mi-ni-ib-du₁₀-ge-ne
   (Haya Hymn = Rim-Sin B 55 OB)

10. šeš-a-ne-ne ku-li-ne-ne èn-tar-re im-mi-in-kúš-ù-ne
    (Lugalbanda and Enmerkar Epic 225-226 OB)

11. "10 gín kù-babbar šúm-ma-ab di ba-ra-a-da-ab-bé-en₆!" in-na-an-du₁₁
    (NSGU 20:6-9 Ur III legal text)

12. níĝ im-ma íb-sar-re-a
    (Letter Collection B 19:10 OB)

13. énsi lú ĝèštu-daĝal-kam ĝèštu ì-ĝá-ĝá
    (Gudea Cyl A 1:12 Ur III)

14. lú é a-ba-sumun ù-un-dù, mu-sar-ra-bi ù ^(giš)šu-kár-bi
    ki-gub-ba-bi nu-ub-da-ab-kúr-re-a,
    igi ᵈNanna-ka hé-en-sa₆;
    lú mu-sar-ra-ba šu bí-íb-ùr-re-a,
    ù šu-kár-bi ki-gub-<ba>-bi-šè nu-ub-ši-gi₄-gi₄-a,
    muš ᵈNanna hé-en-ĝar, numun-na-ni ᵈNanna hé-eb-til-le
    (AmarSin 12 32-49 Ur III)

15. dub-sar-me-en na-rú-a ab-sar-re-en
    (Letter Collection B 1:14 OB)

16 ᴵGú-TAR-lá dumu Saĝ-a-DU Diĝir-ĝu₁₀-da an-da-ti, Ki-lugal-u₅-a^(ki)-a ab-tuš;
    ᴵLugal-nam-tág dumu Ur-ub Inim-ma nu-bànda an-da-ti, Bára-si-ga-^(ki)-a ab-tuš;
    dumu Nibru^(ki)-me Lagaš^(ki)-a ab-durun_x(TUŠ.TUŠ)-né-eš: ha-mu-ra-ne-šúm-mu
    (ITT I 1100:1-16 Ur III)

17 ùĝ-bé a-še-er-ra u₄ mi-ni-ib-zal-zal-e
    (Lamentation over Sumer and Ur 481 OB)

18 ki-kù ki nam-ti-la ĝìri-zu hé-ri-ib-gub-bu-ne
    (Rim-Sin D 33 OB)

19 anše-ba šu hé-eb-bar-re!
    (TCS 1, 72:6 Ur III)

20 Na-ba-sa₆-ra ù-na-a-du₁₁: 5 ma-na siki Lú-^dIškur-ra ha-na-ab-šúm-mu!
    (TCS 1, 150:1-5 Ur III)

21 šu-níĝin 12 igi-nu-du₈ Uru-inim-gi-na lugal Lagas^(ki)-ke₄ é-gal-ta e-ta-è-dè,
    Sa₆-sa₆-ra mu-na-šúm-mu
    (DP 339 vi 1-vii 3 OS, PNN are a king and queen of Lagas)

22 ĝeštin níĝ du₁₀ i-im-na₈-na₈-e-ne
    kaš níĝ du₁₀ i-im-du₁₀-du₁₀-ge-ne
    ĝeštin níĝ du₁₀ ù-mu-un-naĝ-eš-a-ta
    kaš níĝ du₁₀ ù-mu-un-du₁₀-ge-eš-a-ta
    a-gàr a-gàr-ra du₁₄ mu-ni-ib-mú-mú-ne
    (Sheep and Grain 65-69 OB)

EXERCISE 16

PARTICIPLES AND INFINITIVES
Note that several of the following are phrases, not complete sentences.

1   balaĝ-di šìr zu-ne
    (Nippur Lament 119 OB)

2   ^{d}Ba-ú-lú-ti
    (OS personal name)

3   naĝ-ku$_5$ da Umma^{ki}-ka, a-na ĝál-la, Ér-diĝir-e igi kár-kár-dam
    (YOS 4, 235:1-3 Ur III)

4   tukumbi dub Za-ra-ba-am 2-kam im-ma-de$_6$ ze-re-dam
    (PDT 231:6-9 Ur III)

5   dub Ús-mu ù-um-de$_6$ dub Ab-ba ze-re-dam
    (Contenau Umma 51 Ur III)

6   šu nu-luh-ha ka-e tùmu-da níĝ-gig-ga-àm
    (Proverbs 3.161 OB)

7   ĝissu-bi ki-šár-ra lá-a ùĝ-e ní te-en-te
    (Enki and the World Order 167 OB)

8   i$_7$-zu i$_7$-kal-ga-àm i$_7$ nam tar-ra-àm i$_7$-mah ki utu-è igi nu-bar-re-dam
    (Ibbi-Suen B 24 OB)

9   úr-kù nam-ti-la si-a-ĝu$_{10}$ u$_4$-zu sù-sù-dè
    šul ^{d}En-líl-le é-kur-ta á-bi mu-da-an-áĝ
    (Ur-Ninurta A 83f. OB)

10 Hammurapi lugal kal-ga lugal Babila^{ki} lugal an-ub-da-límmu
    kalam dím-dím-me, lugal níĝ a$_5$-a$_5$-bi su ^{d}Utu ^{d}Marduk-ra ba-du$_{10}$-ga-me-en
    (Hammurabi Sippar Cylinder, KVM 32.1197 OB. Hammurapi is speaking.)

11 balaĝ ki-áĝ-ni "Ušumgal-kalam-ma" ^{giš}gù-di mu tuku níĝ ad gi$_4$-gi$_4$-ni
    (Gudea Cyl A 6:24-25 Ur III)

12 šen-šen-na eme sù-sù-e-me-èn, muš-huš kur-re eme è-dè-me-èn
    (Šulgi C Segment A 15-16 Ur III)

13 har-ra-an lú du-bi nu-gi$_4$-gi$_4$-dè
    (Inanna's Descent 84 OB)

14 PN ká ^{d}Nin-urta-ka nam-érim kud-ru-dè ba-an-šúm-mu-uš
    (Steinkeller, Sales Documents 73 n. 209, HSM 1384:20-22 Ur III)

15 ^{d}Šu-ni-du$_{10}$ ì ga-àr-ra du$_6$-ul-du$_6$-ul-e ì ga-àr-ra nu-du$_6$-ul-du$_6$-ul
    ((Lament over Destruction of Sumer and Ur 334 OB)

16 ká še nu-kuru$_5$-da še i-ni-in-ku$_5$
    (Curse of Agade 123 OB)

17 itima é u$_4$ nu-zu-ba ùĝ-e igi i-ni-in-bar
    (Curse of Agade 129 OB)

18   lú tur gibil-bé é dù-ù-gin₇, dumu bànda^da ama₅ ĝá-ĝá-gin₇
      (Curse of Agade 11-12 OB)

19   ᵈinana i-zi-gin₇ an-ta ní gùr-ru-a-zu-dè
      ᵈnin-é-gal-la ki-a súr-dù^mušen-gin₇ še₂₆ gi₄-gi₄-a-zu-dè
      (Inana as Ninegala [Inana Hymn D] 120-121 OB)

20   nam-šub ᵈnu-dím-mud-da-kam e-ne-ra du₁₁-mu-na-ab!
          "u₄-ba muš nu-ĝál-àm ĝír nu-ĝál-àm
           kir₄ nu-ĝál-àm ur-mah nu-ĝál-àm
           ur-gi₇ ur-bar-ra nu-ĝál-àm
           ní te-ĝe₂₆ su zi-zi nu-ĝál-àm
           lú-u₁₈-lu gaba-šu-ĝar nu-tuku"
      (Enmerkar and the Lord of Aratta 135-140 OB)

Printed in Great Britain
by Amazon